D0437712

# Private Heller and the Bantam Boys

# PRIVATE HELLER AND THE BANTAM BOYS

*AN AMERICAN MEDIC IN WORLD WAR I*

## GREGORY ARCHER

Based on the Combat Diary of Private Ralph H. Heller, US Army
Ambulance Corps (1917–1919)

Guilford, Connecticut

An imprint of Rowman & Littlefield

Distributed by NATIONAL BOOK NETWORK

Copyright © 2015 by Gregory Archer

*All rights reserved.* No part of this book may be reproduced in any form or by any electronic or mechanical means, including information storage and retrieval systems, without written permission from the publisher, except by a reviewer who may quote passages in a review.

British Library Cataloguing in Publication Information Available

Library of Congress Cataloging-in-Publication Data is available on file.

ISBN 978-1-4930-1736-2
ISBN 978-1-4930-1737-9 (e-book)

♾™ The paper used in this publication meets the minimum requirements of American National Standard for Information Sciences—Permanence of Paper for Printed Library Materials, ANSI/ NISO Z39.48-1992.

*I'm sick and tired of war. Its glory is all moonshine. It is only those who have neither fired a shot nor heard the shrieks and groans of the wounded who cry aloud for blood, for vengeance, for desolation. War is hell.*

—GENERAL WILLIAM TECUMSEH SHERMAN
UNION ARMY, US CIVIL WAR
FROM HIS ADDRESS ON JUNE 19, 1879

*You can't say civilization don't advance. In every war they kill you in a new way.*

—WILL ROGERS (CIRCA 1920)

*They cry for help, but there is no one to save them.*

—PSALM 18:41

*This book is dedicated to Private Ralph Heller, the Princeton University Bantam Boys, the US Army Ambulance Corps, and every man or woman who has ever gone to war not to take lives but to save them.*

*If we remember old wars, perhaps we will be less likely to start new ones.*

# Contents

# Prologue: The Guns of June

*Thursday, 25 June 1918. Near the Marne River, France*

A misty shroud embraced a mustard gas–tainted, artillery-ravaged wasteland. Nothing survived except for depleted infantry soldiers. Even the rats and birds were dead. A man escaped from this tormented soil only by way of dreadful wounds, pitiful insanity, or a violent death. Most preferred death over disfigurement.

The German Empire and the Republic of France ground each other's armies to dust for four disastrous years. The tragedy continued. The 1918 German Spring Offensive entered its tenth vicious day. To the exhausted French *soldats* in its path, stopping tens of thousands of Germans, *les Boche*, seemed as unachievable as pushing lava back into a volcano.

Retreating from the firestorm was Private Ralph Heller, an American medic detailed to the French Army. He was twenty-six years old, but looked forty-six. A shell of his once 205 pounds of farm-raised muscle, he struggled to steer his M1917 Ford Model T ambulance. His road was not a road. It was a muddy cow path.

Seven filthy, wounded French soldiers crammed into the back of his truck. Two others in dirty, tattered uniforms clung to each running board. One, bleeding profusely from a bandaged facial wound, wits dulled by blood loss, bobbed his head as he rode on the passenger seat. He moaned, "*Ça fait mal! Ça fait mal!* It hurts! It hurts!"

Their combined weight overloaded the deficient springs of the primitive Ford undercarriage. A damaged left front fender rode heavily on its tire, scuffing the tread. Ralph smelled burning rubber. The trapped wheel made the ambulance impossible to turn as it plunged wildly ahead. A blown tire would put his ambulance out of action.

No Man's Land

"Get off my machine!" Ralph said to the young soldier on his left sideboard. The man did not react. Ralph tried his heavily accented French, "*Descendre!*"

Ignoring the command the soldier held tightly to the kerosene lantern. Ralph rocked the steering wheel but the ambulance refused to turn. Artillery shells flew overhead. Bullets plummeted down as if in a hailstorm. Desperate, Ralph shook the soldier on the sideboard and said, "You ain't hurt. Walk! *Marcher!*"

The frightened soldier did little but mutter in indecipherable French and gaze at Ralph with unfocused eyes. Ralph pushed him. The boy tensed his grip on the fragile lantern and clung to the vehicle with renewed terror. Ralph grabbed him by the collar and pulled him closer saying slowly: "*Nours allons mourir!* We'll all die!"

The boy turned his head and cried for his mother, "*Maman!*"

Ralph said, "I'm sorry!" He closed his fist, wound up, and cold cocked the soldier. The boy tumbled off the ambulance, splashing into the mud limp as a rag doll.

Ralph cranked the steering wheel back and forth, regaining some semblance of control. He turned the ambulance and bounced down a small ravine. It was the only escape route Ralph could see.

The gash in the earth provided respite from the bullets. Machine guns no longer barked directly at him, instead merely peppering the rocky bank above. Artillery felt less lethal as it flashed overhead.

He cautiously drove on growing tense and apprehensive with every foot covered. As he searched the periphery for an escape route, Ralph shook his head. Nothing looked familiar. Exits were too narrow for his machine. Retreat seemed foolhardy. The first rule of survival conferred by French Headquarters echoed through his mind: *To stop under fire was suicide*. He had to keep going.

Moments later Ralph saw hazy figures scurrying out of white smoke at the end of the gully. *Is that chlorine gas?* he asked himself. He carried only one gas mask. He then asked aloud in French, "Any of you have gas masks?" Ralph already knew the answer. Wounded men never carried equipment.

The advancing figures were heavily armed, their faces covered by treated leather gas masks. Ralph's heart raced when the lead man signaled to the others to stop by raising his fist. The strange figures froze in their tracks. They looked like a frayed platoon of ghosts floating above the ground in swirls of fog. Ralph then realized these apparitions wore field gray. Their helmets were the shape of big pots, not the elegant form of the French M15 Adrians. He faced not ghosts but German storm troopers.

Ralph jumped on the brake, pinning it to the floorboards. He jammed the ambulance reverse pedal as far as possible, shredding the transmission band. The worn drive train squealed in protest. He tried once more, but Ralph merely scored the useless reverse drum as it threw off metal flakes. Heat poured from the glowing drive train of the dying machine. He now smelled burning oil.

The French soldier jumped from the right running board and motioned ahead. He said, "*Les Boche! Les Boche!*" Barely finishing his shout,

7.92mm Bavarian spitzer bullets struck the soldier's body, contorting him like a beaten dog. The Frenchman took a deep breath as he struggled to remain on his feet. The next shot removed the left side of his face. A blur of red mist engulfed his head as he twirled toward muddy grass.

The storm troopers scrambled for the sparse cover of rocks, dead tree stumps, and water-logged shell holes. They spread in all directions, resembling rats scurrying from a pantry when a light turned on.

Ralph saw soldiers on his flank shouldering their rifles. A grenadier ran bent over, rummaging in his satchel. A tall sergeant glanced up over a stump assessing the situation through the dirty, narrow eye ports of his gas mask. In one hand the sergeant held a 9mm Luger handgun; in the other a long stick grenade.

Ralph continued to battle his Ford's transmission. As he did, Frenchmen scattered off the ambulance, melting into the chaos. The wounded man in the seat next to Ralph dismounted and slowly walked toward the Germans. He seemed oblivious to the danger, and Ralph called to him. As the boy turned back he took gunshot wounds to each leg. Falling to his knees, he seemed not to understand what had happened. Then a bullet exploded through his sternum. He slumped into a bloody heap and tumbled into a shell hole.

Growling with outrage, Ralph fought to control his floundering vehicle. As he watched his young "Frenchie" disappear into the hole, he accidentally bent the Ford's steering wheel. He had strength he never knew existed. But it did him no good. He howled in frustration as several more bullets whizzed past sounding like ferocious bees. He fought the shifter determined to squeeze a final effort out of his machine.

A bullet skimmed off the ambulance's hood imbedding in the wooden framework next to Ralph's head. Another drilled in directly overhead. A burst from a 9mm Bergmann MP 18 light machine gun stitched the ground in front of the car with the speed of a sewing machine needle.

*Tat–tat–tat–tat–tat.*

He shook his fist at the enemy. "You stupid bastards! I'm Red Cross!"

Ralph heard a wounded Frenchman moan in the back of the ambulance. As the man struggled to get up, a stray bullet hit him in the chest.

He cried out, fell back, and flopped like a beached trout. He convulsed no more when he finally bled out.

The two remaining wounded men in the rear stayed put, making not a sound. Their rescuing ambulance had transformed into a splintering coffin, disintegrating under the impact of lead and steel. Ralph sniffed cheap tobacco as one lit up a cigarette and took a long drag.

The Germans continued their attack. A bullet struck the radiator of the battered little Ford. Steam spewed from the overheated engine, whistling furiously as if from a deranged teakettle. Ralph turned and pounded on the wooden backboard.

"She's done for! Get out! *Sortez!*"

As Ralph spoke, an air burst artillery shell exploded overhead. A pressure wave tumbled down on him and slammed his face into the steering wheel. Shrapnel fell. It struck his helmet and peppered his arms with piercing splinters of white hot metal.

Stunned by the blast, Ralph's mind strayed from the onslaught. Seconds passed. His eyes would not focus. His ears could not identify muffled sounds. His nose was bent but he felt no pain. A moment of confused tranquility overtook him.

Looking to the sky he said, "My fault boys . . ."

Ralph pulled an old rabbit's foot out from the upper pocket of his soiled Army blouse. He dangled it in the air with a shaky hand.

He realized his celebrated "Heller Luck" had just run out.

Ralph Herbert Heller, Army volunteer, medical student, YMCA wrestler, entered the war believing he was indestructible. He was immortal. Most soldiers started it that way. None now believed it.

Ralph and his fellow Princeton University volunteers, the Bantam Boys, began with grand dreams of how the Great War would end. His finish was not a celebration where he received numerous medals with proud family members in attendance. Ralph's ending was a nightmare plunge down a nameless abyss. Thoughts tumbled in his head. *This wasn't how it's supposed to be. How could it go so wrong? I loused up everything!*

Ralph felt like a crumpled piece of trash thrown into an incinerator. He had burned so completely not even his soul remained. In his mind the entire war had been futile. Nobility in war was a grand illusion. He had been duped by false visions of glory.

Now he would pay for it with his life.

Overwhelming fatigue gripped him. He didn't know what day it was. He had forgotten the names of the last towns he had driven through. He wondered, *Will anyone know how I died? Would anyone care?*

Ralph slumped in his seat as he dropped his rabbit's foot onto the mud-covered floorboards. He casually flipped the dented helmet off his head and wiped his dirty, sweat-streaked cheeks. His wounded left arm began to ache. Trickles of blood emerged from his punctured eardrums. Artillery explosions were muffled as though he was underwater. The vile odor of one hundred thousand dead soldiers assaulted his nostrils once more.

Suddenly to Ralph's left, a jittery, undernourished German private jumped up. The Boche charged with his bayonet-clad Mauser Gewehr 98 bolt action rifle to within a foot of Ralph's face.

Ralph didn't move.

He stared back at the anxious Boche without enough energy to care or worry. He could no longer even muster hate. If anything, Ralph felt relief.

The two men watched each other; for how long Ralph didn't know.

Colors faded away. Sounds grew nonexistent.

The moment became surreal as if they were in a silent movie like the ones Ralph had watched in the hospital camp cinema room.

The German's bony finger closed on his trigger.

Ralph bowed his head. With his remaining strength, he tried to conjure up a picture of her in his mind. Her photograph, weeks ago, had been obliterated by artillery.

Ralph closed his eyes. Then he could see her.

She looked so pretty in her white nurse's uniform.

Ralph smiled gently. "Love ya, Edyth . . ."

# CHAPTER 1

# Count Me In!

*Wednesday, 20 June 1917. Battle Creek, Michigan, United States*

A festive atmosphere reigned over the hospital property. Forty-eight-star American flags waved in the warm breeze. A well-dressed crowd stood on wooden parade bleachers. A rumpled band of gray-haired men played an enthusiastic albeit off-key rendition of "America the Beautiful." Everyone sang along:

*America! America!!*
*God shed his grace on thee,*
*And crown thy good with brotherhood,*
*From sea to shining sea!*

Standing at attention on Battle Creek Sanitarium's manicured front lawn was a newly minted Private Ralph Heller. He was twenty-five with thick brown hair and a fair share of good looks. He wore an ill-fitting but crisp Army uniform with a waist belt and wide-brimmed hat. Puttees wound upward to his knees from the tops of his spit-shined russet brown boots. Ralph's singing was as off-key as the band.

The US Army Ambulance Corps (U.S.A.A.C.) identification disc Ralph wore around his neck was serial number 102. He was one of the first "chained to his dog tag." U.S.A.A.C. boys chided each other that the metal discs also had the downbeat nickname "cold meat ticket" for the "unlucky mug occupying the same space as a bullet." Gallows humor was in full swing and they hadn't even left home.

The U.S.A.A.C. was formed from the American Field Service and the Harjes units associated with the American Red Cross. The American Field Service was organized in 1914 when Americans volunteered as ambulance drivers for the American Hospital of Paris. The Harjes was named after banker Herman Henry Harjes, whose bank, Morgan Harjes & Co., helped the French finance war purchases in America. Because combat troops had not yet been trained in sufficient numbers, medics, ambulance drivers, and support troops were some of the first American soldiers sent to Europe in 1917.

The previous March, German submarines had sunk five American merchant ships. The British secret service (Military Intelligence, Section 6, known as MI-6) then discovered a plan in which Germany would support Mexico in an ill-conceived bid to recapture Texas, Arizona, and New Mexico. Mexico had been engaged in a low-grade border dispute with the United States since 1910. The US government viewed the German offer of assistance as an act of war.

On April 6, 1917, President Woodrow Wilson, with Congress's approval, declared war on the Kaiser and his German Empire. America joined the Allies. The Allies consisted primarily of the British Empire, France, Russia, and Belgium. The enemy Central Powers included Germany, Austria-Hungary, Bulgaria, and the Ottoman Empire (now known as Turkey).

Thousands of Americans were raring to go fight these outlaw countries. One of the fastest ways to help was to join the U.S.A.A.C. These boys would work with French forces. The Battle Creek volunteers were among the first midwestern inductees.

Ralph stood with a similarly dressed platoon of young medics and ambulance drivers. The boys sang with the enthusiasm of winners of a million-dollar choir contest. Several of the eager faces looked young enough to be Boy Scouts. The group's average age was about twenty years. As most groups of young men of their time, they referred to themselves as "the boys." They ranged in size from the smallest at just over five feet to the tallest, Ralph, at almost six. Height didn't matter now. They stood as high as a forest of redwoods.

As the band completed its lively but dissonant performance, everyone hushed.

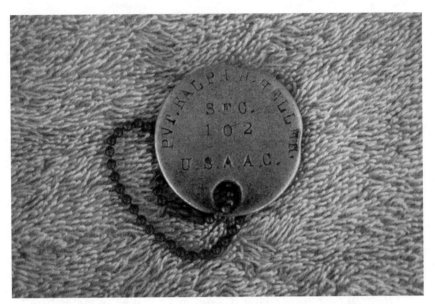

Private Heller's "dog tag"

Captain Case, a tall, stern man, stepped up to a podium in front of the crowd. He had been a doctor at Battle Creek before joining the Ambulance Corps. He joined to lead the "Battle Creek Boys" in Europe. An Army cavalry staff officer reverently gave the captain a rolled paper tied with a red ribbon.

Captain Case called the boys to attention. Case said, "Raise your right hands." He then read solemnly as if from an ancient, sacred document.

In unison, they repeated the captain's pronouncement. Ralph said, "I, Ralph Heller, do solemnly swear to bear true allegiance to the United States of America, and to serve them honestly and faithfully, against all their enemies or opposers [sic] whatsoever, and to observe and obey the orders of the President of the United States of America, and the orders of the officers appointed over me."

Hands dropped when they finished. Case saluted the boys. They saluted back. A cheer went up from the crowd. They were now wards of the US government. "Welcome to the army, boys!" said Case.

In celebration, they threw their wide-brimmed hats into the air. The hats rained down like leaves from an autumn tree. The Battle Creek Boys hugged each other, slapped backs, shook glad hands. The crowd, applauding furiously, washed out onto the parade ground to add their congratulations.

Ralph scooped up a stray cap, tried it on, and smiled. He finally found a hat that fit his extra large head. *Nice!* he thought. Now if he could just snatch an oversized pair of boots for his jumbo dogs he'd be set for life. This was the finest set of matching clothes he'd ever owned.

Out in the crowd, Nurse Edyth Sarah Lemmon, twenty-four, petite, long dark hair wrapped into a bun, dug through the mass to unearth her "Ralphy." She found him horsing around with five of his closest buddies. When the boys saw her, they formed a line and bowed. "Ralph's princess approached." They respected her nursing skills and, on top of that, she was quite the "looker."

One rival once asked, "How did you corral that lovely young mare?"

Ralph merely grinned back.

Ralph and Edyth daintily hugged so as not to appear brash. A quick peck of a kiss ended the embrace. She looked at Ralph with some hesitation. Ralph knew she had mixed feelings about him leaving. Her concerns did not dampen his enthusiasm for this grand and honorable once-in-a-lifetime European adventure. He had to go!

Edyth stepped back and pulled an old, worn rabbit's foot out of her pocket. She held it up high. "Dad said it would get you through anything," she said. "It got his Daddy through the battle of Richmond in the Civil War."

Ralph reverently took the charm. He turned it in all directions, smiled, and said, "That cinches it. The Heller luck can't be beat."

The two met at the Battle Creek hospital. He was training to be a doctor and she was working on a ward. They had an instant attraction. The usually shy farm boy asked Edyth out on a date. To his surprise, she accepted right away.

Since the pair had little money, they enjoyed picnics and walks on the hospital grounds. They had much in common, both coming from rural southern Ohio. He was from Marietta. She was from Cambridge.

He wanted to be a small town doctor. One day Ralph said to Edyth, "You could be my nurse."

"I'm expensive!" she teased.

Several days after the induction ceremony, Edyth bought Ralph a leather-bound diary. She wanted to know the details about his little wartime escapade into the "land of croissants and cheese." She said, "Write down everything you do."

"Everything?" he asked.

When Ralph started writing about "everything," he included early entries revealing his boredom. His stint in the Army did not start with the glory he'd hoped for. Much of what the Battle Creek Boys did was march, shine boots, and wash dishes. Ralph felt like the officers didn't know what to do with their ambulance men. Officers added the heroic act of peeling potatoes to the Battle Creek regimen.

Ralph's biggest fear was that the war would end before he got out of Michigan. An ill-timed peace treaty might rip laurels from his grasp. His wait was, however, soon over. The boys received travel vouchers. They were ordered to pack their meager gear, mount up, and clear out. All marched down to the Battle Creek train depot. Ralph was as excited as a graduating medical student.

As the boys waited for the train, Ralph heard a rumor that June 26th was also the date the first US combat troops were scheduled to arrive in France. He hoped he wasn't far behind. He said he didn't want "fightin' boys to get all the glory."

In a jostling Pullman railroad car Ralph wrote in his diary:

### Wednesday, 27 June 1917. Onboard the Pennsylvania Railroad

*On the evening of the 26th we marched over Battle Creek. Applause went up where ever we went. With Colors flying and the band playing, we realized our boyhood dreams in reality.*

*I'm anxious to be at the front. I wonder how my nerve will hold.*

Ralph recounted in that entry that, at 7:20 p.m., the boys gathered together at the train station. Goodbyes were exchanged with families, friends, and envious strangers. Boyfriends and girlfriends looked into each other's eyes, some for the last time ever.

Off alone together, Ralph and Edyth hugged and lingered for as long as time allowed. The train's whistle blew. Acrid black coal smoke wafted in the sky. The pair let go of each other. Ralph grabbed her hands and pulled them up between their bodies.

Ralph worked up his courage. He then asked Edyth, "Will you wait for me?"

She cupped her hands on his face and looked into his eyes.

"Yes."

From out of his pants pocket, Ralph pulled a small gold fleur-de-lis pocket watch. He pinned it on the left shoulder of her white nursing uniform. He made sure it hung straight and stepped back to admire his work.

"This was Ma's," he said.

Edyth looked at it and stroked it. "Ralphy . . . It's beautiful. I won't take it off till you get back."

"I'll twenty-three and skidoo, and be right back to you!"

Edyth grabbed Ralph's hand. "Be careful. If you get hurt, I'll come over there and take care of you."

Ralph pulled from his breast pocket his rabbit's foot. He dangled it in the air, winked, and said, "Don't jinx me!"

The train lurched forward. Ralph gathered the duffle lying at his feet. He stole a last passionate kiss and jumped on the train as it jerked, wheels groaning. He slipped inside, ran down the aisle, commandeered a window seat, and wedged his upper body out the window. He waved furiously to Edyth. The train clawed the tracks of the noisy station. People cheered for the men on the train.

Ralph cupped his hands around his mouth and yelled, "You'll know me when I return! I'll be the one plastered with all the medals!"

Edyth waved until she couldn't see him anymore.

As she turned away a tear rolled down her cheek.

They would not see each other again for two years.

— ⁓ —

After Ralph left, Edyth grew restless. She did not feel she was doing her part for the war effort. She wanted an Army nursing position and to transfer to Europe to be near Ralph. A local recruiter could not provide any such guarantee. Given her skills, and because Edyth was rather feisty, the recruiter asked her to join the Army Medical Corps. As a nurse, it was one of the few areas women were permitted to work on equal footing with men. There was also an Army nursing shortage stateside. They needed her. Appealing to her patriotism, she reluctantly agreed. Edyth soon dispatched to Camp Upton on Long Island, New York, as a US Army nurse.

During Ralph's absence, Edyth cared for departing doughboys. She also spent considerable time with British and American combat casualties in a trauma rehabilitation unit. Britain's hospitals were so overwhelmed with wounded many were sent to the United States for long-term treatment and physiotherapy.

Edyth found the work fulfilling, but she never saw the shores of France despite multiple transfer requests. She missed Ralph terribly. She badgered her commanding officer so frequently he started locking his door when he saw her.

As the war dragged on, she was increasingly plagued by nightmares. On many a night she dreamt of Ralph wounded on a battlefield calling out her name.

Edyth dashed through the mud to save him.

No matter how fast she ran Ralph always died before she got there.

---

The Battle Creek Boys continued on their exciting cross-country train journey. After a long, restless, and cramped twenty-three hours onboard, they reached their destination on June 28th. After setting up for the night, they got their bearings and a good meal. Several days later Ralph recounted their trip in his diary.

### Sunday, 1 July 1917. Allentown, Pennsylvania

*The biggest crowd I ever saw was there to see us off [from Battle Creek]. Many tears flowed while the band played.*

*Slept little but I like the crowd [that he was traveling with]. Saw Niagara Falls and Buffalo, Lake Geneva and the Le High Valley.*

Nurse Edyth Lemmon, Camp Upton. A copy of the picture Ralph lost in an artillery barrage in France.

*Arrived at Allentown at six o'clock in evening and marched to [the] State Fair Campgrounds.*

    *Slept in a horse stall and believe me the slumber was good.*

    *I never spent a better night!*

The boys entered into the myriad joys of Army life at Camp Crane. Ralph was condemned to several stints on KP or kitchen patrol. He hated it. Scrubbing pots was boring and messy. The harsh lye soap could eat the chrome off a pocket watch let alone the skin off his bones. Every Army recruit got a share of washing dirty dishes. In the bustling camp, dishpan hands were more common than trench foot.

Ralph's soggy mitts soon got a reprieve. Considering his medical training, Lieutenant Chapp, a local by-the-book Army officer, drafted him. Chapp sent him to the Allentown Hospital. At that moment Ralph was sure a benevolent God existed.

At the hospital, he gave inoculations to soldiers and dispensed pharmacy orders. Civilians were also patients on the wards. Much to Ralph's surprise, his first full-time charge was a one-year-old baby. The son of a prominent local banker, the baby had broken his collarbone in a fall. Unsure of what to do, he massaged the crying child's back every night until the little guy fell asleep. Feeling triumphant, Ralph thought about a future as a pediatrician rather than a surgeon.

He enjoyed his hospital duties. His work, however, wasn't without danger. Due to a bout of scarlet fever as a child, Ralph did not hear well. One afternoon, a new captain came in and mumbled, "Where's Lieutenant Clap?" (He meant *Chapp*.)

Ralph thought he said, "Where you tend clap [gonorrhea]?"

He discreetly took the short, plump captain to the venereal diseases isolation tent. There the faces of patients bore forlorn looks. The area smelled of too much bleach. The sheets were snow white—unlike the activities that got the patients admitted.

Ralph wrote that the unit was known as "The Sunday School." The name didn't derive from the fact that Bibles laid at all bedsides. It came about because "noxious treatments of intimate parts put the fear of God in atheists."

Boys on KP: We signed up for this?

Mercury salts, which maim at high dosages, were a favored treatment. To call this medication unpleasant would be an understatement. Adding to the injury, patients would endure living hell from their officers when they returned to their squads. "It was a good time had by none."

The chubby captain blew his top when he realized where he was. Feeling horribly insulted, he attacked Ralph with a tongue sharp enough to gut a rhino. It took Ralph a few moments to sort out the confusion. After his tantrum faded, he was thankful that the captain did not bear a sidearm.

Days later, Ralph was champing at the bit to go to France. He wrote in late July:

> *. . . God help Kaiser Bill. America is waking up. The papers state all within the age limit will be drafted.*
>
> *They say Russia is driving ahead and hint that Germany wants peace.*
>
> *I wonder if we will ever see France.*
>
> *We are drilling a little. Yes, it's a great life if you don't weaken.*

A draft was coming. Despite hundreds of thousand of volunteers, more men were needed. General Jack Pershing, commander-in-chief of the American Expeditionary Forces (AEF) in Europe, on July 2nd requested a million-man army from Congress. Only nine days later, he upped his request to *three* million. Pershing realized this had become a true world war. If America came to the table unprepared, the results could be calamitous.

Training ambulance men was easier than schooling combat soldiers, because there wasn't much ambulance training available. Being some of the first volunteers, officers weren't quite sure what to do. Training routines had not yet been developed.

Ambulance corps "drilling" primarily consisted of marching. The boys didn't even get mock wooden guns to hold. Marching had as much application to warfare as peeling potatoes did to improving self-defense skills. At least it upped their physical fitness. They received, however, no cogent briefings about the Western Front. They obtained no legitimate training beyond the basics: how to dress, how to keep cadence, how to make a proper "Army" bed, and how to make brass buckles sparkle.

Ralph was unhappy. The boys marched back and forth, back and forth until their feet bled. *The war will be over and all I'll get is a bunch of bunions!* he thought.

He still did not have proper-fitting boots. Ralph beat his leather uppers with rocks to soften and stretch them. The result helped but weakened the stitching so water and mud had new entry points. He'd soon regret that experiment.

With a short fuse to the powder keg of his frustration, he was about to blow. Ralph thought to himself, *I gotta do something.* He wasn't sure what to do.

But he wanted out of Allentown.

### Thursday, 2 August 1917. Allentown Military Headquarters

Seeing several groups depart before the Battle Creek, Ralph made a snap decision. He marched into the headquarters and demanded to be transferred to the under-strength Princeton University volunteers. He heard they'd leave within days. Expecting his request to be challenged, he was ready for a fight. He stood up straight and tall.

The gruff commanding officer looked at him and said, "Granted."

*What?* Ralph was taken off guard. He didn't even get to use the long-winded justification speech he'd prepared. *It was darn good, too!* he thought to himself.

The Princeton volunteers had the French designation as the Section Sanitaire Unis 523 or S.S.U. 523 [523rd United Sanitary Section] (America kept the S.S.U. but called them Sanitary Squad Units). Known as the "Bantams and Pigeons," they were lightheartedly named for the chicken coop they converted into a barracks on the outskirts of the university campus. They adopted a white rooster on a red background as the 523rd emblem to spite their detractors. To each other they were known as "the Bantam Boys."

Assembled by Professor Robert Kilburn Root, a noted Chaucer scholar at Princeton, the men shipped to Allentown below their authorized strength of forty-five. Several more members subsequently left for officer candidate school. The unit was nine men short. At the end of July, Ralph, five of his friends, and three Ohio State boys applied to enter the Bantams' ranks. All were accepted.

Sergeant "Gabby" Lee was a wiry fellow with a serpentine walk that caused his head to jerk to the side with every step. He was one of the few experienced non-commissioned officers and in charge of the Bantams. He took his job seriously. He was called "Gabby" because he always had something to say. In doing so, he employed every curse word available to the English-speaking world. "The Sarge" yelled at recruits and other similar species of sub-humans with the gusto of a hungry rattlesnake striking a rat. A boy would rather face a slew of rattlesnakes than one angry Sarge.

A good command sergeant was a combination of sadist, comedian, and ugly mother-in-law. This hybrid personality tortured, ridiculed, and ordered recruits around with impunity. Gabby Lee was all of this with a little sprinkling of street brawler thrown in for good measure. These greenhorns needed his leadership to survive. Even so, "non-coms were as popular as a furnace in July."

The new Princeton boys weren't exactly welcomed with hearty hand-shakes and big kisses. Many of the Bantams came from wealthy families. A few were accustomed to an opulent lifestyle Ralph couldn't imagine. In the beginning, the rich and the poor mixed together like vinegar and oil. They separated. As with all successful armies, shaken hard enough and long enough, they soon emulsified. Sergeant Lee loved "shaking the shit out of college cockroaches." And he did just that.

One commonality, however, among the boys was the unusually high level of education. As college men, this unit was well read and scholarly. They had studied literature, philosophy, and mathematics. Other college-based ambulance volunteer services, such as those from Harvard and Yale, were similarly erudite.

World-famous writers including Ernest Hemingway, e. e. cummings, John Dos Passos, and even Walt Disney were tempered by fire in the American Ambulance Corps. Dos Passos became a Bantam, as did future Hollywood actor John Litel. (John had 215 screen credits, including

*Jezebel* [1938] with Bette Davis and Henry Fonda.) He and Ralph made runs together far more dramatic than any movie Litel ever made.

The US World War I Ambulance Corps was one of the most highly educated organizations in military history.

Ralph was thrilled to be part of the Princeton squad. It was an honor. They, too, were happy to have someone older and brawnier, replete with medical experience.

By joining the Bantam Boys Ralph was sure he'd get to France before Germany surrendered. Glory was within reach of his restless clutches.

He gained acceptance into the Bantam fraternity.

They'd become a brotherhood forged in war.

None, however, expected such violent hazing at the hands of *les Boche*. Or the Sarge.

# CHAPTER 2

# Move Out, Lobsters!

*Wednesday, 22 August 1917. Allentown Fairgrounds, Camp Crane, Pennsylvania*

Lieutenant Lyon, a tall, stately, immaculately dressed officer took command of the Bantam Boys. He came adorned with an eccentric New England habit. After shrilly roaring orders at the boys, he would drolly call them "Lobsters." No one dared ask why.

At ten o'clock on the night of August 22nd, the excitement began. Lieutenant Lyon and Sergeant Lee rousted the boys from their sleep. Lyon blew his whistle and bellowed, "Move out, Lobsters!" Every man eagerly packed his scanty gear.

Sergeant Lee lined up the boys and distributed field rations. Drivers hauled the Bantams to the Allentown Depot in old Packard trucks. They boarded a train and arrived in New York City at five the next morning. Jumping on a ferry they later disembarked on Pier #59 at the Chelsea Piers in Manhattan.

Exhausted and hungry from the nonstop trip, the boys opened their Army ration cans. The contents looked like cat food that not even a stray could stomach.

"What the hell is this?" asked a Bantam. Acquainted with haute cuisine, he marched over and fearlessly complained to the Sarge.

The Sarge stuck his knife in the can and then licked it off. He said, "The great Teddy Roosevelt ate this fine cookery in the Spanish American War. Eat it or I'll pound it down your skinny throat!"

The Princeton Bantam Boys

The boys quickly and cleanly emptied their cans. Ralph said to the guy sitting next to him, "I think that was left over from the Spanish American War."

"Mine, too."

The boys then stretched out to take naps on huge cotton bales. Ralph looked around thinking the New York skyline was both imposing and spectacular. He couldn't really comprehend its scope, having never seen a city larger than Cleveland or Detroit. Later that afternoon, Ralph wrote about his first steps onto a world-class luxury liner.

### Thursday, 23 August 1917. R.M.S. Baltic

*We rested an hour on the dock and then boarded the Baltic. I slept most all day.*

> *We are classed second and have fine, comfortable quarters!*
> *The ship is busy taking on cargo.*
> *It is an English boat of the famous White Star Line.*

Ralph's Baltic pass

The steamship RMS *Baltic* had been an opulent craft before the Great War. At 23,876 tons, she was the largest ship in the world until 1905. She was the third of four ships greater than twenty thousand tons displacement. These ships were referred to as "The Big Four" with the others being the *Celtic*, *Cedric*, and *Adriatic*. The *Baltic* had just brought the controversial commander of the AEF, General John "Black Jack" Pershing, to Europe in a secret May 1917 convoy. Pershing, thought to be a scoundrel by some staff officers, had the audacity to champion the role of African-American soldiers in the US Army.

On the *Baltic*, Ralph was berthed on a ship he could never have afforded. His room was #249, Deck E, Berth 2. Ralph's admission pass was printed: KEEP THIS CARD. Being the good soldier, he kept it for one hundred years.

Like a kid at a circus, he ran around the ship and continued writing about his discoveries:

*The Vaterland [a huge German liner seized in 1917 and renamed US troop ship SS Leviathan] is moored across the bay.*
*We have a base hospital unit and 1700 AEF Aviation and Signal Corps men on board. Some [civilian] passengers are on the boat, too.*

*The cargo is mainly comprised of grain and cotton.*
*There are twelve howitzers on deck which go to Russia. They*
*weigh 36,000 lbs apiece and are powerful eight inch guns.*

The Bantam Boys settled in for the cruise as if it was old hat. For the really rich boys it *was* nothing new. At first, some of them made it known to Ralph and other "late-comers" that being part of *Princeton* meant something big. These few "New Jersey Nutballs," as Ralph referred to them, had snobbery down to an art.

Occasional put-downs were quietly tossed at Ralph's "quaint" southern Ohio drawl. One of his most famous sayings was, "You 'shore' look bad, boy." He would say "shore" for "sure," "git" for "get," and various and sundry midwestern butcheries of the King's English. It was fingernails on a blackboard for some of the Nutballs.

Ralph didn't fret long about their highbrow comments. He had an ace of clubs up his big sleeve: eighteen years of farm work. He was in superior physical condition. His family ate little meat, piled on the vegetables, and didn't take to alcohol. Tobacco and gambling were verboten. Growing up, Ralph would have to toss heavy hay bales into a loft. Running three miles to class through the rain and snow was just an average day. To privileged Bantams, Ralph's life was pitiable.

Ralph watched some Bantams struggle through exercises that weren't terribly strenuous for him. The Sarge conducted bouts of onboard physical training, known as "PT." He ran the boys down decks, and demanded hundreds of push-ups and pull-ups: the latter using overhead support beams. Pull-ups left weaker boys hanging from beams like despondent chimpanzees struggling on metal tree limbs.

Ralph snickered when they ended an afternoon PT. He reminded the worn-out minions that wealth did not procure strength, endurance, *or* eminence.

The only response mustered were a few Bronx cheers aimed in his direction.

Later, the snobs shook Ralph's hand as an equal when he beat the five biggest Bantams in consecutive wrestling matches. Only one man did not get pinned to the deck. Wagers placed on the outcomes led to Ralph's pockets being lined with coins. He had neglected to mention that he had been a YMCA heavyweight champion.

Ralph slept often, ate gluttonously, and strolled leisurely as if on vacation. He gorged on ample meat and fish. He ate anything the servers tossed in front of him. There wasn't a wasted crust of bread outside of what he took on deck to feed the seagulls.

The *Baltic* finally departed on the 24th at 12:40 p.m. An enormous "Hurrah!" erupted from the ship's voyagers. Everyone watched from the railings as "The City" slipped by. Ralph Heller sailed for his first time—outside of a leaky rowboat or a two-man canoe on the Muskingum River. That night he wrote about the ship's exodus.

### Friday, 24 August 1917. Onboard R.M.S. Baltic, New York Harbor

*The sea is smooth and sailing is good. We passed the Statue of Liberty and soon got out of sight of land.*

*We saw one battleship and several cruisers.*

*So far I have not been sea sick. All lights were put out on board.*

*The pulsating of the engines can be felt below.*

*The sea breeze is inspiring.*

*Now I'm tired and ending a perfect day with some sleep.*

Days later, things were not so perfect. Ralph awoke sick. He wrote that he felt like "he had eaten hardtack" (a notoriously indigestible army biscuit). He scurried outside for some fresh air. The ventilation system apparently emitted some type of petroleum fumes, fuel particulates or possibly carbon monoxide. Every boy in second class suffered from nausea and dizziness. The verdict was the *Baltic* suffered from wartime overuse and poor maintenance.

At breakfast Ralph suddenly went pure white. After barely downing his oatmeal, he flew out of his seat bowling over anyone in his way. At the nearest outer railing he bent over and "fed the fishes." Looking around he wasn't alone. The rail was draped with soldiers and they weren't marveling at the waves. Atlantic cod dined well that morning. Some tried napping on deck to "get some air."

That afternoon the boys lingered on deck with plenty of time on their hands and fresh oxygen in their lungs. Many soon lost money shooting craps or playing poker. Ralph spent hours walking around the decks and searching the waves for whales and porpoises. He found some. One dolphin jumped out of the water and nearly gave him a heart attack. He thought it was a German torpedo and he screamed like a schoolgirl. Fortunately none of the boys heard him.

Later that day a stalwart Bantam asked Lieutenant Lyon, "Sir, how are we going to talk to them Frenchies? These phrase books aren't much help." (They received small paper booklets containing French expressions. But no clear pronunciation guide.)

It was a good question. Lyon didn't know if any of the boys spoke French. He gathered the Bantams on the forecastle and asked, "Any of you Lobsters know French?"

Jack Stearns raised his hand. As a short, professor-in-the making, he frequently boasted about his intellectual aptitude. He told Lieutenant Lyon he'd taken language courses. Jack did not, however, reveal his training or designate which languages he had studied. But he was able to say, "*Oui*" and "*Non*." And spell them correctly.

Bingo! That was good enough for Lyon. Jack was now officially qualified to be headmaster of the French maritime language school. Because of its expected utility, practicing French became a popular Bantam shipboard activity. At the first class Jack said to his students, "You be talking French before ya know it."

It was not exactly so.

Under Jack's tutelage, the boys learned to murder the language so expertly that a Frenchman's ears would have bled. They did acquire some vocabulary. For a well-attended class, a British deckhand provided French curse words he'd learnt in Marseilles. Eventually, with pronunciation assistance provided by a French civilian passenger, Jack's lessons taught actual argot. Most boys gained some minimal competence.

The *Baltic* steamed toward Halifax, Nova Scotia, Canada. Arriving safely, the ship anchored in its protected harbor. The Bantams were released like a pack of amorous wolves on shore leave. What happened when they hit dry land is unclear. Unit lore has it that this was a foray from which the local pubs would need international aid to recover.

After that raucous episode the boys were sequestered onboard the *Baltic* until the convoy launched. Impound was dictated by an infuriated

Sarge Lee. Relegated to captive status onboard the *Baltic*, the Bantams fashioned their own entertainments.

Ralph explored navy life. He knew nothing about large ships. A mid-level naval officer willingly gave him lessons on British maritime warfare tactics. He told Ralph that convoys were the main defense against German submarines. Their name was derived from the abbreviation of *Unterseeboot* or underwater boat. U-boot was anglicized to U-boat. The Huns commissioned 375 U-boats of thirty-three different types during the war.

One of the most commonly produced types was the U-93. Twenty-four were manufactured, each seventy-one meters long and displacing one thousand tons. Each U-93 contained sixteen torpedoes in fore and aft tubes with a 105mm deck gun. Prior to convoys, the deck gun was used to sink ships. The submarine surfaced and fired at unarmed merchant ships. Later, when facing destroyers, the subs relied on torpedoes launched underwater to avoid detection. Despite malfunctions, torpedoes were generally rated as effective.

The naval officer told Ralph, "No ship sails alone." The March sinking of five unescorted American merchant ships, which brought America into the war, illustrated the vulnerability of a single craft.

Destroyers and navy escort ships protected convoys on their way to Europe. American and British navy ships frequently worked together as a shield. This tactic discouraged ambushes and massed "wolf pack" sub attacks.

Allied shipping losses decreased substantially from 1915 to 1917. No ship, however, was immune. The *Baltic* had two prior attacks. She was a prime target for Hun torpedoes due to her prestige and transport capabilities.

Rumor had it that the Kaiser ordered her to be sunk. That gossip gave the British officer a peculiar sense of pride. Ralph didn't share that same sense as he pictured himself floating in the ocean watching the *Baltic* sink like the *Titanic*.

Coordinating large maritime convoys took time. The officer told Ralph to sit back and enjoy the scenery. They weren't going anywhere anytime soon.

Back on the second class deck, the fresh salt air and too many hours on their hands invigorated the boys toward mischief. On one supremely notable evening, a grand fête was ignited by illegal corn hooch smuggled on board by sympathetic British crew members. The boys coaxed Ralph into drinking his share. He knew it was a mistake.

Empty booze bottles were filled with slips of paper containing names, relative wealth, and pleas for female companionship. Re-corked, they bobbed in Halifax bay. Singing, akin to the sound of the mass strangling of felines, infused the brisk night air. It carried on until late evening. The impromptu celebration was wholly unappreciated by Sarge Lee. As a longtime man of the military, however, he knew not to confront men when they were smashed. He would smash them when they were sober.

With a smile and nod, Lieutenant Lyon gave the Sarge control of the situation. "Sir, I promise to teach them boys a lesson," said the Sarge.

Lyon folded his hands and said, "Try not to kill anyone."

The Sarge lounged in his quarters smoking cigars and dreaming up devious and sundry cruelties to inflict on the "college knot-heads." The next morning, he corralled his herd of bleary-eyed, unshaven Bantam ruffians. Ralph, not used to drinking, was in rough shape. Looking at the railing, he considered throwing himself overboard to end his agony.

With a smug grin, the Sarge raced the boys up and down the decks. A few hundred push-ups and sit-ups were on the agenda as well. The whole time the queasy boys panted more feverishly than a pack of rabid skunks.

Near the end of the fun and games Sarge Lee yelled, "It's lunch time!"

Ever the humanitarian, the Sarge topped off the morning with specially ordered rye bread sandwiches of butter, limburger, and onion. As the boys choked down their "sangwiches," the Sarge lectured them. "Soldiers need to maintain high standards at all times. Men control their alcohol not vice versa . . . blah, blah, blah."

His head thundering, Ralph rushed to the railing and threw up. He was grateful for another opportunity to nourish the local marine life.

A compassionate but amused woman peered from the superstructure above. She tossed clean cotton towels down to the Bantams. Ralph picked one up to wipe his face.

Seeing the white towel gave the Sarge another stellar idea. Since the boys smelled of rotten tripe, he thought a freshening-up was overdue. The

Sarge grabbed a saltwater fire hose. He took aim and tidied the rabble nicely.

The cold water nearly paralyzed Ralph. The blast left the deck sparkling clean as well.

"Well done!" yelled the Sarge. "Go lay under your rocks, worms!"

Drenched from face to foot, their egos flushed out the scuppers, the Bantam Boys wearily slogged off to eight hours of lock-down in their musty cabins.

Several quiet days later, the *Baltic*'s engines roared to life.

## CHAPTER 3

# Those Devious Huns

On September 2, 1917, the German *Luftstreitkräfte* treated London to its first moonlight air raid via Gotha aeroplanes. The raid caused 152 deaths, 130 of which were naval recruits in a dormitory that received a direct hit. It was the worst single bombing incident of the war. Rigid airships, known as zeppelins, raided England fifty-two times starting in 1915. High explosives and incendiary devices killed over five hundred people in these attacks.

British civilians had entered the Great War en masse. Two hundred and thirty would die on September 3, 1917, in Kent. On the 4th, a German submarine shelled Scarborough on the English coast. "Fortress Britain," a safe and secure island, espoused by so many Ministers of Parliament before 1915, didn't exist as the Bantam Boys steamed toward Liverpool.

### *Wednesday, 5 September 1917. Onboard RMS* Baltic, *North Atlantic Ocean*

Sleek, low-built US Navy Caldwell class destroyers darted about the *Baltic* convoy with the liveliness of mad hornets. Armed with four-inch Mark 9 guns, twelve-by-twenty-one-inch torpedo tubes, and Type D depth charges, they were primed to obliterate any suspicious sighting.

The destroyers joined the *Baltic* at 4:30 in the morning. They terrified everyone by sunrise greetings via salvos off their Mark 9s. The blasts caused Ralph's new buddy, Bill McClenaghan, a lanky and cranky little rascal, to nearly decapitate himself. Bill launched out of his bunk half asleep and dashed headlong into a hardened steel crossbeam. Smelling salts revived him. The moniker "Bonehead Bill" stuck until landfall.

Ralph took solace in seeing the sturdy destroyers and hearing their engines' "throbbing little hearts." Their collections of fierce weaponry, quick acceleration, and Stars and Stripes flags between their smoking funnels made an obvious impression.

As an indispensable ship, the *Baltic* steamed in the middle-forward position of the floating array. She was shielded by nearly a dozen "expendable" transport vessels. In a worst-case scenario, the outer ships were to sacrifice themselves. They were to ram U-boats if the opportunity presented itself, especially if destroyers were out of attack range.

As the convoy proceeded, the *Baltic* left slower ships behind. Higher speeds diminished the possibility of detection by prowling German submarines. Submerged U-boats were slow and nearly immobile compared to the *Baltic's* maximum sixteen knots (eighteen miles per hour). This was also faster than many of the accompanying military transports.

The crew informed the boys that should *any* ship get torpedoed, including the *Baltic*, unarmed ships would not pause to rescue them. Passengers and crew were on their own. To stop only gave the Huns a second target. Therefore, *everyone* was expendable. Ralph was not comforted by the thought that he was now a number—not a man.

Given the danger, the Bantams were issued bulky life vests and assigned a specific lifeboat adjacent to their sleeping quarters. English salts coached the boys on how to set out and release the boats should the ship develop a list. They practiced until each boat crew could do it safely. These boats had survival provisions including water for forty-eight hours. Ralph considered it just enough kit to add a few extra days of suffering in an otherwise miserable demise.

As the lengthening convoy plowed northward on its nine-day trip, the weather deteriorated. The varnished mahogany deck of the *Baltic* heaved underfoot. A strong wind slapped the faces of seasick Bantams. To reduce his misery, Ralph tried to focus on the horizon. It didn't help.

While suffering through their "green about the gills" sightseeing tours on deck, the boys were told to search the sea for telltale signs of German compressed air torpedoes. They'd resemble white streaks heading toward them. With a large ship like the *Baltic*, they'd likely be fired in pairs for a greater probability of hitting the target. Ralph couldn't understand how the Huns could fire a "torp" in such a maelstrom. But he looked for them anyway.

In the capricious north Atlantic, high winds and waves assaulted the ships. Rain came in torrents. Unknown to all, a hurricane born on August 30th in the Caribbean raced up the Gulf Stream to ensnare them. Gusts clocked in at 105 miles per hour.

When the storm hit the ship, the Bantam Boys could barely navigate their vomit-strewn corridors. Some tied themselves in bed with their sheets. A few others, uncontrollably sick or borderline insane, lashed themselves with belts to the outside handrails when the cabin mess and smell became intolerable. Any misstep could cause them to be swept overboard.

Ominous creaks and groans led to talk that the great *Baltic* could break up. To be drowned by a monster storm was something Ralph had never considered.

The land-loving Bantams endured the dreadful ride. Booze could not even provide relief because nobody could keep it down long enough to absorb it. More than a few bruises were raised and every stomach turned. The worst injury among the boys was when Bill took a tumble and kissed yet another well-engineered support beam. Fortunately, neither the storm nor Bill's head caused any fatal structural damage on the *Baltic*. The winds departed as quickly as they arrived. The sea calmed. The boys cleaned up and swabbed their barf-blemished decks.

Land pierced the horizon. Ralph's mood grew brighter. He hoped they had a few days of calm to recover from the debilitating seasickness. As he shook off his queasy condition, he vowed never to become a sailor.

### *Friday, 14 September 1917. Off the coast of Wales, United Kingdom*

Ralph woke up at 5:00 a.m. local time to a clamor on deck. He hurried up a dark flight of stairs, worrying an enemy sub had been spotted. He remembered to take his worn, moldy life vest. He thought its utter uselessness would provide a good laugh as he was drowning amid the *Baltic*'s flotsam and jetsam.

Arriving on deck, Ralph caught his first glance of a British Coast Guard dirigible or blimp. It sailed directly overhead, visible by the early light and departing stars. The outline of the Welsh coast poked up in the distance. He had never seen such a large airship. It was the shape of a Cuban cigar sufficient for a five-hundred-foot-tall Sarge Lee.

Ralph had read about the aircraft and had seen pictures of a German zeppelin. Until now, he never knew how big they could be. He was like a kid watching his first trapeze artist. He thought about possibly joining the flying corps.

As the sun came up, the green coast of Wales spread across the horizon. The *Baltic* neared Liverpool, England. Captivated by the vision, Ralph took in surprising new things to see. Another Brit dirigible was off in the distance standing watch for subs. The destroyers lagged the convoy. The crew laughed more than usual. Ralph believed the threat from U-boats was now over. Another Bantam joined Ralph outside on that leisurely September morning.

Ralph wrote what happened next:

*Lloyd Haupt and I went over the port side of the boat. We had remarked that all danger must be past as we watched a beacon light winking its one red and one white eye at us.*

*Then our attention was drawn to the phosphorus lights [from algae] in the water. I looked up again and the [beacon] light had changed position.*

*I thought it was another and I told Lloyd, "There's another of the lights."*

*He said, "It's the same one," and that we had swung around.*

*"And Lad, look at her swinging now," he added.*

The crown jewel of the British White Star Line, *RMS Baltic*, launched into evasive tactics. The captain set the engines to full speed. He then engaged the rudder to ninety degrees, a very dangerous move. The ship took a hard right turn toward the Welsh shallows with its adjacent jagged landfall. A desperate measure for a massive ship, the *Baltic* could not be righted quickly. Then it happened.

*Boom!*

Ralph and Lloyd "the Lover" Haupt, an always dapper young man who prowled for women like a hungry tiger after prey, heard a deafening noise. It emanated from the opposite side of the ship. They grabbed each other out of reflex. Everyone around them ran toward the starboard railing in the direction of the blast. Ralph pushed away from Lloyd and they were off and running. Arms flailing and Lloyd trailing, they rushed to the opposite rail. Ralph described what he saw when he got there:

> *A rocket and a shot or two from one of the destroyer's main guns showed that spotting subs was guesswork no longer. We were under attack.*
>
> *Three destroyers collected in a spot and circled around it, darting here and there at incredible speed.*
>
> *One started to veil us with smoke but soon stopped. It seemed to hesitate a minute then made a direct beeline towards us. And Lord how she came!*
>
> *She had covered about half of the distance between us when something happened. There was an immense explosion.*
>
> *The ship [Baltic] rocked and vibrated but did not seem to be as loud as I expected a torpedo. The Baltic herself was cutting all sorts of gymnastics.*
>
> *I thought we were badly hit and so did everyone else. The whistle started to blow. Three short blasts and then one long drawn out tremulous one rolled over the deck.*

Ralph saw the crew uncovering lifeboats. He knew that was a very bad sign. "Let's go!" he said.

The pair double-timed it toward their lifeboat station. In the turmoil, however, they got lost. Not sure what to do, Ralph climbed over a railing for a look. He spied Bantam Boys about thirty meters away down the deck. That's where they needed to be.

Ralph jumped off the rail as a crewman sped by. He long-armed the sailor and asked him, "Are we hit?"

The Englishman said, "Yea. In the arse! Get moving ya bloody fool!" The sailor dashed off into a throng of frightened passengers.

Ralph and Lloyd high-tailed down the deck. They barely avoided trampling confused passengers. Ralph was relieved when they "slid into home." The run only took seconds but seemed like one of the longest of his life. He wrote about the sheer uncertainty of the moment:

> *The Baltic stopped and then suddenly proceeded at full speed. We did not know what was going on. But she sure did go.*
>
> *Blowing black clouds of smoke and flaming embers out of her old funnels, she sure did do herself justice. She didn't zigzag either.*
>
> *She was only bent on one thing: to get as many miles between her and that spot as possible.*

Blasts from the destroyer's main guns stoked the fire of disorder onboard the *Baltic*.

*Blam! Whoosh. Splash!*

Shells lofted into the sea at near point-blank range.

Hundreds of passengers struggled to find their assigned lifeboats. Many looked completely lost—sheep without a shepherd. Then all eyes focused on one of the nearby destroyers as a shock wave hefted the destroyer's stern out of the water. It looked as though the unfortunate ship took a direct hit.

*Boom!*

Then another huge blast occurred right after that one. *Boom!*

Massive geysers of water splashed all around the destroyer. Ralph thought those navy boys were doomed.

A civilian on an upper deck screeched, "Torpedoes!"

Unfamiliar with the nature of anti-submarine warfare, the *Baltic's* passengers believed depth charges dropped by the destroyer were torpedo strikes. Three-hundred- or six-hundred-pound canisters of TNT (the chemical compound TriNitroToluene) or amatol (TNT with ammonium nitrate) rolled off the back of the American destroyers. The barrels sank and exploded at various pre-determined depths. The blast sent plumes of water into the air like the Old Faithful geyser in Yellowstone Park.

A U-boat in the blast radius would be destroyed by a hull breach. Outside the death zone, shock waves were strong enough to disable or sink a sub through damage to critical control systems. Even beyond the effective range, a U-boat crew was in for a frightening, tension-filled roller coaster ride they'd never forget.

The stark array of depth charge detonations made it look as if the entire convoy was under attack by a horde of U-boats. The *Baltic*'s jumpy crew screamed orders to ready the lifeboats. The Bantam Boys donned their gear and extra clothing if they had it. They snugged into their life vests. Ralph's chest strap broke as he pulled it tight. *Dammit! Not now,* he thought. The only consolation in his mind was that he was a decent swimmer. What he didn't know is that it wouldn't be much help in the cold, current-raked straits. Few swimmers could survive such an expanse this time of year.

The boys prepared to swing out their lifeboats. The boat suddenly looked remarkably tiny to Ralph. Land, however, was in sight. It wasn't far.

Some of the Bantam Boys were on the Princeton rowing team. They felt they could easily row to land.

"And have a bloody good time doing it! A cake walk boys!" somebody yelled. They encouraged each other and dared to make bets on who would get there first.

Ralph liked the enthusiasm, but he knew this wouldn't be an intramural race on a calm, picturesque American river. People might drown. People might die of exposure. He might be one of them.

The Sarge walked confidently among the boys. He made sure their life preservers were cinched. Once finished, he took out a cigar and lit it. He took a puff and said, "I'll shoot the first dumb bastard that drowns!"

Ralph wondered if he heard him right. A few crossways smiles perked up. Ralph thought, *The Sarge made a joke! The bastard was human after all.*

Tense minutes passed as depth charges and naval gun shells raked the ocean. The boys nervously checked and rechecked each other's boats for provisions and paddles. Ralph tied the broken ends of his straps together in a hopeless granny knot so it wouldn't unwind. As he did so, the rowing team coxswain started barking the Princeton fight song:

> *And then we'll crash through that line of blue,*
> *And send the backs on 'round the end!*

Others boys united in the growing volume and emotion:

*Fight, fight for ev'ry yard, Princeton's honor to defend.*

All the Bantam Boys strained their vocal cords:

*Rah! Rah! Rah! Rah! Tiger sis boom bah!*

The whole side of their ship joined in:

*Rah! Rah! Rah! Rah! Tiger sis boom bah!*

It was as if they were in the greatest game Princeton University ever fought. Pungent gun cotton and cordite stench flushed from the destroyers' main guns blanketed the *Baltic*. Ocean water splashed into great columns all around. The Bantam Boys and the impassioned travelers sang their best and braced for the worst.

They had to win this one.

*Rah! Rah! Rah! Rah! Tiger sis boom bah!*

Ralph found the moment curiously exciting. Huns were trying to kill him. He was enjoying the moment. It was like the thrill of a mountaineering party getting swept away by an avalanche. And living to tell the tale.

Concentrated naval fire added fuel to the tumult. A shell skipped across the water to within fifty feet of their ship and sank. The *Baltic's* survival appeared in doubt. Some boys prayed. They were convinced God was on America's side.

Minutes passed. Eventually the ruckus quieted down. Singing faded away in the stillness. Ralph could almost hear his heart beating.

The "big one" hadn't found its mark. Ralph didn't know how long the wait lasted. From sheer nervous exhaustion the Bantams relaxed.

Not knowing what else to say, Ralph joked, "Those Huns shore are lousy shots."

A few of the Bantams directed funny looks at Ralph.

"That ain't no jinx," Ralph added.

Bill asked no one in particular, "Why do we call them Huns?"

Jack Stearns had the answer to Bill's question. He always had an answer whether it was true or not. This time he was correct. Jack said the origin of "Hun was an interesting lesson in political faux pas. During a state speech, in an especially daft historical analogy, the Kaiser compared German shock troops to the forces of Attila the Hun. It wasn't amongst the best public relations efforts. The jolly old Huns had reputations as cruel, murderous, frenzied invaders."

In short, Jack said the English insult *Huns* stuck to the Germans like cement overshoes. Occasionally, the British would use the name "Fritz." But *Hun* was so much more descriptive.

Jack continued his lecture despite the inattention of his audience. "In contrast, Frenchies prefer the long held Franco slur—*Boche*. Translated to English," he said, "Boche meant: *Ugly little cabbage-munching blockheaded assholes*. French is a colorful language."

As the boys started falling asleep during Jack's political science sermon, Lieutenant Lyon arrived. He said, "Men, I am very pleased to tell you that the depth bombs which your brave comrades discharged sunk those devious Huns. And at the same time caused the explosion which we mistook for a torpedo. We are absolutely untouched!"

Cheers welled up from the Bantam Boys. They shook each other's hands and slapped each other's backsides. Lloyd smoothed his usually perfect hair. Everyone grabbed each other's hands and held their arms up in a victory celebration.

*Tiger sis boom bah!*

Their first real taste of combat was in the bag with no bloodshed. Even Bonehead Bill hadn't crowned himself anew on a bulkhead. The boys were ordered to stand down. They methodically stowed their emergency gear for the last time. The entire ship seemed to sigh with relief.

Within hours the ship docked. Safe on land, Ralph resumed writing the next night with an unsteady hand:

*Saturday, 15 September 1917. Liverpool, England*

*We hear that a ship [they left behind] was sunk today.*

*The morning found us ready to cross the plank and we landed in Liverpool at noon. I slept till four o'clock AM and then got to thinking about our adventure and couldn't sleep any longer.*

*We boarded the little playhouse train and started for South Hampton. Back at Liverpool, we saw several shiploads of Canadians and some Coolie [Chinese] troops headed for the Front.*

*We were unable to get details of last night's adventure. Some say that we got torpedoed. But if we were, the torpedo failed in some way. They say we got the sub.*

What really happened to the *Baltic* that day will never be known. Later published accounts will note this as the most potentially lethal encounter of the war for the White Star ship. German Navy records, however, show no U-boat operating in the area that week. Documents from the era are often incomplete. It is also possible that the Germans did not want to admit to an attack on another liner after having sunk the *Lusitania* in 1915. The loss of the *Lusitania* and 1,198 passengers and crew, including 128 Americans, was part of the reason the United States entered the war against them.

The best explanation for the incident may be that anxious American gunners assassinated a pod of inquisitive dolphins. Alternatively, the *Baltic* may have set off a British magnetic mine or been buffeted by a rogue depth charge.

All the maritime drama was for naught. Tons of ordnance had been expended and no U-boat had been confirmed sunk. Ralph never saw a debris field or the oil slick that usually accompanies a hull breach.

Regardless of the origin of the fracas, Ralph had begun to change. Reality began to take hold. This excursion was no longer a mere vacation.

It wasn't an amusing episode of boyhood fun.

He realized that this journey, for some Bantam Boys, could have no return.

# CHAPTER 4

# Where's the Stupid War?

*Saturday, 22 September 1917. Le Havre, France*

The Lobsters shipped from England to the French coast at Le Havre without molestation from Hun submarines. The nag steamer, the *Antrim*, brought them across the English Channel. The old workhorse was more akin to a garbage scow than a troopship. *Baltic*'s luxury had spoiled the boys.

Ralph was more concerned about the *Antrim* breaking apart than getting hit with Boche torpedoes. "The Huns wouldn't waste a bullet on her," he said.

Fortunately, the trip was short. Channel winds were calm. Two destroyers and a cruiser escorted them over a smooth sea. None became seasick.

Ralph had some spirited conversations with British and Australian troops onboard. He became a "Mate" with an amiable Londoner and swapped an American nickel for an English copper penny the size of a half-dollar. He felt he got the better deal for the massive coin. For good luck, Ralph stowed his penny next to the rabbit's foot in his blouse pocket.

Le Havre was a huge, industrious port. Vast arrays of Allied cargo lay on worn docks. Any manufactured item in the Western world could be found there. Most of these containers, however, were filled with the machinery and materials of war, millions of dollars, francs, and pounds spent in the pursuit of death.

Allied soldiers disembarked from troopships. The Brits looked like lines of khaki ants. As they marched toward town, they were bombarded with flowers and hit with the strained cheers of toothless old men and breathless young mademoiselles. Wine bottles were enthusiastically passed around even though beer was their drink. Soldiers endured wet smooches from the "lasses" for the sake of international harmony.

Upon docking, the Bantam Boys broke a "heavy sweat unloading that smelly, infernal hold" of the *Antrim*. They pulled equipment from the ship's bowels for hours. Despite the toil, it didn't seem like they made a dent in the sizable cargo. Once they recovered all their personal gear, they were abruptly sent off the ship. Ralph was happy to leave but wondered why the quick exit. Many tons of crates were still onboard.

He got an answer. The port authority didn't want any able-bodied soldiers blown up unloading the thousands of artillery shells from the lower level. That was a job for nonessential men: those who could not fight on the front. Many of these men were older or minorities from French colonies such as Indochina. Ralph realized that if the *Antrim* had been torpedoed, he would have "gone out in style" in a bright fireworks display courtesy of over five thousand HE (high explosive) and shrapnel shells.

Sarge Lee chanted cadence like a professional as the Bantams marched several miles across the hectic city of Le Havre:

*March along, sing our song, with the Army of the free.*
*Count the brave, count the true, who have fought to victory.*
*We're the Army and proud of our name!*

The boys refrained:

*Then it's hi! hi! hey!*
*The Army's on its way.*
*Count off the cadence loud and strong!*

Pelted with flower petals and plied with *le vin* by appreciative Frenchies, no one turned down a drink. The Sarge looked the other way. The boys had had no food since the day before. Wine was better than nothing. Even Ralph took big swigs. With all the flattering attention he felt heroic. *This is the life!* he thought. *Maybe I'll make the Army Medical Corps my career!*

The dauntless Bantam stevedores finally boarded third class rail cars. The boys were taken aback; it was as bad as the *Antrim*. The decrepit train looked as if it hadn't been cleaned since the invention of rail travel.

Bill carped, "What a shit hole."

Sarge Lee gritted his teeth. "You boys would have complained if the Queen of England herself had come down to Liverpool and fucked every one of you!"

Jack said, "I heard she's not so good looking."

Lieutenant Lyon accounted for all his Lobsters onboard. None had been stolen away by enamored Frenchie lasses. The boys policed up their areas as best they could and laid down for snoozes. Sleep was the best option since there was no dining car attached or provisions on board, including water.

Ralph said, "Even cattle get water."

The old and ailing train pulled out of the crowded station at a snail's pace. It stopped every twenty to thirty minutes in a painfully slow trek to locations unknown. Much to their ire, the train would jerk them awake when it gruffly restarted for its next undisclosed destination.

The creaking, poorly greased wheels underneath the carriage made it difficult for Ralph to fall asleep. He counted the rhythmic wheel gyrations as if counting sheep. Belly growling and thirsty, he soon fell into a well-deserved but erratic slumber.

Despite their fatigue, not everyone went to sleep. Since Lieutenant Lyon and Sarge Lee were forward in slightly more comfortable second class cars, the Bantams were without parental oversight. Hungry boys get resourceful. Taking advantage of the measly walking speed of the train, they sneaked off when they spied a small town coming up the rail line. Running like banshees, they dashed in any open shop they could find. Huffing and puffing, they threw American money on the counters. French shopkeepers threw broad smiles and open arms right back at them.

Over the next hours the boys gathered bread, cheese, and strips of dried ham or prosciutto. As they soon learned, no French meal was complete without wine. They purchased, or were given free of charge, enough red wine for a brigade. Despite the war, France had no shortage of *le vin* and the grateful Frenchies readily shared it with *les Américains*. No sensible man turned down free wine.

Bill scurried to the rail car with an armload of wine. He had never run that hard during physical training. And he didn't break a single bottle. Divvying up the load, the boys pulled the corks with their teeth or dug them out with pocket knives. Someone spit out pieces of cork from a poorly opened bottle. This inspired act evolved into a game of who could "Hock the Cork the Farthest." Bets were wagered. Money passed hands.

Since most French towns had more wine shops than churches, empty bottles were soon replaced by new. So many bottles appeared the boys lost count—not that they were trying to remember. To the French vintners' credit, all thought it was "damn good." Despite buying commendable food as well, their cheese and bread stocks were insufficient to soak up this volume of wine. Nobody complained.

Feeling inspired by Bacchus, piano player Lev "The Larcenist" Hoffman, a slick and calculating guy, and his harmonious friends were in the mood for some music. They clumsily formed into a circle in the compartment forward of Ralph. Lev and his "Highbrow Lowlife Singing Sensations" decided to put on a little concert. They set the stage by poorly crooning the smuttiest songs they could remember:

*Oh, Mademoiselle from Armentieres, parley-vous?*
*Oh, Mademoiselle from Armentieres, parley-vous?*
*You didn't have to know her long, to know the reason men go wrong!*
*Hinky-dinky, parlez-vous.*
*She's the hardest working girl in town, but she makes her living upside down!*
*Hinky-dinky parlez-vous!*

Their lyrical recall was notable. Had they put that much effort into their studies at Princeton, all would be straight-A students. The blue caterwauling went on for quite a time, much to the consternation of those trying to sleep. When the Lowlifes ran out of pornographic melodies, they composed bawdy new ballads on the spot:

*Oh the wench was hot but her face was not, I stuck her head in a great big pot!*
*Hinky-dinky, parlez-vous.*
*The pot fell down and broke my crown; I danced around like a crazy clown!*
*Hinky-dinky, parlez-vous!*

*I found another but she looked like my mother; I went back and mated with*
*the other!*
*Hinky-dinky, parlez-vous!*
*When I was done, I had to run; here came her brother with a great big gun!*
*Hinky-dinky, parlez-vous!*

It was as if a regiment of tactless music majors had gone hormonal. Lev and his hoodlums free-associated lewd musical selections for what seemed like hours. Sleep was nearly impossible for the weary non-participants.

An anonymous voice echoed through the car, "Shut the hell up!"

Simmering down, several of the Lowlifes grabbed poetry books. They quietly read their favorite selections aloud. This quickly degenerated into a literary duel. Back and forth they went. Louder and louder it grew. The boys sounded like a crowd at a boxing match featuring Emily Dickinson versus Walt Whitman.

"Shhh . . . quiet down boys," Lev soon said. "Dickinson beat Whitman. She smote his Longfellow."

Hearty laughs spewed out of the drunks—along with wine from their noses.

By then Ralph had had enough. He sat up and pounded on a seat. "You loudmouths are shore lookin' to git whooped." Ralph then stuffed his extra pair of socks in his ears and tried to go back to sleep.

The Lowlifes quieted down to a hearty giggle for a few minutes. Then somehow another squabble ignited. A political dispute followed after someone innocently asked, "How did the war start?"

After several misguided attempts at wisdom, Lev put up his arms to quiet his Lowlifes. "Shhh. . . ." He slurred, "I got the real dope on this here war. It's them Royals. Gotta marry their sisters! Unnatural, I say!"

"Hear, hear!" The gang pounded on the seats, whooping like spider monkeys.

Ralph sat straight up and said, "You shore need to pipe down!"

Lev snottily said, "Speak English, Heller!"

The civilizing dam broke and a wave of caste wrath flowed forth. Ralph leapt up. The train needed cleaning and he was a broom. A general roughhouse erupted with Ralph introducing his fist to Lev's chin. Punches flew. Gear fell into a jumble around them.

Alexis "Smart Alex" Kirkjian, a brilliant but small quiet type, tried to avoid the flood of fists. Quicker than a cowboy escaping Indians, he jumped for a window but slipped. Bill was able to cuff Alex as he somersaulted out of the window and nearly tumbled under the train wheels. A moment of panic froze the melee. Boys scurried over to help Bill reel in Alex. Everyone took a breath and lowered their dukes.

"Not so smart, Alex," Ralph said. "Now y'all go to bed before somebody really gets it."

The boys scattered to make their beds.

As Ralph turned away Lev whispered to Bill, "I coulda beat him."

"Yeah, using your face to punch Ralph's knuckles was brilliant."

Around seven the next morning the train parked itself next to the town of Chartres. As the boys were rousing, someone saw the Sarge on his way back to their car. "Inspection!" shrieked Lev.

They quickly tucked in their uniforms and fled outside. The boys fell in line and pretended to be marveling at the large, ornate cathedral near the Chartres railroad line.

Jack nonchalantly said, "The church is built of stone. They started building it . . ."

The Sarge arrived and said, "Attention!"

The boys snapped to.

Having a supernatural sense of smell for the stink of mischief, the Sarge was immediately suspicious. He closely examined the boys. Some had bruises. Some had swollen eyes.

The squad tried desperately to suppress giggles as the Sarge passed stiffly by. After looking them over, the Sarge laboriously crossed his arms and peered menacingly at a bruise-free Ralph.

The Sarge asked, "Heller, were you chowder heads face-fucking each other again last night?"

Ralph's eyes grew wide. "Uhh . . . Sarge, we don't . . ." He couldn't find the words he needed to a question that had no graceful answer.

Bill squeezed his innards with all his might to avoid bursting out in laughter. He grunted and his eyes reddened under the strain of his bridled amusement.

The Sarge stepped back and shot an angry glance at Bill. "You college goofs don't learn very well, do you?"

Bill kept his bulging eyes pointing straight ahead and his mouth clamped so tight his lips turned blue.

The Sarge shook his head. He continued walking the line. "America's finest cretins! Do I *need* to *read* you the riot act?"

"No Sergeant!" the boys yelled in unison.

The Sarge looked down the line. "I should shoot you dickheads now and save the Huns the trouble. But since you dime store whore baits got so much goddamn energy, give me one hundred push-ups. No . . . make it *three hundred!*"

Everyone groaned.

At six o'clock in the evening the arm-weary Bantams arrived in Le Mans. Ralph found out they were heading west toward the French Loire Atlantic coast, the opposite direction of "The Front." Everyone was disappointed when he told them.

Bill said, "We'll never be a part of this damn war."

They camped in Le Mans until the next morning. The train coaled and the engineer repaired a leaky boiler. After settling sleeping arrangements, they debarked to the city for a decent meal and to sightsee. Ralph described the scene:

### Monday, 24 September 1917. Le Mans, France

*We roamed through the town and spent our pennies. There seemed to be many wild women. All the fellows bought dinner but we ate outside on small tables.*

*A bunch of kids came around begging money and tobacco.*

*A French soldier came up and asked me to drink. I went with him and ordered coffee. It was a bum trade. It was the vilest stuff I ever drank. It was thick as molasses and tasted like condensed whiskey. It made me half sick though I only drank a little. I thought I was being poisoned.*

Ralph left his first cup of primal cappuccino and wandered into the public square. There he talked to several people and to an entertaining, curly-haired child. Ralph wasn't even sure if the kid was male or female. They gibbered at each other. He made up words just for the fun of it. Hand gestures helped the two understand each other.

Ralph found that the children understood him better than the adults. That was until an attractive mademoiselle asked to sit with him. Ralph, the ever-courteous bird, invited her to his perch. She didn't speak much English but was so friendly her body language did most of the talking.

With Ralph's basic French, he eventually determined that she wanted him "to take a hack (carriage) ride with her." He was not sure what to do. He had never been approached in such a forward way. Ralph also thought, *That ain't all she wants.*

First and foremost, Edyth was his girl. When he politely declined her proposition, the little lady got rather upset. Apparently she wasn't used to rejection. Her displeased rebuff needed no translation. Ralph got up and found a more comfortable seat.

Looking around the square once more, he became distressed by the clear lack of able-bodied men. The few males were old, disabled, or foreigners. He later wrote, "Everywhere are crippled soldiers. France is a badly stricken nation. England was worse. There are no fathers."

The Bantam Boys returned to their train. Two days later, on a convoluted trip crossing through many small towns, the boys arrived at a spur near St. Nazaire. This was their jumping off point. It was time for them to get "real ambulance training."

The Bantams quartered in an old inn. Ralph became enamored by the French home cooking. He said the meals there were some of the best he had ever eaten. With a new cot and two new blankets, it was as if he landed a VIP suite at the five-star Le Royal Hotel in Paris. Ralph thought, *Life don't get better than this.*

The next great news was that a boatload, literally, of ambulances had arrived at the docks of St. Nazaire. Cargo lorries were being unloaded at the nearby "auto park." The boys were eager to claim their *"Lizzies"* (short for "Tin Lizzie" also spelled "Tin Lizzy," an early nickname for Ford Model T automobiles).

Everyone scurried down to the park like children running to a Christmas tree. When they got there disappointment overtook them. The ambulances were pancaked in *crates*: lots and *lots* of crates. The partially assembled Ford Model T chassis were skeletons of what they should have been. The boys' ambulances had to be put together like kids' bicycles from a box.

Ambulance beds ready for final assembly

Ralph asked, "What do we do now?"

The Sarge provided the answer. "You goofs are going to work!"

Over the next few days, the Bantam Boys spent their time learning how to be Ford assembly line employees. Some of the well heeled were fuming. They thought they should *own* Ford factories, not *work* there. "Mutiny never was nearer."

Sarge Lee caught wind of their annoyances. He said, "Either punch your time cards boys. Or I'll punch your ugly faces!"

Grasping the Sarge's point of view, everyone picked up wrenches and plastered on smiles. Their shift started. The boys eventually figured out how to outfit the naked frames with parts and mechanisms. French and American mechanics directed the chaos.

The boys rifled through and set out components from myriad wood shipping crates stenciled *Ford Motor Company, Detroit, USA.* Related parts were organized into large parcels. A dozen parcels were packed into each crate. Smaller boxes contained oodles of hardware on the bottom.

"It's a lot to figure out," said Ralph.

The scene was a grand cinematic portrayal of American industry—but not necessarily starring its most delighted workers. Many a knuckle was skinned.

The engines, drive train components, and axle systems on the under-carriages were placed in rows. Smaller parts were strewn about in a semi-organized arrangement around the undercarriages. Truck beds were distributed to each frame as a last step. Bantams wandered among the ambulance ingredients looking no more confident than neophyte cooks in a five-star Paris kitchen. The field was a colossal jigsaw puzzle.

Sarge Lee inspected the boys' progress. At least his goofs were intel-ligent goofs. The ambulances were taking shape, looking how ambulances should look. There seemed to be amazingly few mistakes and no incurable mechanical blunders.

When his ambulance engine actually started up, Ralph got tremen-dously excited. He couldn't wait to drive that machine!

There was, however, a fly in the chauffeur ointment. Few Bantams knew how to drive well, including Ralph. Fewer still, despite family money, personally owned luxury brand automobiles, let alone the inex-pensive Ford Model T.

The wealthiest families had drivers for their posh town cars. Few family members drove themselves. The Princeton boys had been given a "driving test" stateside but "you could pass it as long as you were alive." Driving proficiency wasn't something Ralph thought much about. It was just a matter of "Get in and go!"

No it wasn't.

First off, the boys learned basic truck function and maintenance: Gas—ten gallons. Radiator water—three gallons. Oil—until full. The Model-T engine had many machined surfaces and gaskets. It constantly leaked oil. Henry Ford reportedly said, "If it's not leaking then it must be low on oil."

Drivers continually refilled oil reservoirs. Failing to do so would seize the engine, usually a fatal occurrence for the power plant.

They committed to memory the roughly twenty-eight lubrication points and when to lube. Then they had to learn how to fix simple breakdowns. Seeing the ambulances in pieces gave the boys a working knowledge of the machines. They received instruction on how to diagnose a misfiring engine, repair broken parts, and change spark plugs. Cleaning the carburetor was an ever-necessary chore. Dirt was everywhere and got in everything. Clogging a fuel line would kill an engine.

Ralph found out much "could go wrong or get busted." These were far more complicated than feeding and watering a horse. Building the ambulances turned out to be an outstanding classroom. Most passed mechanical muster.

After all that hot, greasy stuff, it was time to drive. It began as a glorious Ford expedition. It ended as a scene out of the Keystone Kops School of Drivers' Education. The first lesson entailed understanding and memorizing the complicated starting sequence. The Ford Motor Company's Model-T Manual gave detailed instructions on how to start a *Lizzie*.

This is exactly what the Bantam Boys had to do to "fire up" their M1917 ambulances (and this is a shortened edition):

*The engine is started by the lifting of the starting crank at the front of the car. Take hold of the handle and push firmly toward the car till you feel the crank ratchet engage, then lift upward with a quick swing . . .*

*Don't, as a usual thing, crank downward against compression—for then an early explosion may drive the handle vigorously backward. This does not mean however, that it is not advisable, when the car is hard to start, to occasionally "spin" the engine by the use of the starting handle—but be sure the spark lever is retarded when spinning or cranking the engine against compression, otherwise a sudden backfire may injure the arm of the operator. When the engine is cool it is advisable to prime the carburetor by pulling on the small wire at the lower left corner of the radiator while giving the engine two or three quarter turns with the starting handle.*

*First: See that the hand lever, which extends through the floor of the car at the left of the driver, is pulled back as far as it will go. The lever in this position holds the clutch in neutral and engages the hub brake, thus preventing the car moving forward when the engine is started. Second: Insert the switch key into the switch and turn the key as far to the left (counter-clockwise) as it will go.*

*Under the steering wheel are two small levers. The right-hand (throttle) lever controls the amount of mixture (gasoline and air) which goes into the engine. When the engine is in operation, the farther this lever is moved downward toward the driver (referred to as "opening the throttle") the faster the engine runs and the greater the power furnished. The left-hand lever controls the spark, which explodes the gas in the cylinders of the engine. The advancing of this lever "advances the spark," and it should be moved down notch by notch until the motor seems to reach its maximum speed. If the lever is advanced beyond this point a dull knock will be noticed in the engine.*

*The spark lever should usually be put in about the third or fourth notch on the quadrant (the notched half-circle on which the levers operate). The throttle should usually be placed in about the fifth or sixth notch. A little experience will soon teach you where these levers should be placed for proper starting. Care should be taken not to advance the spark lever too far, as the engine may "back kick."*

*When the engine is cold it may be necessary to prime it by pulling out the carburetor priming rod, which is located on the instrument board. In order to avoid flooding the engine with an over rich mixture of gas, the priming rod should only be held out for a few seconds at a time.*

Starting an ambulance was that simple.

After plenty of cranking practice, the boys progressed to open field driving. Having not run over each other for an hour or two, the Sarge lined them up. Crossing his fingers, Lee signaled them to follow him. They took off down a bumpy road. Despite being all over the boulevard, driving like drunks, somehow no one was rammed, slammed, or rear-ended. No livestock or Frenchies became hood ornaments, although a woman carrying a basket of turnips came very close. The boys drove almost an hour.

As the joy ride drew to a close, an ambulance driver lost control and went head down into a deep irrigation ditch. The convoy halted. An irritated Sarge and the rest of the boys walked up to the crash site. Dick Brooke, a big-eyed, tall, fun-loving guy, sat in his car in the watery dike. Slumped over his steering wheel, he looked mortified. Joe Swan, his quiet, thoughtful partner, shook his head as he threw pebbles into the water.

Joe said to Dick, "I told you not to brake so hard."

The Sarge tramped up and surveyed the damage. The front end appeared reasonably intact with only minor recently added imperfections.

Dick sheepishly looked up and said, "Sorry Sarge."

Turning to Dick, the Sarge said, "So what gives, Private Dick?"

"It's Brooke, Sarge. Dick Brooke."

"I know who you are, Penis. Why did you hurt my machine?"

"I had to miss that big dog."

Lee looked around. "What goddamn dog?"

Dick turned back. "That one!" he said pointing at a small black and white calf grazing on the side of the road.

"Okay Wisenheimer, get a tow rope and get your stupid blind eyes checked!"

The Sarge turned to the boys standing on the road. He pointed at Ralph. "Heller, pull your broke Dick out."

Ralph didn't move.

Driving the ambulances took experience. The Ford Model-T Manual had a great deal to say on the subject:

Ralph learns to drive.

*Slightly accelerate the engine by opening the throttle, press the clutch pedal half way forward, thereby holding the clutch in a neutral position while throwing the hand lever forward; then press the pedal forward into slow speed and when under sufficient headway (20 to 30 feet), allow the pedal to drop back slowly into high speed, at the same time partially closing the throttle, which will allow the engine to pick up its load easily. With a little practice, the change of speeds will be easily accomplished, and without any appreciable effect on the smooth running of the machine.*

To stop the ambulance:

*Partially close the throttle; release the high speed by pressing the clutch pedal forward into neutral; apply the foot brake slowly but firmly until the car comes to a dead stop. Do not remove foot from the clutch pedal without first pulling the hand lever back to neutral position, or the engine will stall. To stop the motor, open the throttle a trifle to accelerate the motor and then throw off the switch. The engine will then stop with the cylinders full of explosive gas, which will naturally facilitate starting. Endeavor to so familiarize yourself with the operation of the car that to disengage the clutch and apply the brake becomes practically automatic—the natural thing to do in case of emergency.*

To go in reverse:

*It must be brought to a dead stop. With the engine running, disengage the clutch with the hand lever and press the reverse pedal forward with the left foot, the right foot being free to use on the brake pedal if needed. Do not bring the hand lever back too far or you will set the brakes on the rear wheels. Experienced drivers ordinarily reverse the car by simply holding the clutch pedal in neutral with the left foot, and operating the reverse pedal with the right.*

All this was done on unpaved, muddy, and heavily shelled rural roads. Stalling an ambulance while under fire could get the driver and his wounded killed.

A fully reconstructed M1917 Ford ambulance PHOTO COURTESY OF DAVID O'NEAL

While primitive, the Bantam Boys' ambulances were simple and functional. The canvas on wood and composite frame Ford Model-T–based vehicle had a four-cylinder, water-cooled gasoline engine. No gas gauge kept the driver checking the fuel tank with a notched wood stick. The transmission brake was usually efficient, except in deep mud. And mud was everywhere on or near the front. Few roads were paved especially in the rural administrative departments (called counties in the United States).

The three-speed (one reverse and two forward) planetary transmission got the job done. Most modern drivers could not operate the vehicle with its combination brake pawl and shifter, and three pedals on the floor. The pedals were forward, reverse, and a transmission brake. It was more akin to driving a heavy-duty farm tractor than any type of modern automobile.

Steering the ambulances was achieved through brute strength. Power steering would not be available on military vehicles until World War II, and would not hit the civilian market until the early 1950s.

The truck beds were designed to carry two to three 140-pound men prone, sliding them in on stretchers. Alternatively, up to six men could sit three across from one other. A driver with an assistant was the preferred mode of travel. In lean times the driver was alone. In an emergency, three really friendly men could crush together on the front seat.

The cruising speed was twenty miles per hour on smooth roads. It hit a blazing top speed of forty-five if the driver had a death wish. Drivers could expect up to thirteen miles per gallon (mpg) of gasoline. Numbers of gallons consumed multiplied by mpg gave a general estimate of driving mileages. It also helped ascertain distances to aid stations established near no clear landmarks or French survey boundaries. For example, "That post is two gallons from here," meant that it was about twenty-five miles away.

The cylindrical Ford tank was gravity fed. With no fuel pump, when low on gas, Ralph sometimes drove backwards up steep hills. This was another good reason not to run below half a tank. Running a tank dry could plug the fuel line with bottom sediments. The boys were told to *never* run it dry.

Overheating and misfires were frequent problems. The leaky oil system required spare oil to be carried at all times. Most carried oil, fuel, grease, and radiator water in *bidons* (tin cans) strapped to their fenders or in the drivers' compartments.

The twenty-horsepower engine was adequate for its day when mules and horses propelled the majority of transport work. Horse teams hauled nearly all of the field artillery for lack of a readily available mechanical alternative.

The Ford engine had drawbacks. When encountering bad roads, it could not safely move much more weight than a driver, his assistant, and three wounded. Carrying more of a load could strain the engine and cause it to break down.

For a couple of days the Bantam Boys practiced driving their ambulances through numerous towns. They stopped at several Red Cross locations and dropped off supplies. Ralph drove to see the eleventh-century castle in Nantes.

At the main hospital in Nantes, Ralph met his buddies from Michigan. The mass of Battle Creek Boys finally got "over there" several weeks after Ralph had arrived with the Bantam Boys. A grand reunion it was. No glass went unfilled, no hand unshook.

Ralph passed his diary around. He had all of his friends and acquaintances sign it during this whopper of a Red Cross party. (The appendix contains nearly one hundred names and their midwestern hometowns.)

Later, sitting alongside a road, Ralph caught up with his diary. While taking a break from driving practice, he noted some unusual sights he had seen en route.

### Friday, 28 September 1917. Rural France outside Nantes

*All along the way we see crucifixes [on graves]. They are large, plentiful and lonely.*

*In one strange place the people seem to be sort of cliff dwellers. They live in places cut into the rock of the hillside.*

*Beige barrels mounted on flat cars carry wine. They are as big as oil tanks. Everywhere is wine, wine, wine.*

*The French people greet us very friendly. Only one slob in a wine parlor acted smart . . . [Ralph taught him a lesson in manners.]*

*France is a beautiful country and well cultivated. The horses are wonderful. The farms look prosperous and the crops very rich. It looks far better than America does in many places. The French women are attractive and not so bold out here like the cities.*

In early October, driver training continued. Lieutenant Lyon wanted the Bantams to be able to start and drive their ambulances blindfolded.

Except Dick Brooke. He needed to keep his eyes open.

Back at St. Nazaire they also practiced map reading. He required his Lobsters to memorize evacuation routes to areas from as far north as the Somme River to the Marne River in the south. They needed to study the Verdun region as well. It was a good idea in theory—if everyone had a photographic memory.

In practice, there were so many roads it became impractical for them to know everything except the main highways. Many roads were not even on their maps. To make the situation even more complex, ambulance drivers had to learn to meander through pastures. Off-roading helped

A postcard showing a barrage balloon over a graveyard

them avoid getting blown to pieces on targeted supply routes. The Bantam operating area was huge. It was far more complex than Lieutenant Lyon had realized.

Next the Bantams practiced starting and driving their Model Ts without a partner. They worked on driving skills and tactics for different road conditions in the ever-shifting weather. They experimented to gain optimal solutions to restarting cars stalled under fire.

The Sarge held contests to see who could start their car the fastest. To make it interesting, he screamed spirited curses at the faces of hapless boys cranking the engine, putting on as much pressure as possible. The Sarge lectured them, "Being blasphemed with words is better than being blasted by shrapnel shells." He said that not thinking straight could "order up a grave for the brainless or luckless dumbass."

The extended training was overkill to Ralph. He was ready to go! He wanted to help those French. He griped to Bill, "Where's the stupid war?"

The October sky turned cold, windy, and gloomy. Rain was frequent. Driving was best accomplished in full battle dress uniform and clad in greatcoats. Extra blankets helped when it got really bad, which was often.

Bill complained to Ralph who looked twice his normal size, "You got seventeen overcoats on!"

"I don't like being cold." Ralph gathered gear like a pack rat.

The ambulance design with open doors, inadequate roofing over the driver and passenger seat, and no heater made driving in adverse weather miserable. Mud and water splashed through the driver's compartment. Boots got smeared. Puttees got soaked.

Ever-present potholes and washed-out road sections made for added amusement. The boys rigged canvas barriers up from the floorboards. They didn't help much but were better than nothing.

Pounding from stiff truck springs riding over uncountable potholes threatened to loosen the drivers' teeth. It caused Ralph endless backaches. Saddle sores from rough breeches on thinly padded seats were a new-found pleasure as well. Drives were not summer carriage rides in front of Buckingham Palace. They more resembled stagecoach excursions through windswept Yukon floodplains in early winter.

Due to the beating, the thin ambulance rubber tires were prone to blowouts. Repairs were a slow, muddy search for tiny holes in inner tubes. Early car tires were more related to modern bicycle tires than tubeless vehicle tires. The spoked wheel was pulled from the axle, the rubber separated from the rim, the inner tube pulled out, the hole located and patched. The process was reversed to reinstall it. Repairs took time.

New tires and spares were scarce. Flats were frequent. In the beginning not all Bantam ambulances had a spare, including Ralph. Under such harsh conditions the Ford-produced tires would only last about five hundred miles. Many didn't make it that far.

The Bantam Boys became de facto mechanics. Ralph became so good he was officially designated on his French military identification book as: Grade—Mechanic, US Army. This categorization melded with driver, medic, guard, dishwasher, platoon nanny, heavyweight pugilist, wine connoisseur, and expert potato peeler.

Ralph was his own army. Not that's what he had in mind when he joined up.

The positive side of Ford engineering was that the design of the Model T was simple and accessible. Relatively few components were

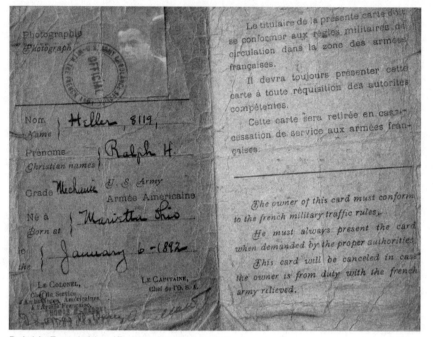

Ralph's French identification booklet

stored under the hood. In part, this was because few mechanical components had been invented by 1917 and these "disposable" machines needed to be built quickly and cheaply.

A mechanic could easily access the motor. Despite careful maintenance, however, breakdowns and mechanical failures were a constant worry for all drivers. An attitude less than a constant willingness to learn all things mechanical could, according to Ralph, get an M1917 driver, "blowed to kingdom come."

The boys did their best with what they had. When lacking official replacement equipment, they obtained "a ready supply of stolen parts." Many were courtesy of Lev the Larcenist and Smart Alex Kirkjian, scroungers extraordinaire. Men did what they needed to do their jobs. French soldiers referred to this forced thievery as "*Systeme D.*"

Ralph had a fair share of "five finger discounts and other newborn subterfuges." He added "cat burglar" to his résumé.

On October 7th, a group of ambulances with Packard and General Motors Corporation (G.M.C.) support trucks containing automotive and medical supplies pulled up to the boys' location at St. Nazaire. In a frenzy of activity taking several hours, a mass of additional officer staff cars formed a huge line.

"*Was this it?*" Ralph wondered.

Twenty-four hours later the order came. "Mount up and move out you Lobsters!" barked Lyon.

Ralph and the Bantam Boys hurriedly jumped into their waiting ambulances. Bill hopped in the passenger side of Ralph's car as partner and geographically impaired navigator. Bill had a hard time with maps. But he agreed to "find where the hell we are."

The two men turned to each other and heartily shook hands.

Bill said, "Drive us to Berlin, Ralphy Boy."

"Look out Kaiser. Here we come!"

It was time to go to war.

# CHAPTER 5

# Where the Hell Are We?

In May of 1917, General Philippe Pétain took control of French Army Forces. A soldier's soldier, he was called "the Lion of Verdun" for his outstanding leadership at that horrific battle in 1916. His artillery men fired fifteen million shells at the Germans in the first five months of Verdun. Together both sides exchanged twenty-three million rounds in what was the largest artillery duel in human history. In one of the most costly battles ever known, total casualties for both sides exceeded 976,000 men. This would have equated to the complete annihilation of 20 percent of the entire pre-war population of Australia.

Unknown to the outside world, from April to May of 1917, French soldiers had mutinied against their prior leader, General Robert Nivelle. Multitudes of soldiers thought he squandered comrades' lives in ill-conceived counterattacks. Upwards of thirty thousand men left the forward trenches and brashly marched to rear lines. They refused to fight after having seen over one million fellow soldiers slaughtered for no strategic gains on the Western Front. Remaining soldiers continued an effective defense but would not "go over the top" to attack. Disaffection spread until half the French Army, fifty-five divisions, refused to fight. After four years of brutal warfare, her military neared ruin.

Pétain handled the matter quietly and fairly according to postwar analysts. Even British prime minister Lloyd George and President Woodrow Wilson never knew the extent of the uprising. All was kept top secret. It would be decades before the entire story was declassified and disclosed to the public.

Pétain assured his troops there would be no more suicidal attacks. He increased home furloughs. He ordered field officers to stop unnecessary

The Bantams Boys ready to go to war

disciplinary actions and augmented rest and recovery periods for active combat units. He guaranteed useless slaughter would end.

Frenchmen returned to their trenches. Over 550 conspirators were tried for treason and sentenced to death. Only forty-three executions were actually carried out. The remaining men were pardoned or given lesser sentences of hard labor. Many accepted grueling labor as preferable to the dreadful life in the trenches.

An incredible crisis had passed. The entire French front was saved from collapse. Secrecy prevailed to an extraordinary level. Throughout the episode, German spies never suspected a ripple of discontent.

No longer would the French Army carry out huge offensives. Instead, Pétain engaged in smaller local battles with reliance on heavily massed artillery. This way he thought he could inflict damage on the Boche but keep his own losses to a minimum. He hoped that he could restore the morale of his troops until significant numbers of American combat troops arrived in 1918. The plan worked.

This change in tactics was great news for the Bantam Boys. Rather than being swept up into massive assaults with thousands of casualties, they'd merely be thrown into smaller set piece or local campaigns with only hundreds of wounded to rescue. It also meant that they could, if the need arose, be sent to any French Army area.

The boys would range in duty from the south of the Somme River, with the French Fifth Army, to as far as Toul, with its First Army. The grid covered hundreds of square kilometers. The boys were going to get plenty of driving experience across a hefty expanse of France. Ralph was more than eager to do it.

To further improve the French situation, the British were kind enough to engage in a third bloody offensive at Ypres, Belgium, from July 31st to November 6th. This action, alternately known as Passchendaele, cost the English Empire as many as 260,000 men. It was one of the British Army's darkest moments. It was the equivalent of a death sentence for 40 percent of the wartime population of Liverpool, England.

Despite little ground gained around Ypres, the effort relieved pressure on the battered French lines in front of the Bantams. German soldiers were diverted northward to take part in the battle, thinning the Marne defenses. "Real" attacks ceased in the south. Diversionary attacks remained common so the French didn't fathom Germany's increasingly precarious manpower situation.

In the ensuing attrition at Ypres, the Boche quickly bled out many of their Western Front combat veterans. The Germans knew large numbers of American troops would arrive the following year. The Empire would be in dire trouble. Berlin High Command fought an internal battle as to what to do next. Reliable options appeared few.

### *Tuesday, 9 October 1917. St. Nazaire*

Grouping at Saint Nazaire, one hundred ambulances from multiple sections of the Ambulance Corps took to the roads. Two dozen Packard and G.M.C. support trucks and British Crossley or Model T staff cars attended each group. All were fueled, provisioned, and given a final mechanical "once over." The Bantam Boys took their place in line. Ralph eagerly sat in his ambulance thinking about how he'd fix potential mechanical problems. Bill chattered on about how many medals he was going to win.

An officer in the first staff car blew a whistle and signaled the convoy forward with a swoop of his arm. One after another the engines were cranked and fired up. Ambulances and trucks slowly snaked ahead in an accordion-like expansion. Some ambulances stalled or failed to start. Boys opened the hoods of their malfunctioning engines. Followers drove around them yelling, "Use more oil!"

Throughout the day the boys drove through numerous stone-walled and concrete constructed villages. Ralph was impressed that these homes were made to last. For many miles they slowly traced each other through a thinly populated corridor toward Chartres.

The quaint countryside, untouched by war, was striking. Ralph had not really noticed the beauty on his way in on the train from Le Havre. He loved "the tour." Poplar trees shaded him during breaks. Local farmers gave the boys endless fruit and wine, and so many waves and broad smiles. It became a splendid ride on decent roads. *Great weather, too!* Ralph thought. It no longer felt like they were going to war.

The convoy never exceeded twenty miles per hour and only drove for short periods of time. Ambulances maintained disciplined intervals of 150 feet. This minimum distance ensured that falling artillery shells would only destroy one car at a time. Fortunately, they were far from the front so maintaining the interval was more practice than useful. It did reduce the amount of dust and engine exhaust they breathed.

The only difficulties arising from their plan were panicked stragglers slowed by mechanical mishaps. Once repaired, many resorted to sprints to catch up to the convoy. That fast pace was tough on new engines. The result was plenty of burned oil.

Blown tires were also a problem and these were "good" roads. Ralph wasn't anxious to see what "bad" meant. Every few miles he could see boys tinkering with their engines or removing tires alongside the road. These marvels of engineering could be less than marvelous. *How will they do under battle conditions?* he wondered.

For Ralph and Bill this was the first of what would become a score of jaunts as partners. As designed, all Bantam ambulances had two men sharing the driving chores. This arrangement avoided excess fatigue for one man. In addition, recovery operations by two would make loading wounded easier and quicker. Finally, if one of them was killed—the other could get the Ford back to the station.

After driving through Nantes and Angers, the convoy stopped at Le Mans. Ralph got "gas, oil and eats." Rather than opening an infamous ration can, the Bantams opted for fresh food. They purchased local fare out of their own pockets. Finding a dizzying menu at a patisserie, Ralph and Bill decided upon half a dozen Massif Central pork belly and Le Mans fresh-baked bread sandwiches.

Ralph said to Bill, "Nothin' beats bacon sammiches."

"Not for the piggy."

Ralph and Bill sacrificed several bottles of beer and wine while dining as well. Alcohol use was standard fare in most combat theaters of the Great War. The British even had a "rum ration" suggested to be about one eighth pint per man per day.

"Rule, Britannia!" Bill once said. "I could be a Limey."

When in England Ralph was taken with the warm but tasty Guinness Irish beer. "That's a drink you have to chew. I might take up the habit!" He wrote later, "French brew is rotten stuff at best." He still drank plenty.

On their trip, Ralph lamented to Bill, "Wine always makes me feel hot and I know my face flushes, partially from shame I guess. It is with a bad conscience that I drink it."

Bill turned his eyes up like an epileptic and asked, "Were you ever a member of the Christian Women's Temperance Union?"

Ralph got angry after disclosing his innermost thoughts. In response, he posed his most famous and oft repeated question: "Have you ever been so bruised you peed seventeen shades of purple piss?" (He loved saying it long after the war according to my late Uncle Ralph.)

Bill looked at him. "I don't know how to answer that. Give me a moment."

Ralph used this warning so often he only had to raise an index finger and say to the offending Bantam: "Seventeen shades . . ."

Unless the boy could run faster than Ralph, his urge for caution was heeded.

In the Great War, French wine was prized as food, medicine, entertainment, and liquid courage. Everyone imbibed from privates to generals. Few Bantam Boys drank water unless its source was known as pure. Ground water was full of gut-busting pathogens. Boiling, brewing beer, and fermenting wine killed the nasty bugs that infected water. British tea was one of the few safe ways to get a non-alcoholic drink.

Ralph drove on with the convoy. On this ride, he delved into a new hobby of photography. He took his first pictures, "one of a windmill and several of buildings." Using his wrestling winnings, he purchased a Kodak Brownie camera at St. Nazaire. Ralph eventually learned how to take first-rate pictures and process the negatives in heavy tents, dark basements, or vacant bomb shelters.

Developing photographs was no small feat in 1917, especially under battlefield conditions. Setting up chemical baths, in a suitable darkroom, took low light, ingenuity, and serious effort. Somehow he managed it.*

The Bantams slept well in Le Mans. Ralph was on guard duty from 10:00 p.m. to midnight but still "got a good night's sleep." A "slim" breakfast was all the Bantams could scrounge up the next morning. Soon they were off down the cobblestones.

Hours later the convoy members pulled into a small town. Ralph and Bill walked up to an open sweet and candy shop. *Don't mind if I do!* Ralph bought a rare half pound of Belgian chocolates while Bill went next door for wine. The two stuffed themselves. They chased chocolate with plenty of red wine in a decadent indulgence.

As they weaved down the two-lane road, a well-lubricated Ralph complained to Bill that he wished Edyth could be there with him. "When I got butter, I got no bread. When I got bread, I ain't got no butter," he said.

Bill said, "Lots of these Frenchie women will butter your bread."

As the journey unfolded, sections of ambulances broke off in different directions at various times. Nobody knew who was going where. They just did what they were told and tried to follow along with their maps.

---

*Author's note*: Ralph took hundreds of photos during his tour of duty. Many ended up in the Bantam Regimental History. An unknown number were destroyed by artillery fire. Over one hundred photographs still exist. Go to drgregoryarcher.com to see more of his pictures. If Ralph ran out of film, he bought postcards to document his location or unusual sites. Twenty of his postcards remain intact.

The Bantam Boys continued on toward Paris. By evening, at a position about fifteen miles past Chartres, rain came down in torrents. Heavy mist and winds slapped the boys in their open cars. Thick mud sucked at their tires. The road *should* have been in better shape. They *should* have been near Paris by now.

None of the area was familiar. They had no guide. Night was falling. Ralph wrote, "Lieutenant Lyon got excited and thought we were lost. He ordered us to stop and he went ahead."

After waiting thirty minutes, "Sergeant Lee told us to go back [to Chartres]. He got in the car with Bill and I went back with Paul Hargreaves."

It wasn't easy turning the Fords on the muddy road. Irrigation ditches lined both sides. The back and forth maneuvering of the trucks ripped up the roadbed like farm plows. While this was going on, Ralph walked down the line of stuck ambulances.

Paul "the Wall Hard-Hits" Hargreaves was about to acquire his nickname. Paul had a nasty habit of hitting immobile objects such as buildings, rock piles, and French national monuments. Though he was suave, debonair, and had a fair bit of money, he lacked innate driving talent. When Ralph met up with Paul, he realized Paul's ambulance didn't have any headlamps.

Ralph asked him, "Where's your dang lights?"

"Hell if I know." Paul pulled out a flashlight. Thrusting it toward Ralph, he said, "Keep me on the straight and narrow."

Ralph knew this was going to be a memorable event. Lacking a safer alternative, he schlepped over and jumped in the passenger seat. Paul tossed Ralph a bottle of wine. "What the heck," Ralph said, looking at a fine Bordeaux.

With the cork out, the bottom went up. Ralph swallowed long and hard. That mouthful cost more than a day's pay. *Not bad*, he thought. He finished the bottle in three fell swoops. Paul looked dismayed as the expensive wine drained away.

Ralph casually pointed the way to the Promised Land by the beam of a battery-powered flashlight. They couldn't see much and the weather got worse. It was much like steering a battleship employing the light of a Detroit streetlamp. He wrote about their intrepid voyage on Thursday, October 11th, when safely back at Chartres:

*. . . such a ride! How he kept on the road, I don't know. Only once did he get way off. We went head over a stone pile. But Paul got the car back all right.*

*About 8 o'clock [we] arrived in Chartres. We had a little trouble finding our lodging place which was a hospital.*

*I got a little supper and then rolled in my blankets in the [Ralph's] old Ford.*

*About 2 o'clock AM I woke with an awful headache. I got hold of Bill's wine bottle and took a pull. I was soon asleep again.*

*I woke in the morning feeling none too good. I took a shower and got my car ready for the day.*

After a breakfast of pork, beans, white bread, and black coffee, the Bantam Boys set off again. The sun started brightly but a rain shower developed in the early afternoon. Bill and Ralph got drenched anew. They were wet more often than dry.

Some hours later along the roadside Ralph saw the "prettiest woman I ever saw." For him to write a note about her, she sure must have been breathtaking. Seeing attractive women made Ralph long for Edyth. He thought about the times they had together in Michigan. His daydreaming didn't last long. He ran over a sharp object in the roadway. Their thirty-by-three-and-a-half-inch tire went flat instantly. The little ambulance shuddered and bucked out of control. Ralph ground *Lizzie* to a halt with the brake pedal.

Frustrated, he and Bill jumped out to diagnose the trouble. Finding the collapsed tire, Ralph muttered, "Flip to see who fixes it?"

Bill said, "Tails."

Ralph pulled out his English penny and tossed it. Catching it he said, "Heads."

Bill trudged over to the toolbox. He got adhesive and a piece of patching material. Turning them over and over in his hand, he looked confused.

Ralph stamped his wet feet for warmth. "What?"

Bill sighed. "When will they issue us a spare?"

"When they promote me to Commander-in-Chief."

Through a dirty and slow process, the duo repaired the tube. With some skillful driving afterward, Ralph caught up with the convoy. He wrote on October 12th:

> *Going out of Versailles we caught a glimpse of Paris. The road was asphalt and smooth as glass. We passed through a forest or park for many miles.*
>
> *The country is rougher than we have been in.*
>
> *At five o'clock we landed at the camp. It is within hearing distance of the line. Those that have come before us have gone already but they left the Fords here. They are standing in rows in a field. There is not much of a camp here.*
>
> *All around are trenches and wire entanglements.*

The Bantam Boys finally arrived in their primary camp post or *Poste* near Épernay. All around the camp were deep trenches. Between the trenches were heavy barbed wire entanglements in various depths and heights. It looked like it was thrown at random. Row after row of wire lined up as if metallic hedges grew in all directions.

An American invention, barbed wire was designed to hold livestock in pastures. It also kept predators out. Here on the front the wire took on a diabolical role that separated hundred of thousands of hostiles. As the first line of defense, wire slowed attackers going through No Man's Land. Taking time to cut through it, the effort left soldiers vulnerable to machine-gun and artillery fire. This was an authentic rendering of the term "Killing Zone."

Barbed wire was effective and inexpensive. Miles and miles of it hung in a nearly impenetrable steel bramble thicket on the entire Western Front. Even artillery often failed to cut it. Shells could pass through and explode under the coils. Tossing them skyward, explosions sometimes balled the wire making it *more* effective.

Facing the Bantam Boys from the German emplacements were interlocking fields of fire from heavy Maxim machine guns or the

*Maschinengewehr 08*, invented by American-born Hiram Maxim in 1884. The 08 number designated the year, 1908, when the German Army adopted it. The German version of the Maxim could fire four hundred rounds per minute of devastating 7.92 by 57mm caliber Mauser bullets from 250 round fabric belts. A water jacket helped prevent the barrel from overheating during sustained fire. Aimed bursts were effective up to 6,560 feet or about two thousand meters.

By 1916, Germany had sixteen thousand Maxims on the front. Many more arrived to bolster defenses and replace worn-out machine guns. A basic gun team consisted of a four-man crew: spotter, gunner, ammo loader, and ammo bearer. If one was killed the next man took over his position. One properly supplied, well-trained machine-gun squad was nearly equal in firepower to a forty-man platoon wielding bolt action rifles.

The problem with the Maxim was it was heavy at 152 pounds (65kg) with the water jacket filled. It could not be moved easily or quickly. This led inventors racing to develop a man-portable machine gun. The Germans succeeded in 1918 with the Bergman MP18 or *Maschinenpistole* 18/I. It was nine pounds (4kg) with a thirty-two-round detachable box magazine. To make it portable and controllable at high rates of fire it used a 9mm pistol round as opposed to the Maxim's rifle bullet (thus it was designated a submachine gun). The Allies scurried to develop similar types of hardware.

The first Bantam post or French *Poste*, as most stations, was behind the last line of French defenses. Beyond them was open country that extended all the way to Paris.

If the Boche got through here, the war, at least for France, could be lost.

The boys received marginal, barely livable quarters. A rusted pot-bellied stove heated their shack. The wood smelled good though. To Ralph it reminded him of the fires back home. The warmth was appreciated. Simple luxuries became important. The usual remedy for cold hands was to place them near a running Model T engine. That wasn't as cheery as a fire even if it was in a "lousy old stove."

However modest these low-grade quarters, they outdid an impromptu bivouac in a pup tent on a wet field. Ralph wrote the likely alternative to a tent was to "catch a few winks in the [driver's] seat." Unfortunately, Ralph and the Bantam Boys ended up sleeping in their cramped cars on more nights than they'd care to remember. For just such occasions they carried extra blankets. Blankets were a "hot" commodity. More valuable than silver coins, wool blankets were a top-notch barter item on the front.

An English-speaking French logistics sergeant major (*sergent-chef de logis*) came up to instruct the Bantam Boys. He briefed them on their meals and emergency supplies. Calling for a powwow, Ralph, Bill, and the other boys circled around the *sergent*.

He blandly spoke as if he had said it a hundred times before. "Food come two time in field kitchen," said the *sergent-chef*. The boys could eat all they wanted. If they'd be gone for a meal they were to take extra rations. "All ambulance carry water canteen two, three bottle of wine, emergency rations two day," he said.

The boys were told to make sure that gas tanks, oil reservoirs, and radiators were full before leaving. "Every time!" Too much could go wrong with the machines. The boys needed to avoid breakdowns and possibly fatal mistakes.

The *sergent-chef*'s advice included, "Keep gas mask. Avoid sniper by drive fast. Avoid artillery by drive fast. Avoid aeroplane by drive faster."

"He think we got racecars?" Bill whispered.

Ralph shrugged his shoulders. All in all, it wasn't the best pep talk ever given.

The next day trench orientation began. Ralph, Bill, Lev the Larcenist, Smart Alex, and Jack Stearns marched up to the front lines with the *sergent-chef*. On the way their Frenchie explained that in most instances, the wounded would be brought to the rear trenches or to aid stations behind the lines. The boys would pick up most wounded at that point. There might be rare times they would have to retrieve men from deep inside the trenches. The boys needed to know how to stay alive. They had to stay alert and keep their heads well below the lip of the trench at all times. Otherwise snipers would "blow their heads off." They'd be dead before they heard the sound of the high-velocity bullet.

The *sergent-chef* explained that most rear pickups were generally safe from sniping. Any distance over sixty-five hundred feet or two thousand

The Bantam Boys getting ready to go up to "The Front"

meters from the German lines was beyond the practical range of the Mauser Gewehr 98 rifles or the Maxims. On the other hand, light artillery could ruin your day at any time if within five miles (8km) of the Hun batteries. Nine miles (14.5km) away wasn't safe if the Huns were shooting the immense Big Bertha howitzers. Even these weren't the most powerful guns. A long-barreled, railroad-mounted rifled cannon could hit Paris eighty miles (129km) away. It was therefore dubbed *The Paris Gun* by the Allies. Firing a 210-pound (94kg) shell, Parisians thought they were being bombed by high-altitude zeppelins because no gun on earth could shoot that far. They were wrong.

The Frenchie *sergent-chef* went on with his perfunctory lesson on how not to die from shellfire. He said there was no practical defense from artillery other than a very deep hole. There was nothing noble about artillery. The front wasn't like Troy where the best men would meet one-on-one in battle where the strength and skill of the best soldier would determine the victor. The greatest soldier ever born could be gone in an instant, killed by an ignorant buffoon firing an artillery piece.

The *sergent-chef* said the boys had to learn what type of artillery they faced at the moment. Otherwise they would be uselessly ducking every time they heard a shot. Every caliber of shell had a unique sound and presented varying opportunities for survival. A favorite German artillery round was known as the "whizz-bang." It was a 77mm caliber shell that flew at such a high velocity that the sound was heard only a second before it exploded. If a soldier was too close he'd only hear the "whizz." Then bang and say goodbye. "Not much you can do," *le sergent-chef* said.

High explosive heavy artillery sounded like hammering a big bass drum. The super-heavy stuff reminded the listener of the sound of a freight train falling out of the sky. These loud, lumbering rounds could be heard from a distance. That meant the boys had time to run for shelter.

If it got too loud, no trench would offer protection. Hundreds of pounds of high explosive could dig impressive holes twenty feet deep. Unless the shelter was reinforced concrete, shells could completely vaporize soldiers. This is part of the reason why so many men went "missing." No identifiable body parts remained.

The *sergent-chef* reassured them. A direct hit probably wouldn't even hurt! Nerve impulses were slower, two hundred mph, than blast waves at over seven thousand mph. "You be gone in second." He went on to say shrapnel shells were different. Those exploded overhead and were similar to falling into a meat grinder. If you did not die instantly, bleeding out from massive trauma could be slow and miserable.

By the end of the discourse, Ralph "didn't feel inspired by the pep-talk."

After the artillery chat the *sergent-chef* corrected the boys' medical terminology. He said a wounded man would henceforth be known as *le blessé*. The stretcher bearers were *brancardiers*. Stretcher cases, men unable to walk, were called *couchés*. Under fire there was no time to waste, no time for miscommunication.

"Everyone speak French," *sergent-chef* said with utmost seriousness.

First aid should have been rendered to *le blessé* by the time they arrived. If not, the Bantam had to work on him. Stabilize the injuries. Then get out. After several complaints about their inadequate medical kits, the *sergent-chef* said, "Do what you can." Supplies were low; shipments unreliable. Just "get on with it" was the message.

After questions ended the "grand trench tour" began. The Frenchie warned the boys to stick together and not get lost. The trenches were a long, convoluted labyrinth as complex as the New York subway system. He dashed forward and the boys followed each other in single file.

Third man in, Ralph became confused by the twists and turns. The farther forward the trenches ran, the earthworks became more elaborate and deeper. The opposing trenches stretched from Belgium all the way to the Swiss border. A soldier could walk nearly the entire distance from Switzerland to the English Channel below ground.

Ralph and the boys entered the reserve trench behind the front line. This held reserve combat troops and matériel for when the Boche attacked. Most of the men there smoked cigarettes. Ralph hated the musty smell of cheap French tobacco.

Scurrying up perpendicular communication trenches, the boys gained access to several layers of fighting positions. German artillery was well timed for their initiation. The ground suddenly shook. Shells exploded around the boys. Bill looked unnerved.

They dashed ahead to the entrance of the front-most trench. They spread out and collapsed against the wall to catch their breath. Shells continued the welcoming party. The noise was monstrous. Falling dirt and rocks peppered them. The stinging smell of cordite, mold, and decay proved indescribable.

By now Ralph was completely bewildered by myriad passages. Despite only covering a few hundred meters forward, it felt ten times longer. He looked up at the steep embankments. He couldn't see anything around their position. He was blind except for a small ribbon of cloudy sky above. Despite his hearing difficulties, explosions were clear as summer thunder.

Sandbags topped the trenches in front of the boys. These front sand-bag *parapets* and rear *parados* absorbed bullets and shrapnel. Properly stacked, the front sandbags had loopholes in them. This was where soldiers would stand to shoot. Ladders lay against the wall when soldiers had to climb out and "go over the top." Floorboards, also called "duckboards," helped keep feet out of the ever-present mud. They were only marginally effective. The trench resembled an oversized city sewage ditch filled with homeless veterans. It smelled like it too.

Walls zigzagged and firebays were cut into the front side under the loopholes. The first line was deeper than reserve trenches by several feet. The zigzag course, which was disorienting, stopped raiders from firing straight down the line at the defenders. It also blocked shrapnel from spraying the trench on direct hits. Listening posts called "saps" were periodically cut forward of the fighting trench. They looked like death traps.

Only now had Ralph become fully aware of the mud-covered combat soldiers. Grimy, motionless Frenchmen sat in dugouts cut into the front side of the trench. They didn't acknowledge their visitors. It was as if they were part of the walls.

Something moved on the ground. Ralph noticed several rats sauntering along the duckboards. The agile little pests showed as much fear of the men as did highly pampered show dogs. A soldier pulled out his bayonet and stabbed one as it happened by. It squealed and writhed as he raised it up. Ralph learned killing them with knives and bayonets was a prime trench sport. The man who dispatched the most got an extra ration of wine that day. It was also said, in lean times, rat made a fine goulash.

This was *The Front* they heard so much about. After months of preparation, Private Heller and the Bantam Boys had finally arrived. Bill sat down next to Ralph. They looked at each other but said nothing.

During a lull in the shelling, Ralph turned and raised himself up. He glanced through a loophole and saw a devastated landscape. Nothing seemed alive. Trees had no leaves or branches. Barbed wire and broken equipment lay scattered everywhere. And what looked like bodies . . .

*Thump!*

A sniper's bullet smacked into a sandbag next to Ralph's face.

*Tat, tat, tat, tat, tat!*

Ralph ducked as a burst of machine-gun fire shredded the sandbag.

The *sergent-chef* rushed over as if possessed. He grabbed Ralph by his waist belt and threw him down in the mud. The previously unflappable *sergent-chef* chattered nearly incomprehensibly: "What I say? You want die? You want die?"

Ralph looked lost. No Bantam spoke. Ralph braced himself up against the trench wall as if resisting some unseen force pulling him toward No Man's Land.

A dozen edgy, battle-worn Frenchmen, seeing all was clear, put down their rifles and leaned back into their dugouts.

They looked like dead soldiers lying back into their graves.

Ralph muttered, "Where the hell are we?"

## Chapter 6

# Pray Like You Mean It

Seven aeroplanes or *avions* zoomed low over Ralph's Post #3. They turned out to be Frenchie hotshots showing off. He picked himself and his mess tin up from the ground. He brushed off. "They're lucky I didn't shoot 'em," he grumbled to himself.

He dumped his butt back down on a box of oil cans and shoved another spoonful of warm spiced beans and ham in his mouth. The field kitchen worked wonders on the ever-changing breakfast staples. "Our food is good but they serve wine and the coffee has whiskey in it," he wrote.

Ralph's coffee tasted better when a logistics officer handed him a letter from Edyth. He dropped his cup and ripped open the letter. In it she wrote that she was busy at work six days a week, sometimes seven. It contained no earth-shaking gossip other than America was mobilizing for war. Camp Upton overflowed with recruits needing immunizations. Edyth was "happy to poke them."

News from his logistics officer was far more exciting. Ralph wrote:

*Monday, 15 October 1917. Poste Trois near the Marne River*

*We are preparing to leave tomorrow. Thirty five will be picked from our section. We will be under French officers. Our own coms [commissioned officers, i.e., Lt. Lyon] will not go with us. Gabby Lee . . . went to Paris to [combat training] school.*

*Four sections will leave.*

The Bantam Boys were split up and sent piecemeal to a variety of aid stations. To his disappointment, Ralph did not depart on the 16th. He

A shell of a church in No Man's Land

went back on despised guard duty where he felt more prisoner than guard. Ralph didn't even have a pistol. He figured they tapped him for security because he was big and "could beat hell out of Boshies."

During his shift, the echo of artillery in the distance intrigued him. *Where was it coming from?* he asked himself. Ralph wanted in on "the action," instead of being relegated to the tedium of watching for nonexistent German spies and infiltrators. He didn't even capture a mechanically inclined grease thief. Ralph smoldered with frustration as he kicked an empty oil can across the depot.

On *Poste* #3 Ralph took charge of one thousand petrol, oil, and lubrication *bidons* or tin containers. *Dangerous duty,* he mused. As ambulance men rolled in for supplies, he wasn't too discriminating about who took what or how much. Drivers got more than they asked for. Ralph pitied the logistics man who would have to balance the post's accounting books. Half his store got emptied.

The bright side of *Le Poste* was everyone on standing duty was issued a new wool blanket. It had been dreadfully cold the last few nights. Ralph couldn't rid himself of a persistent chill. This was odd since he suffered through many winters of extended cold, wet, and snowy Ohio weather.

73

He hoped he wasn't getting sick.

Ambulance drivers from the S.S.U. 528th, Bucknell University (Lewisburg, Pennsylvania) unit limped in hours later. The Bucknell Boys got food, water, oil, and medical supplies. Meal in hand they sat down and chitchatted with Ralph. Their tenor grew serious as the conversation progressed. They said over the last three weeks they "lost 4 men and had 3 more wounded."

A few days before, the Bucknells were loading wounded when artillery began to pound them like snare drums. Chaos ruled as an ambulance took a direct hit and killed its load of wounded. The boys scattered into trenches until the salvo abated. Then they rushed to load up the remaining cars and "drove like their asses were on fire."

They took separate highways to avoid losing the entire team on the next barrage of incoming shells. "She was a bitch." Nobody really knew who made it out okay. Some boys were still missing. (At the end of the war the official Bucknell casualty list included three members killed in action and nineteen wounded or gassed.)

Their thrilling story acted as a tonic to Ralph's ennui. He wanted to ship out with them. Right now! He rushed to talk to their NCO and got stopped in his tracks. The Bucknell sergeant said that no private could obtain authorization to leave his post. That's not how the army worked. "Thanks but no thanks," he said. Dejected, Ralph waved as the "Buckies" stoically drove off to another battlefield thrashing.

Ralph gained his admission to the front on October 17, 1917. The remaining Bantam Boys were told to load up their ambulances. Ralph wrote the boys "traveled like heck all day." They ended up roving through numerous small villages near the Marne River. It turned out to be an unintended lesson on memorizing escape byways. A bit lost at times, they stopped for the night at a small town. He and Bill slept a good eight hours in a horse barn. On October 18th, during a break from driving, Ralph wrote:

*We had a breakfast of apple butter, bread and roast beef. We see many automobiles transporting troops and etc.*

*This is a wonderful farming country. We see many tractors with gang plows on them. We see a good many oxen and plenty of fine horses.*

One of many Bantam Boy *Postes*

The boys resumed shadowing the Marne, driving through various small parishes. Ralph wasn't sure why it was taking so long. He could hear booms of artillery all day long. It was both exciting and unsettling in its intensity. *This is the real deal,* he thought.

The Bantams drove into Châlons situated precariously behind the Fourth French Army trenches. The city was relatively intact. There the boys refueled their cars and "ate a heavy meal." Afterward, they were granted six hours of unrestricted leave as they awaited orders. Ralph, Bill, and a few Bantam Boys explored the energetic little burg.

On their first stop, the boys visited a barbershop. Ralph said he needed a new coiffure to celebrate this momentous undertaking. He looked at a printed diagram on the barber's flaking wall. None of the haircuts illustrated grabbed him. He then came upon a bright idea. To make "a big American impression," Ralph decided to get a Mohawk haircut like he had as a kid. Bill thought he was completely nuts.

Ralph got his Mohawk after minor difficulties in translation. The barber feared he would kill him if he didn't like the outcome. Ralph loved it.

Admiring his mane lines, he thought his row of hair down the middle of his head would provide a cushion for his uncomfortable "Brodie" helmet. The upside down saucer-shaped helmet was fondly known as Helmet, steel, Mark 1, to the English Army. America copied it in 1917 despite its marginal design compared to the encompassing German Model 1916 *Stahlhelm* (steel helmet). Huns mocked the Brodie as the *Salatschüssel* or salad bowl.

While at the barber, Ralph wrote that he also had "the closest shave of my life for 5 cents and I doubt I'll ever need another. I don't blame Napoleon for shaving himself." Ralph feared the barber had cut his throat on several different strokes. He shaved himself from that day forward while in French territory.

Then Bill cooked up a bright idea. "After supper he went down the street and inquired where the Cat houses were. A man took us to one and told us that a German flier dropped a bomb on it last year. The statement was verified when we went inside," wrote Ralph.

Ralph didn't want to enter the "fun house" with the Bantams. Edyth was his girl. "No whore for me," he said.

Bill said, "You don't have to do anything. Stand guard. You're good at that."

Ralph wasn't amused. But soon felled by peer pressure, he advanced inside. Carrying a ton of guilt, he plopped on a threadbare loveseat in the red-wallpapered foyer. He hung his head while the boys ran up a flight of stairs to perform their wayward deeds.

Head still hung, Ralph's fresh Mohawk garnered unwanted attention. An enchanted woman sauntered over and stroked his cranial fur column like he was a poodle. He was *si belle* (so cute). Ralph knew this was going to end poorly. He added this rather unceremonious entry to his diary describing their sojourn into the village tart shop:

### Thursday, 18 October 1917. Chalons

*. . . the whore that came to me was fat. She had been good looking once. She kissed me on the ear when I wasn't looking. I wiped it off with my handkerchief. So she didn't try again.*

*. . . I could feel my face burn and presumed that it was evident that I didn't feel good. The conversation soon lagged and she left me.*

*As far as being tempted was concerned, there was nothing of it. I couldn't have aroused any passion if I had tried.*

76

*That was the first whorehouse I've ever been in.*
*I think it will be the last.*

With an evening curfew looming, the Bantam Boys raced off toward their barracks. They didn't want to risk the wrath of unknown French officers by being late. The boys never knew what to expect from new officers. Most Frenchies turned out to be reasonably amiable and less strict than Sarge Lee.

Of course, Old Testament God was less strict than the Sarge.

Unlike Moses, the wise old Sarge had only three simple proclamations: 1. Nothing is easy for enlisted birdbrains. 2. If something can break, a knuckleheaded private will break it. 3. No plan is foolproof because all privates are goddamn fools. The Sarge was a philosophical genius. The boys awaited the Sarge's return the way colonial troops awaited the onset of malaria after being bitten by clouds of Anopheles mosquitoes in the African jungle.

The momentarily contented Bantams stampeded back to camp led by their Indian guide "Ralphy the Redskin." Jack Stearns, who missed the majestic cathouse adventure, met them and told the boys they would go to work the next day. Jack also passed along that he had talked to a group of experienced French ambulance drivers. They reassured him that their work wasn't dangerous. But Jack couldn't help wonder why most of their ambulances had more holes than the proverbial swiss cheese.

October 19th was the first of many potentially lethal encounters in Ralph's driving career. He was more than ready to get into the field. His newly assigned station north of Châlons was several miles from the front. Operations were full throttle when he arrived. Ambulances and horse-drawn Red Cross wagons flew off in all directions with injured and dying. Ralph was full of nervous excitement as he dismounted from his car.

### Friday, 19 October 1917. Suippes

*We can hear the artillery and see the flash after dark. We see several planes most any time we want to look and two observation balloons . . .*
*Some of the boys tell wild tales.*

French colonial troops doing laundry

One tale was of an ill-fated Frenchie who was firing his rifle through a trench loophole. A nearby artillery blast launched his upper torso skyward toward the Boche. His legs were last seen plummeting in the direction of the French reserve trenches *sans* left boot. Ralph wondered if the poor boy knew what hit him.

Ralph's first orders were to go solo. Bill got reassigned elsewhere in the muddle of the battle. Ralph was ordered to pick up French *blessés* near the front at Suippes. He jumped in his ambulance and flew down a bumpy lane at an engine-straining twenty-seven miles per hour. His knuckles turned white from clenching the steering wheel of his bounding *Lizzie.*

Expecting to find a town at the end of the road, he only encountered ruins. Suippes had been pounded to the ground. The site reminded him of his hometown of Marietta, Ohio, after the epic flood of March 1913. Few buildings were standing. Debris lay strewn everywhere. An occasional chimney stood where a house used to be. Mounds of rotting horse flesh were strewn around in bloody, brown clumps. (In the 1929 book

*Front Memories of a Horse*, Ernst Johannsen estimated that an astounding 9,586,000 horses died of wounds or sickness in the war.)

Heavy artillery shells fell in slow random patterns. The mushrooming blasts, even at a safe distance, made Ralph feel small and insignificant like an ant under a workman's boot. Mud-covered orderlies manned an aid *Poste* full of bloody, groaning Frenchmen. A line of dead bodies lay twenty feet behind them. Greatcoats or pieces of uniforms covered the contorted faces of the slain.

Ralph described more of what he heard and saw in that entry:

> . . . *You could hear the rapid fire [machine] gun's spiteful volley. It sounded like a racing car with the muffler off, that was not exploding regular. The hand grenades have a mean sound, too.*
>
> *A division of French soldiers were preparing near [by].*
>
> *You can hear the artillery all the time. And see the aircraft and hear the hum of the planes' propellers.*

Ralph loaded with badly wounded men and sped back down the road. Within a few hundred meters the wounded soldiers, known as *poilu*, spontaneously broke into a lively French tune. He did not know the title but it sounded patriotic. Ralph had to admire the poor boys being bounced down that dreadful road. It had to hurt. He guessed that their wounds were severe enough that they knew they were going home.

*Poilu* literally meant "the hairy one." The name arose from the universal image of the unshaven French enlisted soldiers or *soldats*. Their beards could be quite substantial and nicely sculpted. Facial hair was one of the few expressions of individuality and pride in the vast waste of the trenches. The risk for the French was that their beards could prevent a close fit on a gas mask. Many sported only moustaches. Liking the look, Ralph grew a moustache in communion with his fellow *poilu*.

While the Bantam Boys weren't combat soldiers, the sight of them heartened the *poilu*. The French knew they needed help and any man was welcome to their side. Language barriers were common at first but eventually overcome. Soon the French and *Américains* interacted

Ralph in full battle dress and brand new moustache

like grade-school buddies. They shared food, wine, and cigarettes when the moment allowed. Ralph felt true friendship. (He called them, "My Frenchies.")

Ralph's next run wasn't so easy. He again loaded at Suippes. This time the Germans had better luck. Long-range, heavy rounds came lumbering in toward the aid station. They hit with the force of an earthquake. Ralph jabbered at the orderlies in tortured French. "*Dépêchez-vous, mes beaux amis!* Hurry up, my fine friends!"

Being used to shelling, the aides didn't seem to be bothered by the falling ordnance. They weren't going to be discourteous to the towering American. An orderly offered Ralph a cup of coffee. Ralph said he didn't want coffee if it had that "slapdash" whiskey in it. He said, "The American state of Kentucky makes good whiskey . . ."

*Boom!*

A huge round exploded about a hundred yards away. It looked like the largest he'd seen so far (possibly a Big Bertha howitzer shell: 16.5 inches [420mm] in caliber and 1,807 pounds [819kg] in weight).

"I didn't care to say no more," wrote Ralph. "That place was hotter than a fresh fucked fox in a forest fire."

October was a particularly violent month. Several days earlier on the 17th of October, northeast of Ralph's position at Soissons, the French and Germans pummeled each other unmercifully. They continued to do so for a week. Neither gained any advantage as they incessantly fired thousands of shells at each other.

East of Ralph near Verdun, however, the Germans succeeded in breaching the French trenches on Hill 344.

Trench assaults began with a "rolling barrage." Artillery ripped up the land in front of advancing troops. This curtain of fire kept the defenders pinned down and masked the attack squad's movements. As sappers and advance men cut the opposing wire, they proceeded until the assault troops slipped into the forward trench. Once inside the enemy's defenses, the fight descended into a nightmarish hand-to-hand death match.

In the confusion of a raid, grenadiers tossed hand grenades ahead of their position. Once the explosion settled, the riflemen rushed forward shooting, bayoneting, or beating the defenders to death with trench clubs.

Some of Ralph's "Frenchies"

Trench clubs were medieval-looking baseball bats that, when properly employed, could *quietly* murder the opposition when the need for stealth arose. On stealth raids the intent was to get prisoners, preferably officers. Men taken back faced torture by the Huns to obtain vital information. Most Frenchies would rather die than be dragged off as a raid prisoner.

Marauding was a terrifying undertaking for attacker and defender alike. If poison gas was used there was even more opportunity for disorder, destruction, and a painful death. Soldiers could barely see or hear and quickly became exhausted. A man never knew if a bayonet was ready to plunge into his body from any direction.

With such ferocity, survival rates were low but usually worse for the attackers. Going over top could be a death sentence. Machine guns and counter-battery artillery had tipped the balance of power heavily in favor of defenders. Modern warfare had returned to the era of castle sieges. Both sides now had underground castles next door to each other and the warring parties took turns beating down the opponent's ramparts. Most attacks were beaten back. The front remained a stalemate for over three years.

In Ralph's recovery of wounded, he found wounded outnumbered killed in action by about three to one. The largest numbers of combat casualties were victims of artillery. About 58 percent of men fell to shellfire. (Later reports stated it took an average of one thousand shells to cause one casualty on the Somme. Trenches were effective although dismal.)

An additional 37 percent of Frenchmen were wounded by machine-gun or rifle bullets. The last 5 percent were gassed, bayoneted, or "fragged" by hand grenades. Ralph learned self-inflicted wounds and suicides were frequent, but the true extent was unknown. Suicides and "death by enemy," where crestfallen men deliberately exposed themselves to rival fire, were dramatically underestimated throughout the Great War.

In addition to wounded, Ralph transported hundreds of sick *poilu*. These men were known as *malades*. The sick were a lower priority for transport but comprised a huge number of casualties, sometimes exceeding the number of wounded.

Influenza, dysentery, and trench fever, the latter caused by lice, were widespread. Trench foot consisted of cold skin virtually rotting off the feet. It could arise in as little as a few days in wet conditions. Even Ralph got a bad case of "hoof rot." Being exposed to so many sick men eventually caused viral or bacterial infections in every Bantam. (Ralph got sick at least five times during the war. He rarely became ill before going to France.)

Ralph continued down the Suippes road on a number of uneventful runs. Some transports were with Bill; others alone. One day, because of a lack of litter bearers, Ralph and Bill performed their first trench rescue. The pair was led down the trench by a French guide, possibly sixteen years old. The kid reminded Ralph of a drummer boy in the American Civil War. An older, heavy *poilu* had taken considerable shrapnel and was a *couché*. His trench mates were having a hard time moving the big man. They needed help.

Artillery fell around the trenches, wafting up in various shapes. Air-bursts exploded like angry black clouds raining steel. Carrying a litter on a furious dash, Ralph, Bill, and their guide zigzagged down toward the fighting trench to locate their man. Artillery hit hard around them. Machine-gun bullets zipped overhead. Ralph tried not to think about it. *Get in and get out. Keep my stupid head down!*

Bill was bent stiff as an angle iron and hardly blinked as he followed Ralph.

Finding their quarry, Ralph and Bill spread the litter. They rolled the injured man onto it. Each grabbed his end and hefted up their 185-pound load. It wasn't easy. They ran as fast as their feet could manage in the water and dirt. As they scurried back through the maze, they heard a shell hit near where they just left. A few moments longer back there and it would have been them showering down.

At that moment Ralph's feet delivered more speed than he ever thought possible. Bill struggled to keep up. Ralph might have accomplished the world's first four-minute mile had he not had Bill in tow.

When the two gasping boys stumbled back to their ambulance, Bill dropped his end. The Frenchie took a painful bounce. Bill fell to his knees gagging like he was going to vomit. Orderlies ran over, took the litter, and put the man in *Lizzie*.

Ralph asked Bill, "You okay?"

"No I'm not okay. Let's get outta here!"

The engine start-up and exit took less than half a minute. Even so, Ralph realized it involved too much time. He decided he'd leave the engine running from now on. He thought, *Better to waste gasoline than us get wasted.*

Under most rescue conditions the Bantam Boys moved *poilu* from the front aid stations to secondary *Postes*. Occasionally they took severely injured men farther rearward to main hospitals. A few lucky boys even got to go as far as Paris if officers needed transport or a critical case needed advanced treatment. Ralph and Bill stayed pretty close to the front lines on most of their runs.

As time progressed, with many runs under their belts, the Bantam Boys received a stark education in how to conduct themselves. The boys learned the main roads and locations of aid stations. They learned tricks to stay alive. For example, jumping into a recent shell hole was pretty safe. When guns fired the recoil changed the aim slightly. It rarely hit in the exact place twice in a row. Not that that was terribly reassuring when one hundred guns were firing at a time.

Despite his rapid adjustment, Ralph hinted that the effort and responsibility of bringing men back alive was already causing physical and mental stress. He hated seeing so much pain. He felt he could do so little for them. The worst part was, "It's a strange feeling when you put a live man in the car and get to station and pull a dead man out." He felt that occurrence was terrible luck. One night he wrote by candlelight:

An area believed to be near Suippes

*Saturday, 20 October 1917. Suippes*

*I slept fairly well but every time I woke up I was thirsty and cold.*
*Even though I don't feel the nervous strain and feel as calm as usual, the physical signs of nerve strain are evident.*
*I notice I always have to drink water at night when I'm worried.*

Ralph kept himself busy to quell his unease. On some return runs, when his ambulance was empty, he would pick up wood and coal for the campfire. Since he enjoyed whittling as well as leatherworking, Ralph "bought a big knife in Châlons," the *poilu*'s favorite—the American Bowie knife, "for the price of 24 cents!" What a bargain.

Whenever possible Ralph gathered unusual pieces of artillery-shattered wood. He carved attractive collections of horses from his raw materials. He kept one masterpiece with him on the car as tribute to the horse. Seeing horses hurt or dead pained him. He sent the rest to Edyth or sold pieces to appreciative *poilu*. (None of his work exists today.)

Ralph was grateful that the machine gun's "spiteful volley" didn't hit him. When well behind the front trenches, he was not in fear of bullets. He thought rear driving was relatively "safe." That was a premature judgment. Ralph discovered artillery was not the only enemy back of the trenches. *Avions* could be anywhere. German aircraft harassed him on several frightening occasions.

Ralph couldn't hear planes while driving. His hearing impairment combined with the noise of his engine masked sounds around him. With his car bumping down the potholed roads, he couldn't "hear shit." To make the situation worse, the Boche *avions* would unsuspectingly swoop in with the sun at their tails making them difficult to see.

When driving back to Suippes, a raggedy, single-seat German Fokker D-II fighter flew down on Ralph's car. The pilot let loose with his twin machine guns. One gun may have jammed, saving Ralph's life. All the while Ralph was happily daydreaming about Edyth while driving alone in his vehicle. Just taking a little drive in the country!

As the bullets smacked the ground, he pulled a Dick Brooke daredevil stunt and drove headlong into a two-foot irrigation ditch. Not knowing what was happening, Ralph jumped out of his car. He hid behind an earthen berm wondering where the hell the shots were coming from. Overhead an aeroplane gracefully rose and turned east toward German lines.

He was furious that Huns would shoot at a clearly marked ambulance. (Red crosses on a white background were painted on the sides and back.) Ralph complained that Hun pilots would shoot at anything that moved, especially if it couldn't fight back. For the first time he thought about acquiring a personal firearm. Ralph, the formerly semi-pacifist (influenced by his vehemently antiwar Aunt Bea) thought, *I could kill that bastard and carry on with a clear conscience.*

Aerial strafing runs did ample ground damage. Large caliber 7.92mm Spandau IMG08 machine guns were air-cooled versions of a Maxim. Loaded individually or in tandem pairs on various Boche planes, they could rip apart a man along with his vehicle.

Interrupter gears spaced machine-gun shots so the pilot didn't chop off his own propeller. Firing sequences were short with limited ammunition and a four hundred round per minute cyclical rate. Most guns had a lone 250-round belt. Some pilots learned the tricky art of reloading in flight and extended their missions. And maybe saved their lives.

The Bantam Boys learned how to "dance out of the way" of strafing pilots. The best survival advice was to run perpendicular to the flight path of the attacking aircraft.

Run as fast and as far as possible.

Don't stop until under heavy cover.

*And pray like you mean it.*

Bill was about to get his initiation into this exclusive Boche machine-gun club.

# CHAPTER 7

# Holy Shit!

During the last week in October, Sarge Lee rushed back to "his goofs." Without resorting to the usual curse-filled greetings, one of his first official acts was to alert Ralph to a "hurry call." That meant someone was in real trouble.

"Glad you're back from Paris, Sarge."

"Never lie to me Heller."

"Lame" Sam Reynolds, who couldn't march in step if the Sarge held a pistol to his noggin, got assigned to drive Ralph's ambulance. The Sarge wanted to give Sam some experience seeing as he hadn't done much driving. Since Ralph was one of the better drivers, the Sarge thought he would be a good mentor. Ralph didn't have a choice. So Sam, with his reluctant passenger and teacher, followed the Sarge.

Right out of the starting gate Sam got behind. He couldn't drive fast enough to keep up with the Sarge, who seemed to think he was entered in the Indianapolis 500. Ralph coached Sam on how to run faster on poor roads: "Stop hitting the dang shell holes asshole!" Sam beat the snot out of Ralph's freshly tuned ambulance.

As the Sarge pulled away, Ralph kept on Sam like an angry Catholic nun. He screeched at Sam to speed up. That made Sam panic and slip farther behind. Cresting a hill Sam slammed on the brake. Ralph launched from his seat and nearly found himself eating sheet metal. As he struggled back to his seat, the Sarge was nowhere to be seen. A fork with two twisting tree-lined roads extended out before them.

Sam asked, "Which one do I take?"

"Pick one, Lame Brain!"

Bantam Boys and Frenchies with their mascot dog (date unknown)

Sam picked the wrong one. After a fruitless hour of searching, Ralph directed Sam back to Suippes. Receiving further errant information there, they redirected toward a far-flung aid station at Mont Frenet. Artillery boomed all along the front. Machine guns were close enough to be clearly heard. Ralph quietly worried they were in double-trouble. He had no idea where they were. Sam appeared nearly paralyzed with fear.

At long last, they entered Mt. Frenet. On the side of the road, Ralph saw dead stacked together side by side looking like a human boardwalk. Dozens if not more French bodies lay in a straight line. What sickened him most was the large number of obese rats. The rodents shamelessly scurried over corpses looking as if they were wiping the mud off their feet on human door mats. One bold rat openly feasted on a dead *poilu*'s ear. Ralph thought if *les mères* could see rats eating their sons—their outcry would stop the war.

Ralph and Sam barely made it to Frenet before darkness fell. It didn't really matter because the Sarge was not there and had not been there. Ralph bristled once more. The Sarge would kill them. Maybe someone died because they got lost. All this from driving lessons for a guy who managed to beat hell out of Ralph's car at the same time.

One of the many roads Ralph drove

He asked Sam, "You ever pee seventeen shades of purple piss?"

Sam froze like stone, looking at Ralph as if he was a medusa. "What?"

Ralph took over driving and hardly uttered a word. He and Sam drove back to Suippes in pitch dark. Ralph wrote about their nighttime ordeal:

### Sunday, 21 October 1917. Chalons

*I drove coming back and almost smashed into a railroad gate. They keep them all closed after dark. I jammed on the brakes and stalled the engine about one foot from it.*

*Sam was afraid to light the [headlight] lamps [Huns targeted lights] and swore when I asked [about] the flash light . . .*

*Sam forgot to bring a flash light [a major error].*

*When I swore back he begged me to stop and almost cried.*

*We got lost several times coming back.*

*We passed 12 or 15 miles of artillery and infantry.*

*We finally went back to Suippes and got the direction home. We carried a wounded soldier and a sick Lieutenant back to a hospital which is only a short distance from camp.*

*When we arrived about 8 o'clock, we made our reports.*

Ralph and Sam received no punishment for their lapse. They were told eat and get some sleep. Their French lieutenant warned them "not get lost again" or they might need an ambulance courtesy of *les Boche* artillery.

At high noon that day, Carey "the Clown" Evans, a shifty little rogue, announced it was his twenty-first birthday. After he "already killed two bottles of champagne," Carey decided to throw himself a party. He promptly gathered cash donations from the Bantams to fund his project. Carey had brains behind a fast smile.

At seven in the evening a rowdy band of Bantams headed to a gin joint in Carey's honor. The owner of the first bar saw the rabble coming and bolted his doors. At the next establishment, the boys bought twelve bottles of the best French champagne in stock. Seeing all those beautiful bottles gave Carey a nefarious idea. Since Ralph had been a killjoy lately, not drinking much wine with the rest of them, Carey decided to get him "drunk as a skunk." Maybe twelve bottles wasn't enough. He bought several more.

Lev warned Carey his scheme wasn't such a good idea.

Carey said, "Come on, it'll be fun."

Lev said, "It'll be fun until Ralph hangs you up on a clothesline and beats you like a dirty rug."

Two sheets to the wind, Carey wasn't too sly about his "alcohol ambush." Ralph, the elder enlisted man, hadn't just rolled out of the cabbage patch either. He knew something was up. He watched Carey and his cronies make a supreme effort to refill his crystal champagne glass. Ralph discreetly dumped the excess bubbly into Lucius Cook's glass. Ever responsible, Lucius had volunteered to aid Ralph in his awful plight as a "safe repository for all liquids intoxicating."

While the ill maneuver transpired, Ralph contemplated punching Carey in the face twenty-one times as a birthday present. "But the skinny Ohio guy is so dang amusing!" He declined to assault "the tricky little bastard." Ralph wrote a long entry the next day:

*Monday, 22 October 1917. Chalons*

*They had it framed up to get me drunk. They think that they succeeded. But I stood back on the edge of the crew and let Lucius Cook drink mine.*

*I drank the first glass. It tasted like pop and came up my nose afterward.*

*Lucius was soon in bad shape. He drank his six glasses and eight for me.*

*When he began to go bad, he came to me and explained that in view of the fact he had helped me out, I should promise to get him home. Alive.*

*Which I did.*

"Luscious" Lucius Cook was a devil-may-care, happy guy who always would lend a hand. Or his glass. But fourteen glasses of champagne on an empty stomach exceeded the alcohol capacity of large draft animals. Lucius didn't know what planet he was standing on when he said, "The big Swede is my friend." (Ralph's heritage was German.)

With champagne flowing deeper than the Marne River, the Bantam Boys had another party to remember. Certainly the locals needed no French translation of the antics that ensued. Almost every boy took a turn at entertaining the troops.

Ralph continued his entry:

*Hank Gillian made a grand speech and so did Lucius.*

*And they tried to get me up there, but a police whistle sounded and everything was quiet. For a while.*

*Then Duke Dennen read a piece [of poetry] called "Dangerous Dan." ["The Shooting of Dan McGrew" by Robert W. Service.]*

*Duke is good! Stewed or not . . .*

*Then we went home. Cook fell flat on his back in a mud hole . . . I saved him.*

*When we got in . . . Duke Dennen kissed all the fellows goodbye and all went fast to bed.*

The Bantams' Main Headquarters

That was one kiss, Duke Dennen, poet extraordinaire, would never live down. It became the basis for jokes and extortion threats for months. When the Sarge later heard rumors of the incident he said, "I don't want no more goddamn information!"

On Tuesday, October 23, 1917, Ralph wrote he "received my first taste of blood." He and Bill were ordered to a village in the Touraine region. As they entered the main thoroughfare, they screeched to a halt. Boche shells came in hot and hard. Ralph feared they had fallen into a trap.

In the roadway in front of Ralph's ambulance were two recently eviscerated horses. Their supply wagon had been blown in half. A filthy soldier was coolly hacking up the carcasses. With a leg propped up on a lamp post, it looked as though a madcap butcher had set up shop in the middle of an artillery barrage. Ralph could hardly believe it. He couldn't stand seeing fine horses slaughtered. One horse still had its gas mask on. (During gas attacks men, horses, and even messenger dogs were fitted with masks.)

The crossroads in the middle of the town sustained heavy shellfire. Ralph counted twenty heavy rounds falling in the first minute. One large shrapnel round fell near the ambulance. It was close enough to kill them if it weren't for the fact that Ralph and Bill were enthusiastically belly-hugging Mother Earth tighter than two garden slugs.

Red-hot metal flew over their heads leaving them relatively unscathed. They only got a few scratches. Later Bill lamented the minor wounds "weren't enough to get a medal." On the other hand, *Lizzie* received a dozen holes in her composite body. Several panels shredded. Ralph felt bad about her damage but the boys were stuck there until she was loaded. Or blown up completely. (Of the 126 American-manned Ford M1917 ambulances destroyed in the war, Ralph lost three of them to shellfire and crashes.)

As the shrapnel settled, they loaded up and scampered away.

Ralph wrote when safe back at his aid station:

*Tuesday, 23 October 1917. Chalons*

*They can be heard coming, making some whirring noise then they burst. The nearest shell was about one hundred feet away from us.*

*They seemed to drop more just as we were leaving. I drove the old Ford home and made no blunders.*

*I swiped a 75mm shell [casing] and took it home.*

*Started to make a vase [out] of it.*

On the 26th, Ralph and Sam Reynolds got partnered again. Ralph was wary but Sam did well. At four o'clock in the afternoon, they took two sick soldiers to Mont Frenet since they knew the route. Then Ralph drove a French flier back to his base.

Returning "home" Ralph ate dinner and hammered on his vase until someone yelled at him because of the noise. He drank a bottle of wine to put himself to sleep. But rains rolled in and woke him up. A leaky barracks ceiling proved impossible to seal. More wine was better than nothing while he lay under his greatcoat listening to the rain drip down on him.

In a fit of military genius, the next day the boys were issued wooden shoes. When he received his pair, Ralph pondered the lumber handiwork sitting in his palms. Wooden shoes in a Frenchie land full of water and mud: "*Brilliant!* as the Brits would say."

He wasn't sure whose bright idea this was.

The intent was to wear these shoes in camp so the Bantams could dry out their main, or only, pair of leather boots. Most boots were destructing from constant wear but they couldn't get replacements. This was supposedly the next best option. The unwieldy clogs, however, tore fragile skin. Soon they too became water logged and heavier than ocean driftwood. Walking through all the mud with wooden shoes made the boys look like they had elephant feet. The good news was that once dried out, they burnt well in the camp stove. Many a Bantam Dutch shoe met an early demise.

With their remaining free time the boys watched silent movies. Many wrote or read letters and books. Mail took weeks or months to arrive. Hometown newspapers could be six months old, but they got passed back and forth anyway. Even if a boy never heard of the town before, he'd read it for "shits and grins."

One old letter that Ralph read on the 26th said Edyth's father was sick with heart failure and pneumonia. This hit him especially hard as he knew this combination of illnesses in an older man was usually fatal.

Ralph feared he'd never meet his future father-in-law.

October waned with added miserable weather. Ralph and Bill got a temporary reassignment to cover an entire outpost station as the sole ambulance. The two drivers left to stage outside of Suippes. "A few arrivals [shells] dropped but none near us."

They spent several days moving several dozen wounded. Being far forward Ralph was delighted that they "experienced no snipers or accurate artillery." At Suippes, the weather turned fair. He took that opportunity to clean and check *Lizzie*. The only problem he encountered was that bloodstains would not come off the floorboards no matter what he did. It wasn't important. *There'd be plenty new to cover the old.*

Later, at nine o'clock in the morning, another car (he didn't write down who it was) arrived as backup for him and Bill. Having a backup vehicle, when they had just been told the unit was already stretched too thin, was not a positive sign.

Seven letters that Ralph sent to Edyth. Many had holes where censors cut out "military information."

Ralph made sure he had plenty of *bidons* of gas and oil. Drivers always avoided going below half a tank of fuel. That meant constant monitoring. Sediment could clog a vehicle's fuel lines. Straining gas helped prevent obstructions but didn't always work perfectly. Fuel was always considered suspect and subjected to impromptu filters. Ralph would use a clean old sock or a hankie when nothing more suitable was available.

The artillery then started in on the two ambulance squads. It came in harder than usual. Their trench Frenchies scrambled to stage a defense. The skirmish grew menacing. Ralph observed the fluctuating situation with French officers as he wrote this entry:

*Tuesday, 30 October 1917. Chalons*

*We saw that something was expected. We thought that they [Germans] intended to get some prisoners. But if that was their real purpose I doubt it.*

*The Germans made an attack and we carried wounded till 2 o'clock [in the morning]. I guess the Boches carried some [of their own wounded], too.*

*We see daily aeroplane fights. Some of the fellows saw a German plane and French one fall today. So far, I saw neither.*

*A German plane brought down two observation balloons yesterday. He dropped bombs into them.*

*A German plane fell between the lines and a [French] brancardier went out to bring him in. The Germans shot the brancardier and killed him.*

A bullet snapped over Ralph's head. The shooter must have been a neophyte sniper or it could have been a stray. To Ralph, the miss meant his rabbit foot was still working strong. Taller than most men, he learned to "keep my head down or it was coming off." When carrying litters close to the fighting, he walked bowlegged like an old miner toting a two-hundred-pound gold nugget. While exhausting, it was better than dead.

No Frenchies were reported missing on this raid; therefore, no prisoners were taken. The Boche probably probed the line to test defenses or created a diversion to cover for their lack of troopers. Thereafter, Ralph's section quieted down as several small attacks went nowhere. The Boche appeared to get the worst of the bargain with numerous dead. Ralph saw that some German bodies out in No Man's Land had stiff arms contorted toward the sky as if praying. He didn't think their prayers had been answered.

Ralph wrote that he and Bill had supper and went on duty at 12:20 the following afternoon. They were ordered to shift their location to an aid station near Verdun. It was a long and unexpected trip that didn't make sense to Ralph. Those were their instructions, however, and he followed them. Like most enlisted men, Ralph often railed against the lack of common sense contained in some orders. He hoped his officer candidate school application would be accepted. Still optimistic, he'd fix some of the silliness and waste.

En route to Verdun, getting refueled became problematic. No one told them precisely where to get gasoline. Ralph and Bill improvised by

A Bantam forward post near Châlons

begging like paupers at every aid station they happened upon. They got fuel, oil, and a couple of substantial meals to boot. The French were always trying to help. For once, everything worked out.

The two boys arrived outside Verdun to a truly ravaged landscape. The Verdun fortress was the site of the biggest battlefront of the war. The area had been obliterated by years of constant artillery duels and failed attacks. Acre for acre, it was one of the worst of the No Man's Land slaughter-houses in Europe.

Ralph learned that the French refused to give ground at Verdun because they felt it would be a tremendous humiliation to leave their prized Fort Douaumont in the hands of the Germans. They let it fall in 1914 without a defense, thinking it obsolete. French soldiers made numerous failed counterattacks to regain it and casualties were stupen-dous. From February to December 1916, the French and Germans lost a combined 750,000 soldiers in what became the single bloodiest battle of the war. In comparison, the United States had 407,000 combat deaths in the *entire* Second World War.

Since 1916, a quarter million more luckless Frenchies and Huns were dead.

Ralph later wrote about the land around him:

*Sunday, 4 November 1917. Verdun*

*It is the wildest place I've been at yet . . . The road was very rough, scrubby pine covers the hills which are very poor and rough. We see many [artillery] batteries covered with pine branches [for camouflage]. Not a single shot arrived but they made things lively with departs.*

*The 155s [mm artillery] roared all night. They seem to shake the whole earth. I thought all hell had broke loose when they began. It was the heaviest cannonading I've heard.*

*Machine gun bullets sang around our ears all day and night. We could hear the French answer with the Benet-Mercies [Hotchkiss-style machine guns].*

*I collected some souvenirs and made a cigarette lighter out of a cartridge.*

*When we were coming home we saw an observation balloon come to earth apparently hit by an aeroplane. We didn't see the plane. The observer escaped in a parachute.*

*We were issued 3 pairs of heavy wool socks and gloves. I took a cold sponge bath and tried on a pair of new socks.*

By November 9th, Ralph and Bill were busy with runs. Rain on the chalky, slimy soil made driving an extra unpleasant, tiring chore. They somehow managed to avoid crashing or sinking into irrigation ditches that lined various roadways. Ralph felt out of control as if skating on ice rather than driving on mud. The chalk did have one redeeming quality: He used it to sculpt little horses with his big Bowie knife.

*Friday, 9 November 1917. Verdun*

*It is white as snow and easy to whittle and nice to carve!*
*It gets slippery as grease when wet and it's wet most of the time.*
*It rains everyday.*

The reserve post at Laversine

Ralph received five letters that week. Three were from Edyth. Her father's health continued to fail. Ralph wrote, "She said her father was very bad. But the letters were old and [I] don't know if he got well or not."

By mid November, Ralph was losing interest in writing. He and Bill had been run hard to numerous outposts. He scribbled, "I'm not very prompt with my diary." Twenty-four hour, seven day a week schedules were standard. Drivers could be called anytime day or night. Fatigue was taking a toll on Bantams across the front. Other boys had been sent to Bussy-le-Chateau outside of Châlons. More were smeared across *les Postes de Scours*, which had ambulance units at Capron, Souain, Madeleine, Paulinier, Cabane, and Boudet. The boys were "all over hell." Every team wallowed in mud toward exhaustion.

Ralph and Bill returned to Châlons. During a lull he forced himself back to his diary. Tired of writing about death, he described hand grenades or "hand held bombs." He said the Germans used a (Model 24 *Stielhandgranate*) "stick" or long-handled grenade dubbed by the Allies a

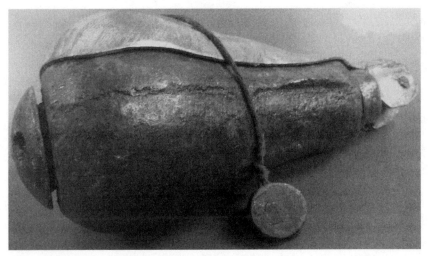

French P1 grenade PHOTO COURTESY OF DAVID O'NEAL

"potato masher." The handle gave more leverage with which to throw. But they were awkward to carry and didn't pack much explosive power.

The British forces' most common grenades were tin spheres or cylindrical shapes. Similar to tin cans they were sometimes called "Mills bombs" after the English inventor. Prior to these reliable 1915 models, soldiers improvised their own grenades using food tins filled with cordite or TNT and shrapnel. The French had several versions of grenades. (Below Ralph describes what is likely the *P1 Mle 1915*.)

*Thursday, 15 November 1917. Chalons*

*The lever is tied to the bomb. When thrown the string that holds it down is broken and a spring straightens out the lever.*

*This lever acts as a rudder and when released also acts as a hair trigger.*

*The least touch or jar sets off the bomb.*

Ralph next got partnered with Lucius Cook. They had a rollickingly good time together. In fact, one afternoon after ample supper and plenty of wine they stumbled upon an unrehearsed Frenchie floorshow. The jaded *poilu* entertained themselves on any given opportunity. This was one of the better-attended events.

Seeing men dressed as women on the stage gave Ralph quite a start. "I thought they were bearded women from the circus." But Lucius immediately got the idea. At the end of the first act, the silly little ham jumped on stage to take his turn at running the burlesque show. Ralph wrote that Lucius "made imitations of foreigners and strange people, Boschies mainly."

Lucius wrote the script as he performed. Being stoked on French wine provided infinite dramatic inspiration. Lucius became quite the hit. Literally. He kicked his heels so high in a German goose step that his right boot flew off and hit a French captain squarely in his perfectly shaved face. With the impact of a leather artillery shell, the captain never knew what whacked him.

The Frenchie crowd froze deathly quiet as the captain shook his head. *Du capitaine's* eyes darted back and forth. He stood up. Gawking at Lucius, he proceeded to laugh himself sick. "*Vous les Américains drôles!* You funny Americans!" he shouted.

Lucius asked Ralph, "Did he challenge me to a duel?"

Upon hearing the captain's response, the *poilu* loosed laughter rarely heard on the Western Front. Tears rolled down their cheeks. Some nearly soiled themselves. Ralph wrote, "Those Frenchmen fell off their benches."

*Poilu* stood up and cheered for Lucius. The opera great Enrico Caruso never received such an ovation. Lucius reveled in the glory of booting an officer. It was an act every enlisted soldier has wanted to do since the beginning of warfare. And he did it right before their eyes! A whorehouse was less entertaining.

The jovial moment was short lived as artillery ferociously dug up the ground around them. Ralph and Lucius sobered up quickly and scurried back to work.

The landscape froze solid as night fell. Shells flew in all directions. Machine guns played their cacophonous tunes. An emergency call went out to Ralph and Lucius.

*Friday, 16 November 1917. Vicinity of Souain*

*At midnight I was awakened out of one of the most peaceful dreams of my life by the yell of "Voiture. Voiture!" [Motorcar. Motorcar!]*

*Got in our wagon and we [with Lucius driving] went to carry a Frenchman with his foot shot up to a hospital on the edge of the ruins of Suippes. It is in an old castle.*

*It was a cold night and the mud was frozen stiff. Our Ford had a hard time shaking its feet loose for Lucius had stopped in the center of a puddle.*

*Lucius passed Souain like a bat out of Hell and he didn't hesitate long at the crossroads at Pethes les Hurlas. That is where the ruins of the old church are.*

*Up the road a little piece we connected with Harvey and Haupt who were returning from Suippes.*

Ralph and Lucius ran into their buddies "Kid" Harvey and Lloyd Haupt on the road. Actually, they *crashed* into each other. Lucius and the Kid barely avoided destroying their ambulances, and everyone else, on the Route de Souain.

"Our fenders lost a little paint in the deal," Ralph wrote in a vast understatement. Their abrupt meeting led to a lively discussion on the meaning of *right of way* as defined by French traffic laws. Lucius and the Kid briskly swore at each other. Each claimed he drove slowly while the other was speeding. They nearly took to punching each other on the nose until Ralph intervened. He held up his fists. Problem solved.

Ralph and Lucius mounted up as did Lloyd and the Kid. Ralph drove back fifteen kilometers on that dark night. They had no lights having just demolished their headlamps. The nearly blind ride ended up well other than tipping over a cow that was blissfully sleeping while standing up in the middle of the narrow roadway:

*Saturday, 17 November 1917. Chalons*

*When we returned all was quiet, not even a depart [-ing artillery round] broke the stillness. But the star shells [illumination rounds] never stop from twilight till dawn.*

*Lucius read a while after we returned to our rat hole but I rolled in my blankets and as soon as I was able to get warmed a little.*

*I fell again into a most peaceful and resting slumber.*

*At 7:30 the cook woke me with our coffee. He is some boy that cook is! Great to talk to and not without brains. I can always understand what he is trying to tell me and he understands my bad French.*

*He had toast and preserves for us besides our coffee.*

Runs continued. But Ralph had time to catch up on sleep and get a little exercise. During a walk, he came upon a French artillery battery. The French officer in charge happily showed the curious American how his guns worked. Ralph wrote about the famous 75mm French field gun, officially *Matériel de 75mm Mle 1897*, and its preparation for firing:

### Wednesday, 21 November 1917. Chalons

*The gunner gave me two empty shells. The shells are made the same as any small cartridge but the "bullet" in the big ones, as [in the] 75's, are explosive.*

*In the end is a primer. Behind this are two aluminum rings which have marks in them. These are set to contain the shell.*

*The timer is screwed in the shell just before it is inserted in the gun. These primers are packed in cotton while not in use.*

*The whole breech swings [open]. When the shell is injected, the hole is plumb with the barrel. Then the breech is swung around. And a solid breech is formed. When the breech locks, the gun is ready for firing.*

*It is a very slick arrangement.*

*Woe be to the one that's in the way.*

Ralph, like a kid wanting a new toy in a store, begged the officer to shoot their gun. "*Se il vous plait!* Please!"

*And they let me! The first shot I fired landed 300 yards short.*

*Well I didn't care. The second was short too but after the third they didn't elevate the gun any more.*

*It is a queer sensation when you let go that cord. All the earth and air seem to cave in on you.*

Interestingly, Ralph worried about having killed some hapless Boche with his errant shots. While it was extremely unlikely he hit anything of importance, his conscience bothered him for several days. He was there to save lives, not take them: at least in theory. He did realize that sentiment did not include Boche pilots. He said he'd like to "pound the crap out of one of those aero-officer shitheads." Ralph was still looking to find a suitable handgun to carry so he could fight back.

The next morning the air was brisk, the sun shone brightly. One of those bold "shithead" German pilots in an Albatross C-III began "nosing around" Ralph's aid *Poste*. The French on the ground turned their machine guns on the Boche. They missed. The pilot rolled his craft back toward the camp. He lined up his plane and let his forward machine gun blaze away.

*Tat-tat-tat-tat-tat.*

Bill, who had just returned to camp, was marvelously unaware that he had just happened through the pilot's gun sight. As bullets flew downward, Bill dropped the bread and cheese he'd been eating. With eyes bulging like telescopes, he screamed "Holy shit!" His voice was so shrill that dogs on Paris streets howled.

He dove for cover but did not clear the immediate line of attack.

A stripe of red-hot lead raced across camp. The two-seat Albatross's Mercedes engine screamed as it dove in at one hundred miles per hour.

Ralph scurried for the ample protection offered by a four-foot wall of solid cement blocks. He balled up, making as small a target as possible. All the while he was wondering what a bullet would feel like as it ripped through him. *That would hurt.*

Fortunately, the Boche pilot stopped firing and veered off under return fire.

Ralph glanced over at Bill. The poor boy clutched his groin looking like a terrified monkey grasping a bunch of bananas. From his expression, Ralph feared Bill was shot. Shot badly. Possibly mortally wounded.

Going into medic mode, Ralph darted over and pulled Bill's arms apart.

Seeing no entry wound, he pulled up Bill's blouse. No damage there.
He checked Bill's arms and legs. Okay there, too.

He rolled Bill on his stomach. His skinny butt popped up. No blood.

Maybe Ralph missed something. *An exit wound anywhere?* He looked.
Nope. Bill's pants were a little browner than normal. But no red.

After several tense moments, Ralph found nothing. Not a bullet hole.
Not a flesh wound. Not a scratch. It was the luckiest day of Bill's life.

"Will I die?" Bill whimpered.

"Only if I kill you. You scared me."

"*You* were scared?"

In the meantime, vengeful *poilu* leapt up and cursed at the pilot with
rare passion: *Con! Con!* (Any of these English translations apply: sod, twat,
pussy, prick, or asshole.) The Boche tried to kill their friendly *Américains!*
They aimed their French 8mm *1886 Lebel* or *1907 Berthier* bolt action
rifles at the fleeing Boche bastard. They let loose with all the rounds in
their magazines. Others tried to redirect the heavy machine guns upward
but were too slow to get a fix.

Ralph described the ensuing duel:

*Thursday, 22 November 1917. Chalons*

*Soon the [ground] firing stopped and we saw a French plane mount
up after the old boy. The rapid fire guns soon began to spit.*

*Around and around they went, going up and down.*

*After a while the Boche started for home. I guess he was hit but he
didn't get far. The Frenchman was hot after him.*

*The guns kept talking faster and faster. Suddenly the Boche
launched to one side, his engine stopped and the guns stopped.*

*The Boche took a drunken spiral course toward the ground.*

*The Frenchmen went wild. And so did we.*

The airplane arced downward. Round it went falling toward the earth
in a death spiral. It hit the ground hard, crumpling in on itself. The wings
broke off. Only the tail section survived. As the smoke cleared no signs of
life arose from the demolished craft. Ralph thought nobody could survive
such a devastating plummet. It was like taking a swan dive off a thirty-foot

Bill McClenaghan and Ralph (date unknown)

platform into a dry swimming pool. But he was soon shocked to find out their would-be assassins were "busted up" but alive. He continued his entry:

> *The Germans began to shell the place where the plane fell. To get the French who went out to see it. But they didn't get any and the bran-cardiers brought the victims in, in about an hour.*
>
> *They took them to headquarters first, to find out what they could.*
>
> *The one was an old man. He wore a captain badge; he was nearly dead. The engine had fallen on his head.*
>
> *The other was a kid. He spoke French and was not hurt bad, however his legs were broken. He played possum while they were trying to question him. But he set up afterward and talked.*
>
> *He said he was 17 years old. I don't believe he was . . .*
>
> *We carried him to a hospital at Suippes. Another car took the other.*
>
> *I got a button off his shoulder for a souvenir.*

It is important to note in the passage above that two broken legs did not qualify as being "hurt bad." Men were tough in the Great War.

As tough as men were, by this time Ralph, Bill, and the Bantam Boys were pretty well "busted up" themselves. They had myriad runs under fire transporting hundreds of French soldiers. They'd experienced thousands of rounds of artillery. They had been in training, on transports or performing continuous duty, much on twenty-four-hour call, for over five months with no break longer than forty-eight consecutive hours. The boys were tired.

Given their time on station, they were entitled to their first "repose" or rest and relaxation period (commonly called R&R in the Second World War). Lieutenant Lyon had made the request three weeks earlier. The Frenchies granted them two glorious weeks off.

The next day the Bantam Boys departed to Paris for a "breather."

What a breather Paris turned out to be . . .

# CHAPTER 8

# The Breast of Paris

*Sunday, 25 November 1917. Paris. City of Lights*

Ralph wandered dumbstruck through *La Ville-Lumière*. Beautiful Parisian architecture and grand monuments loomed endlessly in every direction. It was as if in a child's fantasy where a knight in armor would soon hasten down the street to rescue a damsel. The only impediment to Ralph's dream was the constant pestering by street vendors, begging children, and flirtatious mademoiselles who rarely took "*non merci*" as an answer. He felt like a wounded elk pursued by ravenous wolves.

In an attempt to ditch the hungry pack, Ralph and Bill rounded the corner of a large building. Bill, pickled like, well, a pickle, nearly crashed himself into its stone foundation. He tripped but caught himself before he plunged face first into the bricks. As he looked up, he spied a pair of full-sized, shapely female legs.

Regaining his balance, Bill saw a vaguely attractive, well-proportioned vixen standing inside an ornate arched entryway. A fluffy mink coat adorned her inviting torso. She smiled. Most of her teeth were intact under heavy lines of red lipstick. Too much rouge coated her cheekbones.

Ralph and Bill returned courteous smiles. Bill tipped his hat and nearly tripped again. "Stupid shoes," he said.

Ralph righted him, looked around, and wondered, *Where the heck are we?* They were searching for a floorshow: a place called the *Folies Bergère*. It was rumored to be the Barnum and Bailey of adult entertainment.

"The *best* of Paris!" a French soldier told them in a bar.

At that moment Bill grabbed Ralph and said, "I gotta see that!" So off they went.

Unfortunately, the boys couldn't find the theater. They wasted an hour on their search. Ralph and Bill didn't think to ask this woman for directions.

Gentlemen didn't do that.

A few feet down the alley the woman noisily cleared her throat.

They turned to look. *Did she need aid?* Ralph wondered. The strumpet smiled anew. Striking a pose she most indiscreetly flashed a glorious, gigantic breast from underneath her coat. It was beautifully enormous.

Heat coursed up Ralph's spine. He felt like he was standing on an exploding steam vent. Never having seen such an astonishing event before, his brain poached in the boiling afterglow; his vocal cords were paralyzed.

True to form, Bill fell in love. He eventually said, "You see that?"

Ralph regained his wits and said, "I'm partly deaf, not blind. We don't want to miss our show. Now come on."

"You kidding me?" Bill asked. "Don't ya see?"

He grabbed Ralph's coat collars and became earnestly sober.

"That guy didn't mean see the *best* of Paris. He meant the *breast* of Paris!"

Slapping Ralph's arm, Bill snorted like a feral pig, tickled by his play on words.

The joke bounced off Ralph like rubber ball. "Move it, Vaudeville Bill."

Ralph cuffed Bill's shoulder and dragged him away.

"No. I want to see more."

"You spent all your money and I ain't lending you a penny."

"Bastard. Barbarian. Bamboozler!" Bill protested all the way down the street. He thrashed like a mistreated dog being separated from his favorite bone.

"I hate you Heller, you Boche loving *Schwein!*"

Disappointed in the incomplete transaction, the vixen frowned. She lit a cigarette and waited for the next advertising opportunity to happen along.

Two days before, the Bantam Boys had decided to split their leave between Paris and the coast at St. Nazaire. On their driving trip out of No Man's Land near Suippes on November 23rd, Ralph and Bill passed numerous batteries of 75mm and 155mm cannons. Ammunition caissons and boxes sat piled high under camouflage nets. Stacks of shells ringed the sandbagged artillery emplacements. Alert Frenchie gunners watched for enemy aircraft. Balloons flew overhead.

Ralph had never seen so many pristine guns and so much ordnance in one place. He hoped they wouldn't be recalled from their vacation because of renewed Allied attacks.

The boys pulled into an ambulance depot. They dumped their ailing cars on a bewildered French mechanic. "Fix 'em," Ralph said. "We'll be back in two weeks."

The Bantams walked over to the Red Cross aid station in Châlons. They got a meal of meat, potatoes, and bread. Afterward a train transported Bill, Ralph, and several other boys to Paris. They "scored" a comfortable second class car. Everyone stretched out for naps so they had energy to burn in "Sin City."

Paris rolled out the Red Cross carpet. As the boys got off the train at three in the afternoon, a strapping US Marine sergeant stopped them. He seemed to think they were deserters. After seeing their IDs and passes, he let them go but warned the Bantams to "not get into trouble." He'd "have his eye on them." Bill held his tongue for once and didn't get thrown in the brig for insulting the NCO.

They stopped at Rue Sainte Anne where the American Ambulance Corps and Red Cross administrative headquarters offices were located. Checking in, they disclosed their itinerary so they could be traced in an emergency. After signing voucher forms, Ralph and Bill went to a nearby office. They received train tickets for St. Nazaire for later in their trip. Tickets issued, the Bantams regrouped and marched over to the "American Bar." Emboldened by freedom, the formidable group laid siege to the renowned drinking establishment.

The actual name of this celebrated Yankee tavern was Harry's New York Bar. It looked like New York to Lev and his Lowlife companions. The owner was a famous American jockey. The wooden bar inside was disassembled in Manhattan and shipped to Paris in 1911. It was a favorite watering trough, tall tales podium, and prime meat market for the Ambulance Corps. It's where Ralph and Bill got their City of Lights intelligence reports and formulated their plans for metropolitan conquest:

*Friday, 23 November 1917. Paris*

*We went to the American Bar. A Frenchman who had put us wise to the ways of Paris directed us and asked us to drink. We ordered cocktails and I choked mine down. {The damn thing made me dizzy, too.}*

*Bill disappeared to the toilet when it came time to pay. The Frenchie was going to pay but I wouldn't let him. That one darn bitter sickly dose of poison cost me 6 francs.*

*We then went to the Y.M.C.A. scored a good room for three francs a night apiece. We ate supper at the same place. It cost 3 1/2 francs. It wasn't by far as good as we get at Bussy [le-Chateau].*

*Then we went to a movie. At the show a brat came to me and sat down. She offered all kinds of insults when I wouldn't go with her.*

*No one ever gained anything by making me sore and there isn't a man in France who could say the same things to me.*

The next day Ralph went sightseeing. Despite Paris being shockingly beautiful, Ralph waxed nostalgic about his own country:

*Saturday, 24 November 1917. Walking In a Big Goddamn City*

*At 9 o'clock I rose and walked over a good bit of the town. I found several of the grand arches you see pictures of and many magnificent buildings. They are not white like the buildings in Washington [DC].*

*God Bless America is all I can say. She gets grander and grander to me each day.*

*I returned at 11 o'clock and Bill went out with me to dinner. The coffee was very commendable. It was made with hot milk and syrups of coffee.*

*In the afternoon, we walked a good bit and went to another picture show. After supper we went to the Casino Theatre.*

*Six francs was the cheapest seat we could get. Bill flirted with a woman and finally took her to the show. I sat alone.*

Ralph, a small-town American, struggled to understand French customs and Parisian mores. Most importantly, he needed to discover clever self-defense strategies to fend off the highly skilled ladies-of-the-night. He continued writing:

*While there [at Casino Theatre] I grinned at a female who I saw looking my way.*

*She immediately passed a card with her name and address asking me to meet her there. That's all it took.*

*I see it don't do [well] to smile in Paris.*

*I went home with Bill and on my way was stopped by several [hookers]. I also got lost and had some time finding my way out. But I went home with my head high. And slept a triumphant sleep.*

*Why shouldn't I? I'd faced Paris, the devil's summer palace, for two days and had done no more than drink a cocktail . . .*

Ralph longed for Edyth. He knew chances were slim that she would obtain a transfer to France. Her last letter had stated that she was nearly indispensable at Camp Upton. *Quit thinkin' about it,* he admonished himself. *Enjoy what you got.*

Ralph quashed his growing loneliness by undertaking a historical tour. Being in a dour mood the next day helped him shred a few long-held beliefs. It also ignited a newly glowing ember of distrust for authority figures. As with many enlisted soldiers, his distrust flamed into outright derision for commanders when he realized they treated their men as an expendable commodity rather than a part of humanity.

### Sunday, 25 November 1917

*I rose, leaving Bill asleep, and set out on foot to see Paris. I saw her, too. I crossed the river took pictures of the Eiffel Tower and the Ferris Wheel, relics of the [Exposition Universelle of 1889] fair.*

*Then I visited the [Eglise du Dome Church] Hotel des Invalides, the place where Napoleon was buried. His tomb is impressive. A weird*

*blue light comes in through the stained [glass] windows. A blue, airy
light. Napoleon rests in a mahogany box in the center of a ring. Christ
hangs on a cross above him.*

*I can't say he seemed as wonderful to me as he once did. [Ralph
was a military history buff.] I felt like going out and slipping a brick
in my pocket to bounce down on him . . . [for the hardships he foisted
upon his troops].*

*I reckon Kaiser Bill will rest in a similar place someday.*

After the famous "breast of Paris" incident (the chapter-opening
story which apparently Ralph retold many times—always with a big
smile), he purchased a city map. The next night he and Bill acquired the
correct directions to the *Folies Bergère*. The two boys strolled through
the theater doors without too much hand-to-hand combat with grab-
happy vamps.

The *Folies* theater's stage was ringed with impressive scenery. The colors shone brightly and the props looked charming. It was nothing like
Ralph had ever seen before. Even more charming were the lively dancing girls. They could kick their heels as high as the rafters. Their low-
cut blouses were puffy but revealing. The wild skirts were round as tiny
parachutes.

The prospect of unraveling their costumes made Bill proclaim love
once more.

Frilly ruffles ran up dancers' legs like the best silk hotel curtains. Ralph
thought the ladies were marvelous performers despite being festooned in
all that heavyweight gear. "They were doing it justice," he wrote, "with
enough energy to clear a wheat field."

All the while, Bill reckoned on which one he would marry. He said to
Ralph, "Maybe I'll become a polygamist."

"I couldn't handle anyone more than Edyth."

The show was both spectacular and mysterious. With its fast-spoken
French, enigmatic content, and hyperactive players with bouncing breasts,
Ralph felt like a six-year-old at a college physics debate sponsored by the
Roman emperor Caligula.

Ralph asked, "Why do they keep insulting the Dutch?"

Looking incredulous, Bill turned hard in his seat. He said, "A stage full of titties. And all you do is figure out the story? You're shellshocked."

Ralph, again, failed to be amused. He later wrote:

*Monday, 26 November 1917.*

*It was what might be considered a good Parisian show.*

*All of them [skits] have an American scene and a heap of sarcasm for the Dutch. Why I do not know.*

*One old fool came out and sang a song which ended each verse with "a gig-a-gig." And so on. All laughed.*

*Even les jeunes fils [the young sons] with their mothers [laughed]. ???*

*. . . They said America worships gold. Well, maybe so, but in my opinion even that is far more dignified than all the sexual worship.*

*I say again, God Bless America.*

The following day, Ralph and Bill went back to Ambulance Corps headquarters in central Paris. They were trying to get new underwear free of charge. Free was free. Otherwise they'd have to buy their own and it "wasn't cheap in that town." Turning them "inside out for more traction" was getting old. Nothing was inexpensive in wartime Paris.

To Ralph's utter surprise, he ran into three old friends, Star Windsor, John Cox, and Mitchel Don Whiting. They had joined university ambulance squads and just arrived in the country. They hugged each other like they never did before.

For an old taste of high school fun, "the gang" formed a football team with a few other ambulance boys. They played a hard-hitting game with Ralph as a "bronco fullback." They easily beat the American 17th Engineers Battalion 17 to 0: two touchdowns; one field goal. Ralph scored seven of the points.

A day later, Ralph and Bill traveled to St. Nazaire, the port city where they first acquired their ambulances and primary road training. On the way there, Ralph got a wild hunch. After seeing his southern Ohio friends, he thought he would find his cousin Lew in "St. N." Lew was drafted into the US Army infantry. Ralph worried about him being in the army because Lew wasn't big, athletic, or aggressive. Lew was "a good kid, a farmer not a soldier." Lew getting killed would kill Aunt Bea.

A large number of American troopships had arrived in port. Ralph believed Lew had to be on one of them. After a long search and numerous conversations with French longshoremen, Ralph never found Lew. (Lew survived the war unharmed. He never saw combat at the front. Ralph, Edyth, Lew, and Lew's unknown girlfriend are in a picture together at the top of the section titled Providence, page 281.)

Bill, however, was shocked to discover his boyhood friend "Snyder" (no full name was given in the diary). Snyder, an American navy sailor, had recently docked in France on the USS *San Diego*. The three boys went to a cafe for a gossip-filled reunion over the odd mix of dark chocolate squares, white cheese, and innumerable shots of Irish whiskey. Ralph forgot about his bruises from the football game courtesy of the liquor.

Other than those chance meetings, "St. N" disappointed the two. General Pershing had standing orders for a 9:30 p.m. curfew for all American military servicemen. "You can't even walk down the street with your mother," wrote Ralph.

Pershing also clamped down on the red light district to prevent Americans from entering. Bill reportedly "threw a conniption fit" over the order. While not overly religious, Pershing wanted no hanky-panky on his dutiful Christian watch. It didn't matter. Bill still found ways to hanky his panky.

On the positive side of his humanitarian efforts, Pershing ripped down an "Officers Only" sign at the Grand Hotel. He proceeded to tear it to pieces. The angry hotel manager flew outside and lunged at Pershing. The manager nearly got beaten senseless by the general's entourage and bodyguards. Once he found out he had almost slapped the commander of the AEF, he was profoundly apologetic. Pershing said if the manager didn't allow enlisted men in the Grand, "It would not serve another American for the remainder of the war."

The horrified manager threw open his arms. He shouted for all to hear, "*Américains* all welcome!"

Bill and Ralph sauntered into the Grand that evening. Acting like he owned the place, Bill got the two a nice room. It even had a bathtub. Later, while lying in the tub, Ralph smiled broadly and said, "I'm gonna soak for the rest of my life."

In the lavish restaurant that night, Bill, the man-about-town, proceeded to get played as easily as a kazoo. He wasn't overly sophisticated in his dealings with women. Despite acting like the firstborn of Don Juan, he was as vulnerable to a flirtatious smile as a bear was to honey.

Two French mademoiselles were very accommodating in exploiting Bill's weakness. Lacking a superior means of employment, they were out to scam the boys for all they were worth. Sensing a trick, and for lack of better entertainment, Ralph pretended to play along:

*Wednesday, 28 November 1917. St. Nazaire*

*When we were almost through eating they sailed in bold as brass and sat down by our table. There were plenty of other places but they crowded in back of us. I couldn't figure their game out and every time one looked our way we looked back.*

*Then they didn't . . .*

*There I ate my first crawfish [shrimp] and raw clams [oysters].*

After making plans with Bill, they'd disappear and never keep their date. Bill was heartbroken for a few minutes, until he set siege upon another "female-type woman." Several times *les Mademoiselles* hurried back and resumed their fishing trip. Bill got hooked on every cast. After reeling him in, Bill got left high and dry on the rocky banks of disappointment. Ralph stood back and "felt sorry for the poor dope."

On the third return visit, one of the women pressed Ralph into taking a walk with her that evening. He thought the request was innocent enough. Ralph was lonely so "it was better than washing my new underwear in the bathroom sink." Of course, the gal never showed up. "And it made me sore as a boil," he wrote.

The only thing Ralph could figure was the women must have been hedging their bets. If someone richer, better looking, or of higher rank came along, it was goodbye prior plans. Ralph formulated suitable revenge. The Sarge had taught him well.

The next morning, Ralph noticed the women in the crowded hotel lobby. The two were affectionately sandwiching an American captain. They might have been trying to pick his pockets. The captain didn't seem to mind.

Ralph marched up in his clean Ambulance Corps uniform and saluted the captain. Ralph growled in the most formal, convoluted medical English he could muster, "Sir, are you cognizant of the fact whereby these two harlots remain under quarantine due to virulent and incurable syphilis treponema pallidum?" Ralph dropped his salute.

Americans in the lobby stopped talking, turned, and stared. The Frenchwomen had no clue as to what Ralph said, their English too rudimentary. But the look in their eyes betrayed a realization that they had just gotten tossed into the trash bin.

The captain did not return Ralph's salute. He stiffened and sprinted for the doorway faster than a track star. Before the women figured out what was going on, Ralph scrammed out the door. He thought his speech might end the women's "dating game" for a few days. It temporarily burned their cheat to the ground. Via the Yankee grapevine, the ladies were given a wide berth for a week or more.

Before the boys returned to Paris, Snyder invited Bill and Ralph aboard the USS *San Diego* (also known to the American Navy as Armored Cruiser #6). Snyder was as proud of his warship as if he were the father of a newborn baby. He said the 13,680-ton ship had a perfect escort record. The impressive battle cruiser never lost a convoy ship.

Onboard *San Diego* Snyder showed Ralph and Bill how the fourteen-inch guns worked. The mechanical aiming instruments particularly fascinated Ralph:

*Thursday, 29 November 1917. St. Nazaire*

*The range finder was one of the most interesting things. You place your eyes in a "scope" and shut one [eye]. With the other eye you see your object. As in a spy glass but there are lines running through it . . .*

*When is it not found the halves of the object do not coincide then you open your other lamp and close the one you have been looking*

*through. There you see pointed out by a hand in plain figures the num-*
*ber of yards the object is from you.*

*It is wonderful and the distance proved to be at least three times*
*what I would have guessed it. {I didn't try to figure it out.}*

*We looked over the guns and saw how the lads slept in their*
*hammocks.*

*The boys have some glorious fist fights. When they get into a wran-*
*gle, they go to the deck and fight it out.*

To his dismay, Ralph found out later that on July 19, 1918, while heading to New York, the *San Diego* sank. It was believed she hit a German mine. The blast killed six crew members. Snyder survived a horrific secondary powder magazine explosion. But that detonation sealed the ship's fate with a second hull breach. She went down in twenty-three minutes during a frenzied attempt to save her.

(Snyder apparently escaped in a lifeboat. No others lost their lives as the ship settled on the bottom off the American East Coast near Long Island. The once powerful *San Diego* remains there to this day. She was the only major warship lost by the United States in World War I.)

The Bantams' playtime drew short. It was back to Paris for the last days of the leave. They took walking tours. Bill wanted to see the Breast of Paris once again, especially since he had cash in hand. To his disgust, he never found the magnificent orb.

In "The City," Ralph and Bill met up with Sarge Lee and others at the Red Cross headquarters. They ate dinner together on their final night of liberty. Bill explained "the vixen's massive titty" sighting. Ralph talked about what he did to the two women at the Grand Hotel. Everyone chuckled from their stories with help from plentiful wine.

Even the cranky old Sarge laughed and said, "Heller, you're funnier than a one-legged Boche trying to hop a ten foot trench."

They all toasted a glorious leave.

When it came time to pay up their hotel tabs the next day, Ralph found he had lost, or someone had stolen, his last twenty francs. He was broke. Ralph tried to shake down Bill for some of the haul he had borrowed. Getting money from Bill was harder than getting diamonds from a coal mine.

In a later entry Ralph wrote "Even though he owed me over 100 francs, he wouldn't lend me a cent to save his life. I told him to pay my bills or I'd beat the living Hell out of him." Cash magically appeared for all Ralph's debts.

Thus the curtain closed on Ralph and Bill's Franco follies and Parisian pleasures. It was the only extended non-medical leave for the Bantams in the entire Great War.

Ralph had finally seen Paris. Despite the beauty he gave it mixed reviews. "It was grand. But I'll take my hometown." He did think about bringing Edyth there after the war, maybe for their honeymoon. "That would be something!"

The boys headed back to their south Somme and Marne areas via the same tired railroad they used coming in for the first time to France. Now was the time to return to their *Postes*. The boys weren't anxious to get "home." The "lice and mice, mud and blood, shit and shoved in it," felt overwhelming. Bill nearly wept on the way in:

*Friday, 7 December 1917. Chalons*

*Returning home we saw them shelling a Boche plane and the flare and blare of guns gradually grew nearer again. We saw air scrapes all day but none of them fell.*

*I didn't go out for two days after I arrived.*

*It seemed fine to be back again.*

Ralph was being facetious. It wasn't fine being back. Running around dirt-free for two weeks made him feel human again. He wasn't happy about returning to the misery of trenches and the constant "call and haul. The dead and soon dead."

Seeing the frivolity of Paris, he knew the world had no idea what was going on out there.

Bill was immensely depressed about their return. On the train trip back to Châlons, Bill said to Ralph, "I don't know how much longer I can take this."

Ralph didn't know how to respond. *What could I say?*

Their time away seemed to make Bill feel worse, not better. He talked about dying. That worried Ralph. He tried to cheer up Bill.

Nothing worked.

While the Bantam Boys were off playing, the war had been relatively quiet in their sector. It was as if serious hostilities had patiently waited for their return. This had not been the case for British forces. Their leader General Haig, fearing rumors about his loss of command, was desperate for some type of victory on their battlefront.

British Expeditionary Forces (BEF) launched their Cambrai offensive on November 20, 1917. One hundred eighteen miles (190km) north of Ralph's position, the attack was led by 476 tanks backed by a thousand artillery pieces.

This was the first massed tank attack synchronized with ground troops. British Mark IV tanks set off to crush tons of German barbed wire, crawl over trenches, and attack machine-gun nests. Foot soldiers followed closely behind, defending the tanks and mopping up surviving Boche. This tactic set the framework for *Blitzkrieg*: the combined man and machine operations that were so successful for the Germans in the Second World War. The plan was sound. The British execution was not.

Six divisions of United Kingdom infantry attacked the German Second Army. They were supported by two divisions of British cavalry. German troops holding the trenches around the city of Flesquieres were overrun and forced to retreat six kilometers to Cambrai. It was the largest Hun loss of territory in years.

Church bells rang all over Britain signaling the advent of a great victory.

The celebration was premature.

The BEF did not effectively follow up on their initial successes. The Germans organized counterattacks and fought to recover the lost territory. Twenty divisions of storm troopers struggled for days to stop the Allied advance. They then mounted vicious counterattacks as Boche reserves spilled into the salient.

Losing the elements of surprise and shock, the British attack faltered. In addition, the Germans quickly devised ways of dealing with the "tank terror." Gunners concentrated weapons on the hull of the twenty-nine ton, three-mile-per-hour lumbering land whales. Boche field guns and machine-gun fire could breach the frail 6.1mm (15/64 in) side armor, usually at the riveted sections. Finding the tank's fatal flaw, the Huns fully exploited it. British tank crews were massacred.

Bullets penetrating the armor plates "looked like sparklers" as they bounced around wounding and killing helpless crew members. A direct hit by a 77mm field gun or a larger round could ignite the fuel and ordnance, burning the crew to death before they could escape. While airplanes were called "flying coffins," British tanks were referred to as "copper coffins."

Accurately firing one or both of the Mark IV "male" tank's 57mm "six pounder" guns (the shell weighed six pounds) could only occur when stopped. (The lighter, so-called "female" version of the Mark IV carried only heavy machine guns.) That made a target engaged tank a sitting duck for the most minimally skilled Hun artilleryman. A glancing hit on tread mechanisms or engines could disable the tank. Once completely immobile, the tank was virtually defenseless. Crews abandoning their tanks were often shot dead by German troops, even if in the process of surrendering.

Through breakdowns and combat losses, only half of the original tanks were functioning after *one* day of the attack. Half again as many were out of action the next day, and so on. English losses mounted in a disastrous spiral.

Driving the poorly ventilated tanks was extremely debilitating to crews due to leaking carbon monoxide from unshielded engines. The extreme heat and noises inside were almost unbearable. The crew had to shout into each other's ears to transfer orders. (A later study showed that gunfire combined with carbon monoxide, heat, and stress of battle incapacitated 100 percent of tank crews within four days of sustained combat.)

By the end of the battle on December 8, 1917, the Cambrai fight had pedaled backwards to another bloody draw. All the territory gained by the Allies was regained by the Huns. It was one more Great War disaster. In the morass of destroyed armor and broken men, the BEF lost nearly forty-five thousand soldiers. In comparison, this was roughly 78 percent of the number of Americans killed during the ten *years* of the Vietnam War.

As Ralph and Bill headed to their railway destination, the fighting flared up around them. Artillery sounded close. Some of the noise was the

Ralph back "home"

echoes of slaughter at Cambrai. "I feel a little blue tonight," wrote Ralph. He had no idea such a hideous fight raged north of him.

At least the ambulance boys had returned safely. Everyone arrived on time.

They needed rest and got it. Ralph reaped memories to last a lifetime.

Smatterings of the boys had gained back some of their lost body weight. Ralph had not. He was still down about fifteen pounds. *I shore feel skinny*, he thought.

Outside Châlons the Bantams left the train to search for their ambulances. The ambulances had gotten time off to be pampered by the French mechanics. The abused machines needed it. Several cars had been bent up in accidents. Most of the Ford transmissions were ailing. All had excessive wear and tear from the harsh weather and ruthless driving conditions. Ralph was determined to get a spare tire even if "I have to steal it out from under a mechanic's fat ass." He got one.

Ralph took a deep breath as he walked toward the depot. "It" was starting all over again. He knew the suffering at the front would not end quickly. The war appeared to him to be growing in its abject cruelty.

That night he had a dream of a maniacal French chef dangling a writhing lobster over a pot of boiling water. The lobster bore Ralph's face.

And *le pot* was labeled *la Marne*.

# CHAPTER 9

# For One Night the Killing Stopped

*Saturday, 8 December 1917. Poste Marne*

Cold, wind, and snow added to the misery of Ralph's depleted Frenchie troops. The *Deuxième Bureau de leÉtat-major général* (Second Bureau of the General Staff; the French intelligence service) warned that the Germans intended to take Châlons by Christmas. The front commander admonished the *poilu* to fight to the death so Mother France could live. Soldiers wrote letters to their families. Some placed goodbye letters in their Adrian helmets to be mailed should they be killed.

While Ralph was in Paris, the French bolstered their Marne defenses. More artillery pieces were ordered up and expertly camouflaged. None wanted Boche reconnaissance *avions* spying on their activity. At least one thousand rounds per 75mm cannon were procured and cached for immediate use. Bulwarks were constructed around the emplacements. Tenderfoot gunners practiced loading and unloading their weapons. They strove to get faster so they could fire quickly, but not so rapidly as to melt their barrels.

The French 75mm cannon could safely fire fifteen rounds a minute (once every four seconds) and up to thirty per minute for short periods of time. Hydraulic recoil systems kept modern artillery pieces on target unlike old wheeled iron cannons. High explosive TNT had replaced black powder and made shrapnel shells especially deadly to the infantry. In 1914, the 75mm was one of the best field guns in the world.

Many types of Allied and Central Powers aircraft overflew the area. Each side observed and taunted the other with daring maneuvers and bursts of machine-gun fire. An occasional dogfight would send a pilot to his death. A hero's funeral awaited him no matter whose side he crashed on. The Red Baron of Germany, the greatest ace ever who scored eighty kills, was given a full Allied military funeral. He was shot down on April 21, 1918, by Australian ground forces—not by an enemy fighter pilot.

Upon the Bantam Boys' return to Châlons, each was reunited with his cleaned-up ambulance. Ralph looked over *Lizzie*. She had received an oil change, lube, spark plugs, and transmission repair. The finicky transmission had given Ralph momentary doses of panic at the least opportune times. Occasionally her wheels refused to roll when Hun artillery paid a call. Mud jamming the axles or tires might have been the culprit. Gunk got scraped from every orifice. The source of the problem wasn't clear, but the mechanic proclaimed her "cured."

*Lizzie* was a tough old girl but weak in the belly ever since Ralph got her. He vowed to pamper his dear girl even more. Speeding over treacherous roads, potholes, and debris had nearly ripped out her innards. He'd watch every inch of road from now on. No more "high centering" or catching her drive train on obstacles.

Now she looked good—as good as a beat-up truck could. The only obvious defect was her composite bed was splitting apart like pages in a book. Thumbing several edges, Ralph realized the fraying "composite" was actually a shoddy material that looked like compressed papier-mâché. (Later Ford ambulances were required to have durable wooden beds.) There wasn't a thing he could do about it now.

On returning to camp, Ralph was treated to yet another thrilling visit from a marauding Boche *avion*. He did not recognize its type. It was fast and agile. Happily, its pilot's aim was not good as he and Bill jumped into a nearby shell hole. The machine gun's glowing tracer bullets missed their mark once more.

The boys pulled themselves out of cover and brushed off. As the Boche raider disappeared, Ralph looked down at his pants and puttees. The hole was flooded and muddy as a pigsty. He shook his head and thought, *Already filthy and not even home.*

A few miles later they were back to their picturesque medley of shell holes and jumbles of barbed wire. It looked like enough steel to ring all of

Battle Creek twenty times over. The craters were sufficient to make a convincing museum exhibit presenting the moon's surface. Above it all wafted the stench. *Who could forget the awful stink?* Even in the cold Ralph could smell it. His Frenchies sometimes valued chlorine gas attacks because the shells killed some of the stench along with a fair number of the rats.

After returning on December 8th, Ralph and Bill "visited all of the primary posts" during the ensuing weeks. Ralph put in so many miles he thought he could become a postwar tour guide. He wasn't sure how far they drove because he failed to keep count of his fuel usage. It was nearly one hundred gallons or approximately 379 liters of gasoline. They might have gone as far as a thousand miles. (Fuel economy on some of the worst mud-filled roads could be as low as six miles per gallon. In the bitter cold and while under heavy fire, sometimes engines were left idling for faster getaways. Thirty minutes of idling could burn half a gallon of gasoline.)

Most of the first men they carried were sick. They'd sit the *malades* in the back of the ambulance, side by side. Having no way to isolate them, the men swapped germs. If they had to throw up, Ralph requested they tap on the rear wall. He would stop for them to leap out. He said, "*Pas de vomissements dans ma voiture.* No puking in my car."

As Bill and Ralph loaded the sick, the ill men coughed and hacked. Bill and he soon ended up with a general malaise they thought was fatigue. In reality it was likely another low-grade influenza but not the virulent "Spanish flu." They had lost count of how many times they had been ill. Aspirin chased by red wine was their only reliable medicine. Ralph forced himself to eat even though he had no appetite. He drank all the clean water and hot British tea he could get his hands on. "Tea is good."

The boys worked steadily, splitting the driving load so neither got too worn out. Ralph and Bill then received a spate of night runs. They could be up all hours of the night. The nocturnal drives soon evolved into a new exciting amusement. Every drive was fraught with unpredictable dangers and near lethal consequences.

Most of the Bantam Boys' primary roads were encumbered with artillery and ammunition convoys. In the 1800s, a cannon in battle shot an average of sixty rounds per day. By 1914, the French were firing up to six hundred shells per day per artillery piece. Each gun required twelve fully laden ammunition wagons. A standard six-gun French battery, therefore, needed seventy-two wagons per day of combat. This did not include food and water for the men and horses, shovels, sandbags, mail, or spare parts. Or ambulances.

A musketeer in an 1800s skirmish fired an average of twenty rounds of ammunition in total. In the Great War, a determined infantryman could fire two hundred rounds in fifteen minutes. A modern infantry column required 120 wagons with six hundred thousand rounds of rifle and fifty thousand rounds of machine-gun ammunition per battle, minimum. Having this many horse-drawn or mechanical transports on inadequate roads caused incredible traffic jams.

Tired soldiers clogged the roads as well, sometimes stumbling around as if they were drunk. Some were. Others struggled with wounds, trench foot, and frostbite.

Close to the front, no driver used headlights because Hun artillery spotters could range on the lights with optical equipment, then rain holy hell on them. Snipers were a problem as well. When obstacles appeared, if they had not already been hit, a flashlight was used to see around them. The Bantam Boys had to develop a form of nighttime clairvoyance to avoid destroying themselves and their wounded. How more men weren't injured or killed was a divine wonder. Ralph once wryly said, "Absence of vision is a hindrance to good driving practices."

A further exhilarating complication was French colonial drivers had a habit of driving on the wrong side of the road. Ralph never figured out why. A number of these drivers came from African villages that sported single-lane roads or none at all. A few colonials had never seen a truck before. A donkey with a cart was a luxury in their world. An ox made a man rich. A truck was nothing short of "magic."

Bill was at the wheel one night in mid-December when a battered *Latil* cargo truck driven by a French colonial magically appeared before him: smack in his lane. It looked like a dusty brown Rock of Gibraltar rolling toward him. Bill screeched like a night owl. He swerved off the road as the *Latil* took his left fender as a souvenir.

Ralph, sleeping next to him, awoke startled not knowing where he was or what was going on. "What? What?" he asked as he tried to find the flashlight.

"Why do those fuckers drive like that?"

"What fuckers are ya fucking talking about?"

The boys learned that their dainty 1,680-pound (762kg) *Lizzie* was no match for a fully loaded, several-ton cargo truck. A 3,400-pound (1,542kg) 75mm field gun with additional weighty ammunition caisson drawn by four stout horses was found to have the flexibility of a brick wall. Therefore, plowing into either one with Henry Ford's prized ambulances was not heartily recommended.

Ralph and Bill avoided at least three head-on collisions at night over the course of a month. The lack of a fatal accident was especially remarkable since supply vehicles and gun platforms traveled swiftly in order to get to their destinations before dawn. They didn't want to be spotted by daytime Boche aviators. This "game of chicken" (whoever turned first "lost" the contest) got worse near the front. Sharp flashes of the artillery nearly blinded Ralph. The continuous roar made it near impossible for him to hear traffic ahead of him. He marveled at how he didn't "end up flatter than a flapjack."

Mostly sick were transported at this time. Artillery didn't take down many of their industrious Frenchies who furiously toiled on fortifications. Ralph and Bill only made a dozen runs with wounded. These tended to be daylight jaunts where Ralph could see where he was going. The disadvantage was daytime artillery tended to be more intense since balloon or *avion* spotters could correct incipient fire to hit fleeing targets. No matter. Ralph preferred day runs because poor hearing was a bigger handicap at night.

Since there had been comparatively few casualties, Ralph wondered if the intelligence service's prediction of a large attack was wrong. Maybe it was all disinformation. He thought, *Me and my Frenchies might live to see Christmas.*

When the weather cleared the usual cat and mouse aircraft game played out overhead. "Air scrapes" filled the entire month. Dogfights were a common spectacle that fascinated Ralph. One especially glorious fight involved five Boche and seven gritty French. This fight with its dozen planes looked like a swarm of hornets trying to sting each other to death.

In most dogfights, pilots picked their prey and tried to get on his tail. Lining up the target using the aircraft controls, the attacking pilot let loose with his machine guns. (Forward machine guns were fixed and could not swivel.) Using short bursts, he attempted to find the sweet spot to hit the target. In practice, this venture took considerable skill and coordination. Aces learned fast. The rest died.

Unwilling to cooperate with its destruction, the target bobbed and weaved to the extent of its design maneuverability. Gun sights had to be repositioned with each change of direction. Around and around they went at each other. Predator could become prey. Prey could become predator. Nobody was safe in the air. But a pilot's flight skills with a dab of luck usually determined the outcome of a fight.

Attacking pilots needed to maintain situational awareness—lurking enemy aircraft could send them flaming to the ground if they weren't careful. In a clawing swirl dogfighters rolled. The struggle continued until one fell, they ran out of bullets, or fuel got low. Many clashes turned out to be draws.

All pilots needed to conserve enough fuel to get back alive. This included compensating for wind speed and direction, and wind drift. Fighting in variable winds could push aircraft miles away over enemy territory. A strong headwind could greatly increase fuel consumption on the return trip as well. Good combat pilots were virtual trigonometry mathematical machines. Or they were really lucky.

Miscalculating fuel usage led to impromptu landings. Even the best landings on prepared runways could result in barely controlled crashes. Landing in an unmarked farmer's field meant the pilot was taking his life into his own hands. He could not see over his engine and hoped nothing substantial was in his way. If the ground harbored uneven or potholed areas, they could rip off his stiff landing gear. Abrupt stops typically led to injury or death in the unprotected canvas cockpits.

In the fight this day, two Boche and one Frenchman punched their admission tickets to the Great Beyond. A Boche *avion* lit up from ignited gasoline. He spiraled to the ground like a flaming brick. In his smoke trail, small pieces of aircraft fabric fluttered down behind him like a tribute of burning confetti. Another arced to the ground in a slow but steep

A dead aviator

angle dive. His dead hands probably never left the control stick until he slammed into the earth like a meteor.

Few pilots lived long. Despite the dangers, most ground men had dreams of flying: Ralph included. As he watched the spectacle he said, "Any idiot can ride a cavalry horse. Few can fly an aeroplane." That gave him another famous idea. Still aggrieved about being shot at by the German pilots, Ralph filled out an application to join the American Flying Corps. *Them Hun pilots shore need to be taught a lesson*, he thought.

Because he held a critical job, Ralph was unlikely to get into flight school. Despite the odds against him, he filled out an application. Lieutenant Lyon reluctantly signed off on the paperwork. He sent it floating down the vast Army bureaucratic channel with its banks of red tape. The water in this canal ran so slowly, no one knew when or if Ralph would get a response.

The average life span of a front-line combat pilot was around two weeks. That's about the length of the existence of the common tomato fruitworm moth that Ralph had the pleasure of smashing on the family farm. A newly christened pilot could be dead before his flight school graduation letter got home to America.

That didn't discourage boys from signing up.

Off duty for eight hours, Ralph and Bill visited some nearby machine-gun nests. Ralph took photographs of the activity. A French executive officer stopped and interrogated the two boys. He wanted to make sure they were not German spies or perfectly cloaked *Frontschwein* ("front hogs," Boche slang for trench soldier). After reviewing their papers, he determined they were not a threat. But the name *Ralph Heller* sounded "too German" to him. (That's because Ralph's parents were from Germany!)

"No is *bon*," said the French officer. "Could be *bon*."

The French officer thought for a moment then put his hand on Ralph's left shoulder. He tapped his left then right shoulders, knighting him. "You now *Ralph Hellier*" (he pronounced it in French as *Rălf Ell-ē-yay*).

The name took a moment to sink in. As it dawned on Ralph, he liked it! He was an honorary Frenchie. *Merci beaucoup!* (The *Hellier* spelling followed him throughout the rest of the war and ended up on his French Government citation for valor.)

Bill chuckled to himself, entertained by Ralph's delight over his new *nom de guerre*. When they got back to their quarters, Bill told the Bantams what had just happened. The bemused boys hopped in on the act. They proceeded to unmercifully twist Ralph's name further. After coming up with numerous hideous nicknames, they landed on a new appellation: *Raff*, as torn from the word "riffraff." It was the final salvo of hostility in the class war of Princeton, New Jersey, versus Marietta, Ohio.

*Raff* fired right back. "Purple piss boys . . ."

The Bantams scattered. But the mold was cast. Whenever Ralph needed cheering up or tearing down, they called him *Raff*. It always spiked his blood pressure and helped the Bantams to improve their one-hundred-yard dash elapse times as Ralph chased them wielding his Bowie knife.

In retaliation, Ralph put some fresh horse poop in Bill's helmet one afternoon. Ralph rushed to Bill and pushed it in his hand. Ralph hurriedly said, "Incoming artillery!"

Without thinking, Bill slapped it on.

Citation for Private Ralph *Hellier*

"Steaming justice has been served," Ralph said as he sprinted away. Bill headed for a shower since Ralph still had his knife.

Later in the day the clouds cleared. Ralph wrote sometime around December 19th, "I filled a whole roll of pictures that day for it was bright and sunny." Aircraft took to the skies. The entertaining "air scrapes run all day but none of them fell."

The endless cycle of war continued. Deaths were accepted as easily as telegrams.

Cold, gray December days slipped by. While no *attaque en force* erupted, each side seemed to be constantly probing the other's defenses. Trench raids and silent prisoner abductions killed and stole men from both sides. German gas shells landed without accompanying heavy artillery or infantry attack, a rather fruitless tactic. Nobody understood why. (As stated before, the Germans were attempting to mask their existing lack of manpower as they built up for the Spring Offensive.)

Recovering sick and wounded kept the Bantam Boys on edge. The random gas shells caught some Frenchies by surprise. "Gas cases" were especially difficult for ambulance men to tend. Each case differed in symptoms depending on the agent employed. These boys were gassed with chlorine, a very nasty substance. If they were to live, Ralph had a lot of work ahead of him when he set out on the hurry call.

As described in *Medical Diseases of the War* (Hurst, 1917):

> . . . *the first effect of inhalation of chlorine is a burning pain in the throat and eyes, accompanied by a sensation of suffocation; pain, which may be severe, is felt in the chest, especially behind the sternum.*
>
> *Respiration becomes painful, rapid, and difficult; coughing occurs, and the irritation of the eyes results in profuse lachrymation. Retching is common and may be followed by vomiting, which gives temporary relief. The lips and mouth are parched and the tongue is covered with a thick dry fur.*
>
> *Severe headache rapidly follows with a feeling of great weakness in the legs; if the patient gives way to this and lies down, he is likely to inhale still more chlorine, as the heavy gas is most concentrated near the ground. In severe poisoning unconsciousness follows; nothing more*

*is known about the cases which prove fatal on the field within the first few hours of the "gassing," except that the face assumes a pale greenish yellow colour.*

*When a man lives long enough to be admitted into a clearing station, he is conscious, but restless; his face is violet red, and his ears and finger nails blue; his expression strained and anxious as he gasps for breath; he tries to get relief by sitting up with his head thrown back, or he lies in an exhausted condition, sometimes on his side with his head over the edge of the stretcher in order to help the escape of fluid from the lungs.*

Transporting men with these painful symptoms made Ralph particularly angry. He felt gas was not civilized. It was not honorable. He hated the man who invented artillery. But he hated the inventor of gas shells even more.

After taking eleven gas cases to the hospital, Ralph suddenly discovered it was Christmas. He'd lost all track of time:

### Christmas Day, Tuesday, 25 December 1917. Chalons

*I've been to Menehould. I didn't know it was Christmas till this evening.*

*I haven't had any mail for a week. I hope tomorrow will bring a letter at least. The Lieutenant received a letter concerning my transfer. It looks a little more encouraging. I may make an aviator yet.*

*We have expected an attack for sometime. Everywhere we see preparations.*

*The Boche have been using gas.*

*We carried 12 cases yesterday afternoon but had no calls at night. One fellow was brought in but he promptly died and saved us a trip.*

*The gas cases did not look serious.*

On Christmas evening a number of French soldiers arrived at headquarters (HQ) to entertain the Bantams. They brought "a fine orchestra and one Grand Opera singer." To accompany them, Lev's six singing Lowlifes, who originally formed up during the raucous train trip to St. Nazaire, were redubbed the "Killjoy Quartet." They joined in.

The good music was much appreciated by all. The boys listened intently and many more sang along. Then the band struck up "God Rest Ye Merry Gentlemen." Everyone stood and heartily chanted:

> *God rest ye merry, gentlemen*
> *Let nothing you dismay*
> *Remember, Christ, our Savior*
> *Was born on Christmas day*
> *To save us all from Satan's power*
> *When we were gone astray*
> *O tidings of comfort and joy,*
> *Comfort and joy*
> *O tidings of comfort and joy*

When it ended, not a dry eye remained in the HQ building. Ralph sat down in a corner and laid his head on his diary. He never felt so close and yet so far away from others. His emotions both perplexed and fascinated him.

Keeping with Princeton tradition, the Bantam Boys bought a "huge" amount of champagne for the Christmas celebration. Ralph stayed away from the crowd to write in his diary. He was thrilled to have received a book by Kipling (no title was noted—he was Ralph's favorite author and one of the most popular writers of the day). Edyth sent it months earlier so it would arrive on time. He sent her a French shell casing vase he had decoratively etched using a fire-hardened steel spike. Edyth later wrote back that she liked it. (Edyth donated the casing to a metal drive in 1943. Its brass was melted down to make American shells during World War II.)

On top of a HQ desk, the boys bedecked a small Christmas tree. They lovingly hung champagne corks, jagged shrapnel, and large bullet casings as ornaments. Someone had brought it to camp earlier that week but forgot to sit its bough in water. Its weakened spine bent under the weight of the metal decorations. Lucius Cook propped it up using a barbed wire "scaffolding" that looked ornate enough to be wrought iron from a classy New York high rise apartment. The boys stood back and admired their work.

Looking at it, Ralph had never seen a more beautiful Christmas tree.

The Bantam Boys' grandma

As the boys sang songs with their Frenchies, they saluted each other with fine champagne. They toasted each other to continued good luck. Some danced together. The sullied Duke Dennen had a hard time finding a partner after he had kissed boys on a prior drunken binge. Jack grudgingly agreed to a liaison if no smooches were involved.

They were joined by their gracious *Grand-mère* et *Grand-père* (grandmother and grandfather). Several Bantams were shocked to find the eighty-year-old couple starving in a blown-up house two days earlier. Their family had abandoned them, thinking them dead. The boys brought the refugees back to their aid station. They put them up in a nearby house and fed them. Ralph had taken the grandmother's picture and made her a copy. She was delighted. (The boys cared for the couple for three months.)

By the end of the night, the boys took time to be alone with their thoughts. Despite all the heavy libations, everyone grew quiet. For many of the men, Ralph included, it was their first Christmas away from home.

Most went off to sleep. Some wandered outside alone in the cold and the stars.

No hurry calls came in to their aid station.

*For one night the killing stopped.*

All through the last week of December the days were wet and frigid. Sometimes snow fell. Sometimes sleet pelted down like sharp gravel. Ralph had had three major runs, two of them to Suippes. On a run to Menehould, a French major named Pique, a physician, befriended Ralph after finding out about his medical career aspirations:

*Friday, 28 December 1917. Menehould*

*Last night Major Pique had some friends here. He came by and caught me reading a French book on medicine. He put his arms around my shoulder and looked at my book.*

*I thought it was Bill and when I looked around I was somewhat surprised. I started to rise to salute but he held me on my seat and spoke very pleasantly to me. I told him that I expected to be a surgeon some time . . .*

*The Major was very pleasant. He took me to his room and showed me his books and gave me a cigar, which I gave to Bill.*

The major offered to loan Ralph his medical books. He borrowed all he could carry over the intervening weeks. Reading occupied his spare time in learning about the emergency medical side of the war. It seemed to give Ralph a sense of mastery over a situation that dispensed no control to anyone living on the front.

Wound treatment as described in *Medical Diseases of the War* consisted of:

*Removal of loose and fixed bits of obvious foreign, and dead matter is, of course, essential. Ample exposure and drainage of the wound is necessary, and those wounds which are too extensive after the above treatment to retain a drainage tube do better than those in which a tube is necessary on account of their depth and narrowness. By this procedure the wound is put in the best possible conditions for the bactericidal actions of the tissues and the outpoured lymph. It is important to remark that it is not wise to impair the resisting and offensive powers of the artificially obtained healthy tissue surfaces by the use of strong or injurious antiseptics.*

Despite the best of intentions, the practice of medicine was crude. Effective medicines were few. Sutures consisted of catgut. Opium and cocaine hydrochloric were plentiful and characterized as universal pain treatments. They were freely distributed to patients like candy, and unfortunately, drug dependency became the next battle for many injured soldiers.

The Great War, out of necessity, spawned medical innovation. Splinting and blood transfusions were used extensively for the first time. Splinting limbs avoided further injury, tissue destruction, and internal bleeding during transport. Transfusions propped up blood pressure. The latter technique helped wounded survive catastrophic circulatory failure—what is now known colloquially as "shock." Before stabilization efforts, trivial injuries could lead to death. Nobody knew why. Loss of oxygen to the brain was the culprit.

Thousands of faces and limbs needed to be restored as well. Artificial limb manufacturers sprang up all over Europe. Suturing huge wounds became a flourishing art, which later led to the medical specialty of plastic surgery. Ralph strove to learn basic suturing by following written descriptions in his borrowed books. Dr. Pique critiqued his work and offered suggestions to improve Ralph's handiwork. He got pretty good by practicing on moldy pork chops.

One morning Bill saw Ralph sewing away. With a cynical smile on his face he asked, "*Raff,* you putting a pig back together out of guilt for eatin' bacon *sammiches?*"

"Sap head, you wanna learn how to replace your two front teeth?"

Between Christmas and New Year's John Litel and Don Casto were at Capron. A long line of French cars pulled up to their aid station. An older man in a smart business suit got out and said to them in perfect American English, "So you are the Americans?"

The boys weren't much up for a conversation, but they talked about several subjects including their work and their hometowns. Don was from Columbus, Ohio. The old man said he had visited Columbus some years past. Don told the man what had changed in the time since the Frenchman had been there. It was a nice, neighborly talk.

Eventually the old man asked, "Do you know who I am?"

Both admitted they did not.

The man said, "I am Clemenceau."

Don and John nearly fell over dead. They were talking to *Le Tigre*— the Tiger, Georges Clemenceau. As prime minister he was one of the most powerful men in France. The boys didn't know if they should bow, salute, grovel, or wet themselves.

They just stared with mouths half-open.

Clemenceau laughed as he shook their hands. "Thank you," he said as he left.

Poor year-end weather and effective artillery fire played havoc with Bantam operations. The indiscriminate chlorine gas shells continued unabated. To top it off, Bill was having a rough, sullen period. He didn't want to talk about it. Ralph tried to give him a break by doing most of the driving. Ralph's fatigue was dulled by ample leftover Christmas food and wine. The best solution to any problem on the Western Front: eat hot food and drink cold wine. Sometimes they heated up bottles over a fire or mulled the wine with spices when they wanted a hot drink.

In between runs Ralph wrote Edyth over a dozen letters. He wanted to know about her Camp Upton Christmas. He wrote his ma as well. He wanted all the details about the family's Christmas. It would be months before he got responses from either.

Ralph and the boys had more driving problems the week between the two holidays than in recent memory. Drivers were getting serious crash injuries. Ralph was afraid somebody was going to get killed. He was right.

Ralph fatally wrecked his *Lizzie*, re-designated *Lizzie #1* (there would be three more). He had just survived a crash into Lloyd Haupt. Later that same day an exploding artillery shell caused him to lose control and hit a house. The impact crushed the radiator, knocked the engine off its mounts, and ended *Lizzie #1*'s transmission woes forever. She was dead. He was aghast at her demise. It was like killing the family's favorite horse.

Ralph didn't get away unscathed either. He found himself thoroughly bruised as if he had been a tackling dummy for the Princeton football team. His legs were black and blue. His head hurt. Ralph's cuts, in his dirty uniform, soon festered despite the cold. *I look worse than bully beef,* he thought.

Safety devices did not exist in any motor vehicle of the era. Fenders prevented tire and vehicle damage at low speeds. Despite this so-called protection, a speedy fender bender could cause a serious driver or passenger injury. The driver could get thrown onto the hood or impaled by the solid steering column.

Ambulances did not have windshields. Rain and snow made it difficult to see. Wind perpetually dried out the boys' eyes. Some of them wore aviator goggles if they could buy or steal a pair. Safety glass had just made its way into the eye ports of military gas masks. It would be 1927 before reinforced glass windshields were required in civilian motorcars.

After acquiring *Lizzie #2*, Ralph took hurry calls with Bill to Suippes. They were forced to drive around in a powerful snowstorm. They practically froze to death. That fun little spree nearly ended in a disaster as well:

*Monday, 31 December 1917. Suippes*

*We made the trip in less than an hour.*

*Coming back, Bill got to going pretty fast and attempting to turn a corner skidded and we landed in the ruins of an old house.*

*It was another close one but no one was hurt and the Ford wasn't damaged to any extent. That is the third "close one" I've come through . . .*

*Lloyd Haupt knocked me clean off the road the other day. A stone pile saved me from climbing a tree. Now a stone pile is no cushion. But if the stones are small it's preferable to [hitting] a tree or a telephone post . . .*

*One day at Suippes we—I have a new car now—took four maladies to Croi Champagne. The load held the Ford to the road going and although the road was covered with ice. The sleet cut my face and blinded me. Even froze ice sickles to my eyebrows and froze my eye lashes together.*

*I made the trip fast enough.*

*But returning I was forced to creep all the way. It was so slippery that I couldn't hold back on the hills.*

*But we got back safe.*

Thus ended the glorious year of 1917.
December drew to an unceremonious close.
It had been a very long year.
Incredibly, all the Bantam Boys had survived.
In 1918, they wouldn't be so lucky.

# CHAPTER 10

# Screwed, Blued, and Tattooed

*New Year's Day, Tuesday, 1 January 1918. Châlons*

The year rang in with endless runs in terrible weather. The bright spot was the holiday cuisine continued to be exceptional, some of the best meals Ralph had eaten. There was plenty of it. Jarlaud, the French *chef de cuisine*, had outdone himself. At least food provisions were dependable. At the moment. Wine was never in short supply.

Ralph, the currently svelte wrestler, gorged and drank to regain his former heavyweight dimensions. He eventually got back to a sturdier 195 pounds but fell short of his wrestling weight of 205. It was close enough. Constantly lifting men was as good as lifting barbells in the gymnasium. His upper body strength remained respectable despite the cold, sleepless, hair-raising grind he had endured.

Ralph received a postal package from a hometown church. (No church name was noted and he didn't disclose its contents.) He had hoped for a letter from Edyth. There was none. That made him "a little blue." He got out his Bowie knife to whittle. Piercing cold prevented any attempt at photography. Leather froze in his hands as he tried to craft a wallet. He mindlessly whittled away on artillery-ravaged tree branches instead.

The Red Cross gave the Bantam Boys a cotton bag filled with tobacco, cigarettes, candy, toothbrush, soap, and towels. It was a highly prized holiday treasure trove. Ralph wrote, "I gave mine to a Frenchman who had his leg shot off." The man looked like so many of the boys he had hauled to the aid stations. He felt it was the least he could do.

Ralph tried to trace what happened to some of the men he had transported. He rarely knew what happened to his men after they left his ambulance. If a boy died in his car, Ralph would often bury the body himself. But too many wounded clogged the aid system. Record keeping was not a priority. Most of the time, Ralph found out nothing about "*ses garçons,* his boys" during his follow-up searches.

"It would have been nice to know how many lived," he once lamented.

A Bantam driver named Davis, who Ralph didn't know well (forty-four men were in the original group at Allentown; not everyone worked together), wrecked his ambulance. Ralph wrote "he wasn't hurt bad." Given Ralph's Great War standards that probably meant Davis's skull was partially crushed. He was admitted to a hospital for an extended recovery. That left the Châlons main aid post without an ambulance.

Lieutenant Lyon tapped Ralph for another solo adventure.

Driving into the main square at Châlons, Ralph heard heavy artillery "off to the left" or approximately northwest in the British Somme sectors. "It sounds rougher than any I've heard yet." What it signified, he didn't know. He wrote, "We have had quite a bit of gas near here." Gas *and* high explosive artillery shells together were an ominous sign often portending large infantry attacks.

He was worried that this was the big battle they had been warned about.

While most soldiers thought the Germans used gas first, the French actually beat them to the punch by shooting tear gas at the Boche in August 1914. The Germans took the lead from there. The Boche put serious resources into the development of poison gases. While tear gas was noxious and temporarily debilitating, chlorine, phosgene, and mustard gases could be fatal depending upon total dosage received.

Mustard gas was difficult to defend against because of internal and external blistering actions. A few hours after exposure, painful symptoms would arise on the affected area. Inhaling even a minor quantity could destroy lung tissue and cause respiratory distress or sudden death.

Charcoal or chemically treated filter gas masks generally provided effective breathing purification for most gases. The French M2 gas mask was used from 1916 to 1918. Ralph kept his M2 close at hand. It was effective for longer periods of time than the British small box respirator (SBR). But the M2 could fog up from water vapor in the soldier's breath. The only way to clear the mask was to take it off—which was not a smart move when steeped in poison gas. The US Army issued its infantry both the British-made SBR (or the American-modified SBR version) and an M2.

Exposed skin had no protection. Painful yellowish scabs formed on uncovered body parts. With sufficient absorption, death followed hours or days later as tissue broke down and lungs filled with fluid. Soldiers could be asphyxiated as the fluid or lung tissue clogged airways. Essentially, they choked to death.

Men survived gas attacks, but some never fully recovered. Estimates of gas casualties include eighty-eight thousand men killed and 1.2 million injured in gas attacks against both sides during the war. In comparison, the United States lost only fifty-eight thousand (total deaths including combat related, sickness, and accidents) in *all* wars in the eighty-five years prior to the American Civil War from 1776 to 1860. (Nearly 84 percent of those deaths were from disease.)

Gas masks had significant drawbacks. When Ralph drove with a mask on, he couldn't see more than ten feet up the road through the tiny eye ports. Bulky leather or rubber gas masks properly secured restricted breathing and impaired hearing. Communication was nearly impossible when artillery was falling and rifles were firing. Restricted sensory input could produce an overpowering sense of claustrophobia. Some men ripped off their masks despite the gas and died because of their panic.

Having such limited perception, trench soldiers never knew if the enemy was nearby or coming over the parapets. Gas, smoke, and dust made it impossible to see much. Hand-to-hand fighting in full combat gear with a cinched mask in a gas-filled trench must have been indescribably terrifying.

Mustard gas could remain active for days depending upon level of saturation, humidity, and weather. Because of its longevity, capturing or occupying a fouled trench could be harmful or fatal to an unwary attacker. Before the unprotected soldier knew what was happening, his lungs could fill with pulmonary fluid. The Bantam Boys were warned to carry an M2 under all circumstances and don it immediately if they felt any unusual symptom.

No gas casualties fell into Ralph's hands on January 6, 1918. He was especially happy since it was his twenty-sixth birthday. He didn't tell any of his Frenchies, desiring no attention or celebration. He just wanted time to carve a new wooden horse and get some sleep. Unfettered evening hours provided time to do both.

The next day Ralph visited La Cheppe. The *Lafayette Escadrille* was based there. The *Escadrille* started out as a section of the French Air Service officially called the *Aéronautique Militaire*. It was primarily composed of American volunteer pilots. They first took off in French airplanes and uniforms in 1916. A screaming Native American Indian head adorned the sides of their fuselages. They registered fifty-seven confirmed enemy kills by February 1918.

Within months of Ralph's visit, the *Lafayette Escadrille* would be re-designated as the Air Service of the AEF. No longer part of the French military, they would be the precursor to the US Army Air Forces of 1941. After World War II, in 1947, it became the US Air Force (USAF), the third branch of the American military in conjunction with the Army and Navy.

Ralph wrote that the *Escadrille* "has about 20 large hangars and about 100 planes." He had conversations with many of the pilots. They talked tactics, machinery, and weapons. Ralph anxiously inquired about their training.

From their description, he thought he could pass muster and get into the *Escadrille*. "I got good eyes. Ears—not so good. Eyes beat ears hands down in the air," he joked. Ralph had not yet gotten a final response to his air service application. All the talk excited him. He was going to talk to Lieutenant Lyon about hunting down and pushing through his pilot request.

The *Escadrille* first flew the single-seat French-made Nieuport 11 fighter. A biplane, the Nieuport's top wing spanned twenty-four feet, six inches (7.5m) and weighed about eleven hundred pounds (500kg). It was driven by a nine-cylinder, eighty-horsepower LeRhone rotary engine. On 30 October, 1916, the first Nieuport 17's began service. They were slightly larger with more robust 130-horsepower engines. The aircraft could fly up to 110 mph (177kph) and get to over ninety-five hundred feet (2,896m) in altitude.

By mid-January, Ralph had been on continuous hurry calls through ice and snow. One in particular was enormous fun. He had heard about the sport of skiing. In France, Ralph got his first opportunity to do so. And he didn't even strap on a pair of skis.

On a solo trip, he hit a patch of ice halfway down a Marne department hill. *Lizzie #2* decided to take off like a ski jumper. Feeling spritely, she added a 360-degree turn to her routine. Like a ballerina in a pirouette, she spun elegantly.

Ralph hung on for dear life. He had no control whatsoever. He was afraid she'd flip and dump his cheering wounded *poilu* all over the snowy landscape. (Apparently his Frenchies thought Ralph was showing off like a teenager doing doughnuts in a high school parking lot.) He didn't want to do something drastic, make a mistake, and kill him and his wards. *Lizzie #2* was moving fast. The brake was useless.

On the final degrees of her downhill turn, he rocked the steering wheel violently. The front wheels found purchase on dry ground, almost flipping his girl in the process. Within forty feet or so, he got her going straight. She slipped and slid, then chattered to a stutter-stop at the bottom on a gravel siding. From the heavy vibration, Ralph thought he had destroyed her transmission. *Hell's bells!* It would be a long, cold walk home that day. His wounded could freeze to death.

His Frenchies nevertheless clapped in appreciation of his high performance. Ralph felt more like cleaning his underwear than doing a curtsy.

Looking *Lizzie #2* over, he found no major damage done by the violent skid. Ralph couldn't believe it. Still puffing from the thrill and exertion, he was saddened that Bill wasn't there. He could have confirmed Ralph's story of extreme driving prowess and skill to the Bantams. *It was one heck of a ride!* He avoided that hill in future snowstorms.

During January, the Germans shelled regularly and effectively. Rumor had it they were specifically trying to kill Americans. The Boche apparently reasoned that if they sent soldiers' bodies back to America, the

United States would quit the war before they sent more men. Like many militaries, they underestimated their foe's determination.

Targeted or not, Ralph felt considerably less safe. A number of Bantams decided to stash handguns in their tunics or under their driver's seats. The gun the Bantam Boys prized most was the outstanding American Model 1911 Automatic Pistol, one of the best firearms ever designed. (The handgun was issued by the US military from 1911 to 1985—an extraordinary seventy-four-year history of service.)

The Colt .45 caliber slug was revered for its "stopping power." That is, it could stop a charging soldier dead in his tracks. The easily exchanged seven-shot magazines offered up considerable close-range mayhem. Ralph decided he'd get one by whatever means necessary. His Bowie knife was not enough. Not all Bantams decided to carry weapons. Lieutenant Lyon told them, "It's your choice, boys. I can't tell you what to do."

One night that week, Ralph heard a ruckus. Knife in hand he slinked off to investigate. He wished he had already gotten a Colt. He thought the strange noise could be Germans sneaking up on their camp. He was ready to stab a rotten *Frontschwein*.

When Ralph got to the source of the rattling noise, he found a little brown kitten with its head stuck in a half-opened salmon can. He freed the tired feline and took the dirty kitty back to his barracks. He gave it a hot bath, brushed it with his comb, and glossed its ragged claws with medical balm.

Ralph put the cute little thing inside his tunic so it could sleep on his warm stomach. The kitten fell asleep. When he awoke the next morning, the kitten was gone. Ralph immediately searched the camp end to end. He put fish out on a plate for days to lure it back to his tent. He never saw it again. Neither had anyone else.

Heartbroken, Ralph feared it had been eaten by one of the camp's monster-sized rats. The thought tormented him for days. In the following weeks, Ralph beat a horde of rats to death with a trench shovel or stabbed them with his knife. He often burned the rat remains in the campfire.

One day after Ralph had pounded a dozen rats into the ground, Lyon asked, "You okay, Heller?"

He never answered.

Ralph then ran multiple trips in and out of Suippes. Two of his cases were trench boys who "cracked." These were his first experiences with "shellshocked" troops:

*Friday, 18 January 1918. Suippes*

*We had some close shells. A piece hit one of the English ambulances there.*

*We made four trips, one at twelve o'clock with one like an epileptic. He was tearing everything up. It took four men to hold him.*

*The weather is warm and the mud is knee deep. I had to push Lucius out of two holes.*

*We carried another boy who had gone bad in the head from an artillery camp near Perthes [Seine-et-Marne]. We could get a full view of the German line there.*

*If the Bad Lands of Dakotas are one half as bad a scene of desolation, it must be some sight.*

*At night it looks more desolate than ever. You see the battered skeletons of trees against the horizon when the star shells [illumination rounds] loom up.*

Shellshock was being identified as a medical diagnostic category. It was thought to be caused by pressure waves from exploding artillery impacting the brain. Thus, a shell "shocked" the outer cerebral cortex, causing little hemorrhages or bleeding within the skull. This supposedly induced fatigue and bizarre psychological symptoms seen on the battlefield and in returning combat soldiers.

In World War II, the term shellshock was renamed "battle fatigue." Most recently the condition became known as post-traumatic stress disorder (PTSD).

In 1917, the term shellshock was quietly banned from British military documents including medical journals. The extent of the problem was minimized. But by 1939, at least 120,000 former British soldiers had financial awards or pensions for psychiatric disabilities from the Great War.

Soldiers subjected to more than one hundred days of sustained combat would, more often than not, develop symptoms of shellshock.

Types and duration of symptoms were highly variable including anxiety, depression, memory loss, hallucinations, and/or exaggerated fear responses. Many afflicted boys responded favorably to food and rest, and subsequently recovered. Others would never recover—no matter what the treatment.

Rates of shellshock from the ceaseless trench warfare in the Great War were exceedingly high and not clearly estimated. Had more men survived, most would have been afflicted with degrees of shellshock. The British reportedly dealt with eighty thousand cases by the end of the war including notable poets Siegfried Sassoon and Wilfred Owen. (Owen died tragically a week before the end of the war.)

Near the end of January, Ralph had a special patient. One of the Bantam Boys (who shall remain anonymous) developed a raging case of syphilis. (Not Bill. By some divine intervention he never got anything worse than dysentery. That, however, wasn't much fun either.) The origin of the VD case was traced back to an expensive drunken debauch in a Paris brothel. Now the bill was overdue and debt collectors were banging on the boy's proverbial barn door. It was off to the hospital for him.

An unidentified Bantam wag said, "Siff was Love that never dies."

Beyond that, little else occurred out of the ordinary in runs for Ralph. That break gave medical officers time for an overdue classroom lesson. Too many wounded patients were coming in to the aid stations only to die. Scarce resources were being wasted on mortally wounded men. The Bantam Boys were more expertly instructed in the art of *triage* in several lectures by French doctors.

Triage techniques prioritized transports. First conceived in the American Civil War, it was fully implemented in the Great War. Patients were separated into categories: 1. Men who should live regardless of the care received. 2. Men who are likely to die no matter the care they received. 3. Those that immediate care might save their lives.

Soldiers who would benefit from immediate care, of course, were sent first. The dying were left in place and made comfortable with a wine or pain medication if available. The rest waited until triage level #3 patients were taken back to station. They also became "walking wounded" and struggled to the rear on their own two feet. (If they still had two feet.)

The key to successful triage was to know how to judge the lethality of wounds. That took significant anatomical knowledge. Ralph was the only medical student with any significant prior training. He didn't look forward to the implications of this lesson. He was going to be forced to make decisions on who lived and who died.

The boys learned that triaging wounds was easier said than practiced. The severity of a wound was usually rated by an experienced front-line doctor. It was never an easy decision because much was guesswork—unless the wound was substantial, clearly visible, or damaged a vital area, it could be like throwing dice. Minor scalp wounds might gush blood like the bullet went clear through the man's skull. Severe crush wounds could look like a simple bruise. Much of triage, Ralph found out, was guess-work. There were no crude x-ray machines in the field. There was no time to surgically explore wounds.

In a few instances when doctors were absent, Bantam Boys made the decision. Ralph did not want any part of the "God role." He already had a difficult time forgetting the pitiable faces of the boys he left behind. *What if I made the wrong call?* Luckily for him a doctor was almost always available. (Ralph never wrote in the diary about any of his triage decisions.)

During this time, the boys finally got a smattering of pay from Uncle Sam. Like mail, pay could be weeks or months behind. Sometimes back pay came in substantial amounts and was distributed in lump sums. Much of that cash washed into the French economy or was shipped back home.

Some of the Bantam Boys were used to spending large piles of money. They never stopped their habit in France. Ralph shied away from spendthrift ways because he needed his money for medical school. With cash on hand and no banks nearby, he became the banker to overdrawn Bantams, Bill especially. A separate accounting note in his diary's margin showed that Ralph had loaned out over 400 francs (about $1,500 today). All of the cash was provided at 20 percent interest.

He beat future Wall Street bankers at their own game. And he loved it.

With warming weather, Ralph took pictures and developed nega-tives in a canvas tent turned darkroom. Unfortunately, his Kodak camera shutter mechanism broke. He had a hard time fixing it. The intransigent

A stylish John Litel

mechanism almost led to the camera being bashed to pieces against a stone wall. Ralph's warehouse of patience bordered on bankruptcy.

His mood brightened when a belated Christmas box and five letters arrived from home. He spent the rest of the day excitedly reading and rereading each letter. Socks were his favorite present. His feet looked like they had been run over by tanks. Trench foot did its dirty deed no matter how often he washed his toes. Good socks were as important as food and water. Putting on new socks was a nearly spiritual experience: The sudden warmth landed mightily upon his beaten paws. *Oh . . . this is good!* he thought as he pulled them over his swollen ankles.

Ralph carefully maintained his boots. Unfortunately, the constant wear on his lone pair left them splitting like hobo shoes. Even with great care, all the Bantam Boys' equipment was wearing out, much of it virtually destroyed. The conditions were so harsh all the boys requested new boots. Almost nobody got replacements in a timely fashion. Good leather was more valuable than gold. Trench soldiers didn't hesitate to take a decent pair of boots off a corpse, or from a man who was wounded severely enough he wouldn't be returning to the front. Men did what they did to survive. Ralph kept a keen eye out for oversized boots for his hinky feet. He never found a spare.

John "The Actor" Litel now partnered with Ralph. He was a good-looking guy with a prominent forehead and longish nose. The New York matinee idol was revered for his puttees. Beautiful leather-wrapped wonders made his shapely calves "the section's pride."

The two had multiple runs between Châlons and Suippes and everywhere in, out, and around those locations. Wherever they were needed, they went. Bill had disappeared so John took over. Ralph couldn't remember the date of the last run he and Bill had taken together. Lieutenant Lyon reassured Ralph that Bill was not wounded or dead. His absence gave Ralph one more thing to worry about. He found the whole incident peculiar but gave up any further inquiry because Lyon scolded him to, "Let it go."

Ralph should have been worrying about fuel consumption. He nearly ran out of gas on two occasions outside of Châlons. That could have had catastrophic results for him, John, and their many sick and wounded. Ralph briefly explained between runs:

*Tuesday, 22 January 1918. Chalons*

*We had several trips. The last was at three o'clock [AM] . . .*

*The Germans had a coupe de main [a sudden attack in force] about midnight but failed later . . . [with considerable loss of life].*

*The French had one [counterattack] and took 27 prisoners. The French lost two men and had five wounded . . .*

*I slept so hard that I didn't even hear the cannons.*

*They have been making vast preparations.*

*We can see that something is about to happen.*

Ralph and John also transported a number of dead or *le morts*. When no wounded needed transport, dead commissioned officers, usually of high rank, took a trip back to fancier funeral parlors. Most enlisted *poilu* on the front were buried where they fell or directly behind the trenches. As in all wars, rank had its privileges.

Surprisingly, the Great War was the first time armies spent significant resources to recover and identify their dead. In previous European wars, corpses were left for the local and often destitute population to dispose of. The French *Le Ministère des Pensions* (the American equivalent was the Graves Registration Service created by General Order #104, issued on August 7, 1917) was so far behind on body identifications that tens of thousands of men were temporarily interred with "Unknown" written on a small wooden cross, if they had any markings at all. Artillery churning up graves further confused later identification and reburials when proper cemeteries were being established.

The warring nations established grave registration units and postwar treaties for protection of burial sites. With so many casualties, vast national cemeteries had to be designed. It took years after the war to find, attempt identification, and re-inter the dead. Remains are found to this day. On the European continent alone, at least 940 Great War cemeteries exist. The neat rows of crosses seem to indicate a specific resting place for a specific soldier. In reality, some of these sites were mass reburials of mingled soldiers' shattered remains.

Numerous memorials to the combatants were also created after the war. The United Kingdom alone has over sixty thousand Great War memorials at home and abroad. Understandably, France had some difficulty allowing German memorials on her soil.

Resembling two abused horses, Ralph and John were "rode hard and put away wet." They'd been beaten up by back-breaking work. There was a reason bodies are called "dead weight." Picking up a corpse is like trying "to grab a 140 pound newborn baby." If not frozen solid, they flop around like jelly once the stiffness of rigor mortis has lost its hold on muscles at twenty-four hours postmortem.

Ralph wrote that they carried more Germans than French. The two boys collapsed early the next morning when renewed shelling ended their mortuary chores, and almost their lives. Having forgotten to eat in the past twelve hours, they scrounged for "grub."

Ralph and John drove to the hospital in St. Hilaire. They left their ambulance at a depot for repairs after having an earlier crash. While they visited troops, the pair rested and ate heavily. Afterward, they received bad advice about a "short cut" back to their base. After a few hours on foot, they found themselves twenty kilometers "farther away from home." Some skillful inquiry for directions from the locals finally got them back.

Ralph wrote the next day, "I was good and tired when I blowed [sic] into camp. Lieutenant gave me enough canned goods to feed a regiment. I'm a little sore in the calves today."

The two boys recovered *Lizzie #2* and drove to Suippes. On the way Ralph read letters while John took the wheel. They arrived casually as if on a Sunday stroll. The front was calm so the two got twelve hours off-duty. Delighted, they "hopped it back to Chalons for a blow [rest]."

Through the end of January and early February, the long-awaited Boche attack in their sector had not occurred. With few wounded to haul, Ralph gathered three ambulance loads full of wood for their aid station stove. He also studied up on the design of regional water pumps for lack of new diary material. Ralph thought about engineering as a profession. On one slow afternoon, he wrote about pumps and drew a crude picture of the mechanism in his diary. "They work with a geared flywheel and have a chain which is encircled in a spiral spring. The spring carries up the water and does it well."

Somehow Ralph was again condemned to kitchen patrol or KP. He hadn't done that in months. He didn't think a medic should be a busboy. Making the best of it, Ralph reasoned that scrubbing pots was preferable to picking up corpses.

The lull continued. Even the *avions* were absent from the fight. Despite the lag, it was curiously tense on their front. Ralph worried that this could be a build-up before a main attack rolled over them and pounded them into the dirt.

Back at his primary station near Suippes, Ralph could hear minor shellfire in the distance. He was not sure where it fell or where it came from. He asked around, "Ours or theirs?" Nobody knew.

One section of their main road had been especially heavily shelled in the past months. A lively new French officer decided the idle Bantam Boys should repair it while they had the opportunity. For Ralph, dirty roadwork was worse than KP.

In that sector, there weren't any genuine construction materials to build with. So the boys lined the roadbed with wet, decaying firewood. Since it wouldn't burn well, it was worth sacrificing. The lifting and digging was grueling. Ralph hated it. He only worked "when I can't dodge it anymore." He volunteered for KP as much as possible and chopped wood for the cook's fire. That was one way to stay off the "chain-gang." He also did some work on his Ford after ignition system misfires sent vibrations through the engine block, and after another minor accident bowed *Lizzie #2*'s front end. The latter was harder to repair. Ralph made sure he took his time and fixed it right:

*Thursday, 7 February 1918. Poste Suippes*

*. . . hammered around on my Ford to try to make it hit on four [cylinders].*

*Straightened the axle that I bent the other night on a stone pile.*

*It's been raining a little all day. We saw eight big guns go up to the lines. They were long 155's. We expect all hell to break loose in a month or so.*

*The hills are completely covered with barbed wire entanglements and wire nets.*

*They [French] are placing anti-tank guns every day.*

Tanks were becoming an ever bigger player in the game of war. The heavy British Mark IV tank came out in 1916 and the lighter, faster (eight mile per hour) Medium Mark A Whippets birthed in 1917. With four British Hotchkiss .303 machine guns and three crew members, Whippets were designed to defend the Mark IV tanks and demolish machine-gun nests. Actual combat results were variable but generally deemed as effective.

The French developed their own versions of tanks in a poorly considered design effort. Of the many options, the agile and light Renault FT was one of the most successful. Its fully rotating top turret with a 37mm gun was revolutionary. A rotating turret became standard design on all modern main battle tanks.

Initially, the German High Command was not enthusiastic about the "ugly" tank. They wasted time developing massive, impractical vehicles such as the thirty-six-ton *Sturnpanzerwagen A7V.* The result was an imposing mountain of metal and scary to the uninitiated. But a child could outrun it. Putting a 75mm French artillery round directly into its belly could turn it into a crematorium. Thus, Germans made few tank attacks during the war. Ralph never saw a Boche tank engaged in battle.

A mediocre German corporal named Adolf Hitler would not repeat that mistake when he ordered *panzers* back onto the French frontier in 1939.

By mid February, the Bantam Boy sector was heating up. Multiple, lower-grade skirmishes and heavier battles flared up. Into this fray, America was finally showing her combat presence. Ralph noted his first contact with US artillery crews:

*Friday, 15 February 1918. Poste Suippes*

*Time goes fast.*

*The winter has been quiet, the spring is opening up and so is the war. We've had several coup de mains. The French have been successful as a whole and have taken many prisoners. Most of which seem young.*

*A few days ago the division next to us made an attack and took a small hill near Capron. They also took a hundred or more prisoners.*

*A battery of American heavy artillery {the guns were French}
came up to bombard the Boche.*

*Last night a gasoline explosion made six blessés for me to carry to
Mt. Frenet.*

The six soldiers injured by the explosion had hideous, painful burns. Their moaning was particularly gut-wrenching for Ralph. He always made an effort to keep his wounded comfortable at all times. He stole many blankets for that purpose. But burns and mustard gas were the worst sorts of wounds to contend with during transports.

Ralph heavily wrapped their wounds in gauze until the burns stopped leaking serum. He then cocooned men in blankets to keep them warm.

No matter what Ralph did, when his ambulance set off on those bad roads, the men in the back got pounded by the ride. All Ralph could do was to drive as fast as possible and get them to an aid station before they died. He did not want any more men to die in his car. For Ralph, deaths on his drives were "bad luck for sure." He tried to forget how many men died in his *Lizzies.*

Large area burn injuries were generally rare compared to artillery wounds. But burns grew more frequent because of flamethrowers. Huns used them for the first time against the French at Malancort on February 26, 1915. As expected, it caused a major panic. Six hundred and fifty-three flame attacks followed throughout the war. Fortunately, early types of man-portable fuel tanks had a short duration and limited range. Known to the Germans as the *Flammenwerfer,* it was so devastating a man could never hope to survive a direct blast with the ignited fuel oil pressurized by nitrogen gas.

Like dying victims of flamethrowers, the six men from the gasoline dump looked like lost deer caught in a forest fire. Ralph marveled how some of them were still alive.

He knew that most would never see home again.

Ralph said to John as they drove off to the aid station, "These boys shore are screwed, blued and tattooed."

Bantams were about to suffer a similar fate.

# CHAPTER 11

# Springtime Slaughter

*Monday, 18 February 1918. Suippes*

February chilled Ralph to his core. He got sick twice. Most every Bantam Boy got hit with something. Dysentery was especially debilitating. Diarrhea caused by viral, bacterial, or parasitic infections was usually mixed with blood. The loss of fluid caused Ralph to be fatigued and led to a renewed weight loss. Stomach pain and fever usually accompanied it. Trying to rest between drives was all he could do to cope with it.

On some runs Ralph would slam on his brakes and dash for the nearest bush. Wounded in his ambulance knew exactly what was happening. They had experienced the same symptoms many times before. Some of the wounded would jump out and grab their own bushes. "Never pass up a potty break" was the general consensus. Dysentery usually lasted at least three days. Respiratory infections could last weeks. The boys had plenty of both. Ralph had more sicknesses during his year in France than in his entire life growing up in the United States.

The nights were so cold much of the camp firewood was burnt. Coal put out more heat per pound than wood but remained scarce. Their quarters were uncomfortably cold. Ralph tried to remember what warm felt like as he shivered all day. The boys picked up and burned any trash or flammable debris they discovered along the roadways. They found twigs and branches on their dysentery dashes into the countryside.

Ralph soon tussled with a logistics officer in requisitioning new blankets. He wanted more for himself and his Frenchies. Ralph explained

Off at dusk on another night of endless runs

just how cold it got in the back of his ambulance. "Wind blowin' on the wounded freezes them," he said.

The logistics men "were stingy skinflints." New blankets weren't readily doled out. But they didn't help anyone sitting in a shed. Ralph thought Lev and he might break into the depot and steal some the next time the Boche raised a ruckus. Bean counters were the first ones to fill a shelter or *abri* when shells popped overhead.

The boys had an opportunity a few days later and stole four blankets each. Ralph wore his M2 gas mask during the theft to avoid identification (despite being one of the largest, most recognizable men in camp). It was a perfect crime with no witnesses coming forward. He thought about becoming a master thief in Paris after the war.

One night the clouds cleared and the new moon shimmered with an unusual bluish tinge. The soft glow dulled the tormented landscape. That exceptional night inspired the boys to sit around the barrack's tiny fire and sing their favorite songs.

In the distance they could hear heavy guns. Frenchies, singing along with them, were on edge more than usual. The only good information was nobody reported gas shells landing in their sector. The night was serene except for a few sad songs.

Ralph took a large number of runs over the next few days to avoid being "frozen to the ground." Driving around what was left of Suippes, he marveled at the absolute tonnage of shells dropped on the position. He couldn't find a square yard of land that didn't have some sort of damage or shell hole. He had to carefully avoid shrapnel and metal shards so he didn't cut down his worn tires. A big slice could not be patched. One spare is all he had, and he guarded it like it was solid gold.

Dud shells were everywhere, sometimes hidden underground. Stepping on one was a bad move. It could blow up any time, especially if a curious soldier seeking metal souvenirs got too curious. Many men did. One of the Bantams twisted the old "curiosity killed the cat" adage into: *Curiosity killed the chap. But satisfaction couldn't put him back together.*

Bomb craters could be up to twenty feet deep. Many of the big shell holes were pitted with smaller caliber holes. Some sat adjacent to one another, weaved into an impassible shell-formed trench extending into the distance. Ralph had to drive around them. Driving directly through them was a great way to get trapped or snap a Model T frame.

Some efforts were made to patch other important roads. Many were blown up again in the following days or weeks. Ralph carried a trench shovel to dig himself out and pitch in on repair efforts whenever he had the time or energy or gumption. Results were generally inadequate. It made for an extra bouncy ride, and many ambulances got stuck if it got warm enough to melt the snow and soften the underlying mud.

Many areas were so barren they were proverbial moonscapes. On various roads it was impossible to miss shell holes. Ralph couldn't avoid *Lizzie #2* "being beat to a pulp." He would get seasick weaving his way around hundreds of the smaller-caliber pits. From all the ordnance expended here, Ralph believed the newly released Army medical statistic that it took one thousand shells to kill a Frenchman. The farmer in him also thought that this metal- and poison gas–polluted farmland would be dead for the next one thousand years. He believed the poor owners would cry when they saw it.

Ralph spent most of his remaining frigid, wet February around Suippes:

### Friday, 22 February 1918.

*I've been at Suippes today and am [on] K.P. tomorrow.*

*Jack Stearns received a letter that some one has beat [sic] him out of his girl and he's been drunk as a fool all day . . .*

*I was made a first class private this month.*

*Gabby Lee [the Sarge] received a commission.*

The most grievous sin a woman could commit during wartime was to break up with a soldier while he was overseas. A relationship termination letter became known as a "Dear John Letter" around 1945. Jack's abominable letter prompted the Bantam Boys to stage a "Floozy Flogging" (FF) in his honor.

FF was a long-held secret Princeton fraternity practice never before disclosed to the outside world. John Litel invoked the "FF protocol" in a most stately proclamation. It was familiar to him. He'd walked down this road when a beautiful blonde ex-girlfriend said she decided to marry a "corporate man not a thespian." (She probably regretted that decision when he became a leading man in Hollywood.)

FF commemoration required the former girlfriend's picture to be glued to an obese cloth effigy. The dumped guy hung it up, usually with a hangman's noose, and set it on fire. He then assailed it with a stick like a Mexican youngster thrashing a piñata—no blindfold required.

The smoldering bits and pieces of the effigy falling to the floor were doused with copious alcohol-infused urine from all members present. The celebration ended with resplendent drinking at a local pub until one man remained standing. It was his job to get the offended man back. Alive. Which John did.

Jack said he enjoyed his party. At least what he remembered of it.

Ralph's promotion to Private First Class meant he'd have a whole *three* extra dollars in each month's paycheck. With the interest from his loans, he was rolling in dough. He sent a number of clean francs to Edyth in a letter as a souvenir. He converted $100 worth to US currency. He telegraphed that fortune to his mother via Western Union on a quick trip to Paris. That would pay a fair share of his medical school tuition. He also bought Edyth a gold wedding band at a jeweler. With all these assets, he was sitting pretty.

The final note in Ralph's previous diary entry, the Sarge being given a commission (i.e., promoted to lieutenant), evoked unit pride but also a crisis. Gabby was on his way to command another unit. While the Sarge acted like the mean, eccentric uncle who should have been committed to a mental institution, he always looked after his college goofs. The boys didn't know what would happen without him. They also didn't know what would happen to him. Lee had "to become an officer and a gentleman."

Lev said, "That's like making the Pope convert to a Rabbi."

Gabby Lee's officer's commission, although well deserved, could be trouble. They were losing their most experienced NCO. Ralph was worried. He felt that he as the "Old Man" at age twenty-six was going to have to take more responsibility for "the younger kids." He rethought his application for officer candidate school. Command was not nearly so inviting when men could die from his decisions.

These changes occurred as the Boche generals grew increasingly desperate. The Germans knew they could not hold out against millions of American soldiers flooding into France. Their leaders prepared a last, risky gambit.

The initial plan would be to expend all remaining resources to split the English and French armies on the Somme. Then the Germans would drive toward Paris. They believed the French would fall back to protect the city. The trench stalemate would be broken. Allied armies would be flanked, the opposition routed.

No effort would be spared as few other military options existed.

The attack started when Hun *avions* returned to the skies en masse. This was the first time Ralph wrote about being hit by regular flights of German fighters and the menacing but unwieldy Gotha bombers.

The Gotha GV was a heavy, long-range bomber that had flown as far as London. It was a two-engine biplane with steel framing and fabric skin. It had a seventy-eight-foot (24m) wingspan and weighed over six thousand pounds (2,730kg). It first took to the skies in August of 1917. A three-man crew dropping fourteen sixty-pound (25kg) bombs caused sizeable damage for the era. These were primarily night bombers, so it was unusual that Ralph was hammered at mid-day. The bombers must have had fighter protection. That was the only way they could have survived an onslaught of attacking enemy aircraft.

### Monday, 25 February 1918. Suippes

*We have had quite a bit of excitement lately. The French made an attack in the sector next to us near Capron. They took a hill and straighten out the line.*

*The Germans made two counterattacks but failed. In one, they retook the first line trenches but were driven out again.*

*The French took about 100 prisoners and they claim that their losses were small.*

*We have had two air raids on Suippes and Somme Suippes this week. The first was on the night of the 17th. The avion dropped five bombs on the railroad station. Only one did any damage. It hit a kitchen and wounded 3 men. The others fell in an open field to the right of the station.*

In the ground attack, the French initiated a rolling barrage. They quickly followed with infantry into the first line of defense. German storm troopers were able to recover the trench, but French reserves beat them back after a second thrust. The Germans lacked coordinated artillery and their own reserves became depleted. Their zone crumbled. The French consolidated gains against the weakened Huns and established a new trench line. Ralph had casualties to transport. But he took more Germans than French to aid stations.

Given all the new activity, the boys were warned to be on alert for attacking aircraft. Dogfights occurred overhead when Ralph was in Bussy-le-Chateau. He then went to Suippes and back to Châlons alone. At his last destination he experienced one of the greatest absurdities of the war: Ralph got busted for *speeding*. He was hailed for excessive speed, in an ambulance, while carrying sick soldiers—to a *hospital*.

Ralph was chased down on foot by a French cop in Châlons. Wartime gendarmes were not known for their outstanding intellect or sharp comprehension of English. Ralph had no idea what was going on. Once the panting, fat cop caught his breath, he yelled at Ralph to slow down. He would write him a citation. But since he was a benevolent officer of the law, Ralph could instead pay *une amende* (a fine) right now.

*A bribe?* Ralph thought. *This rear echelon asshole is trying to swindle me!*

He exploded more violently than a Big Bertha shell. Ralph let loose employing some of the Sarge's best curses. "You rat bastard! You pile of steaming shit!"

The surprised constable leapt backwards. His eyes grew large. He understood Ralph's English clearly. "*Pas besoin d'être bouleversé.* No need for being upset," he said.

Ralph flew from his seat. He left few swear words unspoken. He thought about strapping the gendarme to the hood of his ambulance like a trophy deer. Before Ralph could grab him, the cop stampeded off. The Frenchie didn't stop until he was out of sight.

The *malades* in the back of his car nearly suffocated from laughing so hard. He wrote:

### Thursday, 28 February 1918.

*I got a trip to Chalons at 2 o'clock [pm] but I was loaded so heavy and the roads were so rough that it took me an hour and a half to get there.*

*Then I had to take the maladies [sic] to different hospitals in Chalons.*

*While running around the streets, a cop called me for going too fast. God dammit . . . I wanted to beat him.*

*. . . But gee, there's a lot of pretty girls in Chalons . . .*

The pretty girls likely heard Ralph's tirade and wondered what was going on. Ralph tipped his helmet to one and proceeded on his way to the hospital with neither a ticket nor a fine. He drove as fast as he could to spite the cop. He never got stopped again.

In March, all hell broke lose. At dusk, Ralph kept watch on all the confused activity. Later, he wrote:

### Tuesday, 5 March 1918. Chalons

*After supper I started to write a letter to Edyth and before I was through the fun began. First we heard a 75[mm] bark and the shell burst overhead. By that time we were all outside.*

*Searchlights were scanning the sky and the anti-aircraft guns were going [off] on all sides.*

*The rapid fire guns were sputtering and sending out phosphorous [tracer] bullets to show the direction. Rockets and fire balls were going up in all directions.*

*We could hear the avion shooting his rapid fire rifle and his propellers humming.*

A demolished building near the Marne

*The guns threw a barrage over the station. For that was [the] point of attack. Once we heard a buzz of something falling. Lev Hoffman thought it was a bomb and in getting under his Ford, bumped his head.*

*Everyone was calm up to this time. The thing [that fell on them] really was shrapnel. Another failed to burst in the air came down as it went up. And exploded when it struck the ground. It fell behind a house across the street from us.*

*Then the whirr of the propellers stopped and there was some confusion. The Frenchmen ran in all the directions possible at once. They didn't seem to know where they were going. And while the confusion still continued there came an explosion that shook the earth.*

*That brought to my mind [that] we were there in an abyss and I got as near to the center of the earth as possible.*

*And stayed there too, till the thing was finished.*

*He dropped five bombs and came back later and dropped five more. All he hit was a hospital at Somme Suippes.*

*Some of us didn't sleep very well that night.*

That was one of the closest encounters with aerial bombing Ralph had experienced thus far. He picked up a piece of *éclat* (shrapnel) and put it in his pocket next to the rabbit's foot and penny. *One more good luck charm*, he thought.

During the bombing, Lev ran to his ambulance for protection. He slid underneath and hit its undercarriage so hard "he knocked himself all the way to stupid." Ralph drove him to the hospital for evaluation of a concussion. Lev's hard head turned out to be okay. No other Bantam Boy got injured in the encounter. Lev didn't remember a thing about it. He thought he had been drinking and had a headache from a hangover.

The attack left a lasting impression on all the Bantam Boys. By now, Ralph had combat nightmares that disrupted his sleep. Others complained about them too. The usual medical advice was, "Drink wine."

Runs continued. Showing considerable wear, the Bantams were soon granted a short leave. Ralph was overdue for a break. Other boys with "less driving time" were sent back to nearby aid stations as reserve crews. All were given ample food, wine, and rest—the standard treatment for overworked soldiers.

Ralph and the "full repose" boys went to Épernay via Bussy-le-Chateau. Ralph rode with Carey Evans most of the way. The ambulance broke down on the outskirts of the town. Ralph got in with another driver, Don Casto. The two drove to a camp at Vertus. They'd send help back to get Carey.

Casto, too, had problems. A tire blew and the engine was running rough. Ralph fixed the tire in no time. He also adjusted the carburetor while he had his tools out. It still didn't run perfectly. They limped in to their billet.

Don and Ralph dumped the ambulance on the first mechanic they could find. Don also searched for a spare. Ralph told him his tire carried too many patches. "You can't patch a dang tire forever," Ralph said.

After procuring an acceptable tire replacement, the boys went sightseeing:

*Tuesday, 12 March 1918. Vertus, Marne Department*

*Vertus is a nice little country town situated in a valley to the South and West in a chain of hills which are mainly formed by a peculiar limestone.*

*Yesterday was Sunday and we visited a cave where the stones had been cut out to build the castle of Rheims.*

*It was one of the prettiest places I've ever seen.*

*Monday we hiked to an aviation camp about six kilometers away. Both [our] Lieutenants went with us. It is an American camp but run on French ideas.*

*We saw some American boys there. Hobey Baker was there. [Hobey was considered the first American superstar in ice hockey. He was killed on December 21, 1918 in Toul, France, in an air crash.]*

*Sunday one [of their] Lieutenants flew over the German lines and did not return.*

*Tuesday we hiked to Broyes. I bought a camera from a Frenchman and have been taking some pictures.*

*Across the street from where we stay are some English girls in a canteen. They have a picture show, a lunch counter, and reading room. They seem pleasant but I haven't seen much of them.*

*We also see some pretty peasant girls.*

*The last night I spent at the front [before repose] was the wildest yet. On the second hill near Capron a shell burst and killed 3 horses on an ammunition wagon. I was there with Davis [a Bantam].*

*There were many shell holes in the road and we carried many gas cases. A shrapnel [shell] burst so near us that it made our ears ring.*

*How long we'll stay here no one knows.*

*We are all waiting [sic] pay day.*

*I entered [an] application for an officers training camp today.*

Up until now Ralph hadn't heard about his flight training application. Finally the Army bureaucracy cabled a refusal for Ralph's transfer request to the Air Corps. Ralph was upset. Despite his reservations about command, he filled out another officer application: for the artillery corps. He decided he liked firing that French 75mm cannon. With all his applications, Lieutenant Lyon was getting frustrated. "You're using up all the paper in France." He asked, "You want to volunteer for submarine duty?"

Ralph said, "I would but I don't like tight spaces."

While on leave at Vertus, Ralph struck up a friendship with a Bantam by the name of Herman "Boche" Richter. Richter, a stoic, fair-haired kid, couldn't escape his Hun ancestry to save his life. The Bantam Boys kidded him unmercifully about being sent to them as a spy before the war started. Boche could speak passable German. The boys joked that "through secret research" they determined his great-grandfather, a Bavarian noble, "was some sort of Kaiser-related crook."

The boys, chiefly when wine was imbibed, interrogated Boche by using poorly crafted English accents. John Litel faked it well. The rest were awful actors. (The other boys wisely chose business or writing professions after the war.)

They'd ask such probing questions as: "Have you ever found lederhosen to be stylish? Are you fond of wiener dogs, old boy?" The most curious question was: "Do you have an Iron Cross tattooed anywhere on your person?"

Boche said he'd drop his pants for examination. No one took him up on the offer.

On the 16th Ralph and Herman had breakfast then rented two bicycles to ride to Soulier. It was a pleasant trip through lands untouched by the war. There they got a tour of the local champagne caves. The owners welcomed the Americans with open bottles. Ralph didn't say how much they sampled but "it was damn good stuff."

Feeling no pain, both managed to pedal back to their quarters without getting lost, crashing their bikes, or being flattened by a Frenchie tank:

### Saturday, 16 March 1918

*Herman and I have been biking together a lot lately. We rode to Éper-nay on bicycles one day and saw there the great champagne cellars. Moet and Chandon have 35 kilometers of cellars which are stored with wine, some as old as the 1890's. The wine has been tested and re-corked every so often.*

*Some of the boys have gone on permission [extended leave] and some have just returned. We expect to stay here some time ...*

*We do most as we please and play games in between [eating] times. And oh such eats!*

A postcard depicting the German General Staff

*. . . I've been taking some pictures and as a rule they have been fair. I like my new camera well.*

*This afternoon I will go to Épernay with John Litel. They have had bomb raids at Épernay most every night.*

*At one place they hit a brothel and killed two soldiers and girls in bed. They did the same thing in Chalons.*

Some guys are *really* unlucky in love. "Bombed in a brothel," Herman said, "that's one way to cure VD."

Hun infantry attacked in force north of Ralph's base on March 21st. The Allies called it the *Second Battle of the Somme*. The Germans named it Operation *Michael*. (The first Battle of the Somme was fought between July 1 and November 18, 1916. It was one of the longest battles of the war with one million casualties.)

The Bantam repose was cancelled and all the boys were recalled to the front. That was ominous for Ralph. He thought this was the beginning of the end. But would it be the end of the Germans? Or theirs?

The collapse of the Russian Army on the Eastern Front released thousands of veteran Hun *sturmtruppen* and divisions of crack infantry to the Western Front. The clandestine transfer of these troops to France gave the Germans a temporary numerical advantage against the Allies.

General Ludendorff, the German top general, knew he had to obtain a quick victory. There were over three hundred thousand Americans in France already with millions more on the way. He could not win a protracted struggle against so many fresh troops no matter how his seasoned veterans fought. His Western army was exhausted and morale had flagged. Time was running out.

As the French before, sections of German front-line soldiers were on the verge of mutiny and rebellion. On the front lines and back at home, common Germans were disillusioned with the war and angry at the Kaiser. They wouldn't take much more hardship and privation. Further adversity could result in a civil war. Communist agitators were at work, following the lead of those who had succeeded in Russia.

Ludendorff thought this was his last opportunity to capture Paris. By grabbing Paris, he could try to negotiate a French surrender or an armistice. That way he could salvage the effort and keep the Allies from invading the German Fatherland. Maybe he could even win the war. All remaining Boche combat reserves and artillery were committed to this last deadly maneuver.

When the Bantams received their recall notice, they beat a hasty return to the front. Their departure did not go well. They proceeded toward their previous camp assignment. But after only twelve miles the entire convoy was forced to turn back. They had taken a secondary road that turned out to be so mud-covered further travel was impossible. Ruts were cut so deep the ambulances became stuck. The boys got out their shovels and dug them free in a grueling effort.

With makeshift tow straps, the Bantams managed to haul everyone back to an unmarked turn-off. Fortunately, there they were met by a frantic French messenger who said they could proceed no further. The main road had been taken by Hun cavalry.

The boys had narrowly avoided capture. Everyone appeared shaken knowing the lines had moved so quickly. It was unbelievable that the long static front was now so fluid they might be standing in captured German territory. The messenger also said that the enemy was heading down this very road toward the Bantams. They had to flee.

Lieutenant Lyon had a crisis on his hands. He gathered the Bantams around and said, "Boys, prepare to defend yourselves."

Taking stock of weaponry, the whole party had only five Colt .45 handguns, a revolver, and about seventy rounds of ammunition in ten box magazines. Eleven knives including Ralph's were on board the ambulances. They wouldn't last long against a Hun patrol or cavalry armed with Mauser rifles. Again, Ralph wished he had acquired a Colt. When he made it out of this mess, he'd "get one no matter what."

Lyon said each man had to make his decision on how he wished to conduct himself if confronted by the Boche: fight, surrender, or flee. No one elected to surrender. They would head back toward their lines and would turn and fight if fired upon. The lieutenant warned them they could be shot for resisting.

Lyon wished them luck and saluted the boys. They returned the salute. The Bantams mounted up their vehicles and sped off behind Lyon. The lieutenant aimed for the hills where he thought the French would have the best defensible positions.

He made the right call. After heading west, they drove to the top of a hill. There the boys met up with ragged French forces. A cavalry formation galloped past the anxious drivers. "Horse Frenchies charged" into the attacking enemy force, wrote Ralph. Both sides took heavy casualties. Without Maxims for protection, many Germans fell within a half mile of the boys. Following the French horsemen, numerous *poilu* marched past the boys in a continuous line displaying grim eyes and tired faces.

Ralph sensed many knew they were going to die.

He could see the French soldiers fix bayonets and charge the storm troopers out in the distance. The fight degenerated into a hand-to-hand bloodbath. As if going back to the first battles of August 1914, bayonets clashed and rifles filled the air with bullets. *Poilu* shot down German cavalry horses. It made Ralph sick, but he knew there was no other way. Men fell in heaps. Soldiers fired until there was nothing else to fire. The remaining men traded bayonets. A few Huns were in the process of surrendering.

Most of those still alive were French. They had won the day. They had taken a near triumph away from *les Boche*. But none cheered. None smiled.

The boys triaged wounded until they could carry no more. They retreated farther to the rear, overloaded with wounded. Ralph took so many men *Lizzie #2* threatened to snap in half under the weight. He later wrote:

*Easter Sunday, 31 March 1918. Retreating South of the Marne River*

*We saw French cavalry going out to meet them [the Boche].*

*One place we saw an armored auto towing an observation balloon. We saw many other armored cars throughout the day and many French and colonial troops going up . . .*

*I took a picture or two this morning . . .*

*Though we heard heavy artillery all night I slept like a rock.*

*Today it is cloudy and fair; the rain has stopped.*

*We hear little and see only a few planes and balloons.*

While momentarily reassured of the safety of their sector, the overall battlefield situation continued to deteriorate. The Bantam Boys retreated even farther down the road taking everyone they could. As they picked up severely wounded men, some of the lesser wounded had to give up their space on the Fords. Ralph did not like triaging men or ordering them off his ambulance. He did it out of a sense of fairness. "*Si vous pouvez marcher, faire.* If you can walk, do it," he said. He only wanted *couchés*, stretcher cases.

Within the hour, their vexed French liaison officer, Lieutenant Motte, finally found the Bantams. He had been searching for them all day and feared they had been killed or captured. He advised Lyon that the reserve Bantams, who did not go on the latest repose, and other ambulance drivers, were getting "shot to hell." They needed immediate help.

With their survival as an ambulance group in question, Ralph gave up his car. He volunteered to drive back in the staff car with Lieutenant Motte and find his boys:

*About noon Easter, Lieutenant Mott [sic] came to Bouzy. He said the boys were at the front and having a heck of a time. Several had their autos hit.*

*In fact, I found none that hadn't been hit when I came up. He [Motte] took me back with him in the staff car.*

*We passed through many towns which had suffered from bombardment. McCune was driving the car and he connected up with our staff car.*

*That caused a little conversation but no harm.*

*Then we came to Aubérive where our boys were. They had been through something for sure. Practically every machine had been hit and some looked like sieves.*

*Bucksnyder's [a Bantam] gas mask saved him. They had been in a retreat and had lost all their goods.*

*They had seen the British give way and the French come up and save the situation. The Tommies told the boys not to go up. "He's a coming on."*

*They'd yell at the fellows "Don't go up there." But he [the Huns] hesitated when the French met [the] Hun. He's stopped now.*

*God how those French boys fight! They never retreat except when they can do more deadly work by retreating.*

*One place a German plane was shot down by a rifleman.*

*In places, the Germans are six feet deep rotting on the ground.*

Several grueling days later, Ralph described what he had been through. Once more he escaped death by the virtue of his celebrated "Heller's Luck":

*Date Unknown. (Probably 3 April 1918.)*

*I didn't sleep much the first night. And about 4 o'clock Davis woke me, for the shells were coming close to us. There was a heavy battery near us and they had been shooting all night. I heard the return shells before Davis woke me but [I] thought it was still the [Allied] guns.*

*I went to an abri [shelter] where there were two or three girls and an old woman, who not knowing where to go, had stayed there.*

*We stayed there till daylight then I went on post with Buck and Paul Hargreaves. I was with both all day. We were at Gille.*

*While there an escadrille of Boche flew over us very low shooting their guns. No bullets came near us but soon they began to shell our abri. One shell hit it fair but didn't cave it in. The abri is an old wine cellar deep in a hillside.*

*It seemed miraculous that we were not hurt.*

*The shell exploded just ten feet from where I was.*

*We had several trips and I think that the Boshes [sic] shelled us for the shells came uncomfortably near on the road. But even at that, it wasn't so bad. I missed the best. Though I was lucky to save my baggage [i.e., wounded].*

Ralph saved some of his personal gear as well. But his only picture of Edyth was obliterated along with many of his handmade trinkets and various combat photo negatives. He took the loss of Edyth's photo especially hard. In his next letter, he asked Edyth to send another. (A new picture never arrived.)

The Boche shelling intensified. The boys had no alternative but to keep working and hope for American reinforcements. They fortified several more *abris*, deep trench shelters. Ralph's newest plan to help the Bantam Boys in case of emergency nearly got him killed. He eluded the grave not once but twice on the same wet spring day:

### Thursday, 4 April 1918. Poste Unnamed

*The lines have not moved for some time. Yesterday it started to rain and has kept it up. We were shelled so heavy on the morning of the third that we moved and are now near the hospitals.*

*The shelling started about 2 o'clock [AM] and continued till daylight. They dropped rows of shells across the place where we were stationed. One exceptionally near one bust [sic] and scattered éclat all over our house, breaking the windows and roof tiles.*

*Several hit neighboring houses. We soon went to the dugout and I went to a little one that I had found. I thought that if a direct hit came there, [to the main shelter] I ought to be someone to dig them out.*

*But it was me that needed to be dug out!*

*A shell hit the arch of my abri and filled it with fire, dust, stones and iron. I'm a little sore in my muscles and chest but otherwise unhurt.*

*I had another close call on post. A shell hit our dugout direct.*

*I was sitting within 10 feet where it burst. A piece of stone wall saved me from éclat.*

*More than a thousand shells fell in the neighborhood of my post on the 4th. Five [French] were killed and 20 [were] wounded.*

The fight became a springtime slaughter.

# CHAPTER 12

# A Time to Die

On April 4th at the Battle of the Avre, the French and British repelled an attack on Amiens, 85 miles (138km) north of Ralph's position. Fifteen Boche divisions attacked seven Allied divisions east of the city and north toward the Avre River. This battle was the first time both the Allies and the Germans used tanks simultaneously. Spirited night counterattacks by the British halted the enemy. A final push by the Germans failed when Australians fell back but retrenched outside of Amiens. They stood their ground and would move no more. The Hun assault collapsed.

On April 5th the battle at the Ancre marked the official end of Operation *Michael,* the first of three major German spring offenses. The British 3rd Army with its Australians finally brought the German juggernaut to a halt on the Ancre River near Albert. The fight was brutal with heavy losses on both sides.

Over the duration of these battles, 177,739 men of Britain and the Commonwealth were killed, wounded, and missing in action. This figure is over three times the number of casualties (both North and South armies combined) in the largest American Civil War battle at Gettysburg, Pennsylvania, the 1st through 3rd of July, 1863.

On the 5th of April, the invulnerability of the Bantam Boys also ended. Carey Evans was dead.

Ralph was both disheartened and enraged when he heard. Carey was following Ralph's lead and thinking about going to medical school. Ralph was flattered. He thought Carey would make a good doctor.

Carey's death left the bitter taste of Hun hatred in Ralph's mouth. Carey had been a friend. He was from Ohio. He was one of the youngest "kids." Ralph was so upset he could only write briefly about what an unholy mess that night was:

*Friday, 5 April 1918. Suippes*

*Carey Evans was killed at Passel while loading his car. Dick Brooke his pardner [sic] was shocked. I took his [Carey's] place at the post.*

*Two French soldiers {and an officer} were killed by the same shell. The night was dark as the devil and the éclat rained on every side.*

*Herman Richter ran in [to] a 75[mm cannon] on the road and Murray Smouse [a Bantam] busted a spring in a shell hole.*

Carey was loading his ambulance with the help of two orderlies. Shells were hitting all around. A French lieutenant dashed toward the ambulance, probably because he was going to tell Carey he had more wounded for transport. The lieutenant didn't make it. An artillery round exploded and tore his right leg off in midstride. He was dead before his mutilated body tumbled to the ground.

Shrapnel from that same shell bowled over the two orderlies from behind, killing them instantly. Standing on the other side of the ambulance, a large piece of *éclat* ripped through Carey's abdomen knocking him on his back.

Regaining his senses, Carey sat up. Realizing he had a bad abdominal injury, he tried to hold his stomach to stop the bleeding. The wound was far more serious than a mere cut. He held tight to keep his intestines from spilling onto the ground.

Dick Brooke saw all of this from a safe distance. He ran over to Carey as fast as he could. Carey was still alive but bleeding out quickly. Dick knelt down and started talking to him. He was not sure what was said. He grabbed Carey and rocked him in his arms. Carey never cried out. When he moved Carey's arm to assess the wound, Dick was bewildered. He knew little could be done. Knowing he had to do something, Dick tried to put pressure on the wound with some bandages.

Carey died several minutes later. His last words are unknown. Dick was too distraught to remember what Carey said. Dick became nearly catatonic for several days afterward and had to be led around by the hand.

Dick Brooke

Lieutenant Lyon gave him two days of leave after he felt Dick could take care of himself. Dick never fully recovered from the experience while in France. He mostly stayed on mechanic duty thereafter.

Ralph thought, *This isn't supposed to happen!* Carey the Clown did not deserve to die like this. Ralph had rarely known such anger. Bantams were "the good guys" doing honorable work. The good guys were supposed to ride off into the sunset with girls in their arms. They weren't supposed to be carried off in coffins at dawn.

The Bantam Boys buried Carey at the military cemetery in Ribécourt. Nobody knew what to say. As officer in charge, Lyon felt obligated to speak. He said, "Every man will face a time to die. Some will have more years behind him than others. It is not that we die. It is how we die. The memory of this boy can't help but make everyone who knew him a better man."

Several others said short goodbyes. Ralph was going to miss that "amusing little bastard." He took a picture of Carey's grave with his

Carey Evans's gravesite

camera. A few of them had a good cry. All helped cover the coffin with earth. Ralph went off. He sat behind a stone wall and cried. He hardly ever wrote another word about Carey.

But many wounded needed help. It was back to work for two miserable weeks.

### Monday, 22 April 1918. Poste Ribécourt

Ralph and Jack Stearns were in Ribécourt-Dreslincourt near Compiègne. Ralph took pictures of a crashed Allied plane and a French 75mm cannon that had taken a direct hit. He also found a big rock with a chiseled inscription. Written by Boche soldiers, it lay near some old 1916 trenches and damaged bunkers.

With the help of a multi-lingual Frenchie, they were able to translate it to English. The insolent rock message appeared to be:

*See what the German barbarians accomplished out of uninviting roughness and made into a livable place.*

*You may destroy or criticize but you can't alter the fact that in this cave-town on French ground, the Germans wrote battle orders.*

Ralph wrote it down and took a picture. He decided to send the expertly carved rock back to the Boche via air mail. With the help of a sapper, the boys wrapped it in twenty pounds of TNT and blew it sky high. Ralph got to light the fuse. He found the activity favorably instructive. He decided he "liked blowing-up shit."

After that delightful diversion, Ralph wrote about his work, his new location, and strange tragedy at the end of April in three extensive, undated entries:

*. . . Four French avions were brought down in a fight and two Germans.*

*We carried one [French] in. He was shot through the arm and leg and seemed happy. He fell a long distance and his plane hit upside down. He said there were two American pilots with him.*

*It was the hottest air fight I ever saw. Some 12 planes were mixed up in it.*

*That was the only trip we had.*

*The cave where we now have our post is on the top of a hill and some 15 kilometers long. It is formed by mining out the chalk for building. We had a heck of a time finding our way about. They have quite a hospital there and will soon equip it fully.*

*At present, things are fairly quiet. A shell occasionally drops near our barracks. One next to the road yesterday killed a horse.*

*Our priest was killed at Dreslincourt. He was standing near the mouth of the cave when a piece of éclat struck him in the stomach cutting him half in two.*

The corps priest was standing outside his *abri* near a 75mm cannon battery. He was marveling at the warm morning sun. An artillery round exploded right in front of him. The priest's body was tossed in all directions, a hideous jumble that looked like a biblical scene from hell. A Catholic Frenchman fell on his knees to pray when he saw it. Several Bantams shook their heads in dismay. One threw up. Two French gunners were also killed by the shell and added their mutilated corpses to the butchery.

Ralph couldn't believe that a priest could die in such a horrific way. He had recently taken the priest's picture. He was a fit and handsome man, well liked by men of all religions. "He was one of us." Ralph thought having the picture was terrible luck. He made a print anyway. "Maybe someone would want to remember that padre someday," he said.

The death of their clergyman hit the Bantam Boys as particularly ominous. That was wrong. Carey was bad enough. But if a priest got "cut in half"—what chance did an ordinary man have? Everyone, Ralph included, became increasingly superstitious. Nearly everyone acquired a magic charm like Ralph's rabbit's foot or a St. Christopher medal for protection. Not all charms lived up to expectations.

The Bantams' sector soon went critical. The shelling was some of the most intense in months. Ralph recounted his wildest adventure to date. It was his longest continuous driving experience. He explained in stark

The Bantam Boys' priest

detail how he nearly got himself killed in a huge conflagration of artillery while hand-delivering bandages to a besieged French combat outpost:

*Paul Hargreaves and I spent a lively day at Passel some time ago. We were on post 36 hours and were on the road 30 out of the thirty-six. We carried some forty men all told.*

*Three attacks occurred in the 36 hours.*

*The French opened the day with an attack and then the French finished it with another. Neither gained much.*

*A night attack is something to be remembered. They woke us at 3 o'clock to evacuate the maladies. We had been in bed about an hour. They told us there would be an attack and to be ready.*

*We made our trip and on the way back we decided they were right. Such a noise no one ever heard. All the guns were roaring.*

*When we passed Thierry there were about a dozen rapid fire guns sputtering. We didn't know what to make of it. Both Paul and I thought that the Boshes [sic] were advancing. Not many arrives [Boche shells] came over however, and we found out that they use the mustard [gas] for barrage.*

*We were busy all the rest of the night and a little after daylight the Boshes attacked. Then was when we had our picnic.*

*The road was shelled for fair. One gun continually played on the cross roads where we turned off. Paul looked at me and asked what to do. I said, "Wait here till the next comes and go like hell." Just then one hit beside us in the wheat field. Believe me, Paul took the rest of my advice.*

*Shells were dropping like hail everywhere. We pulled into the first abri and didn't attempt to run over to the east of Secours.*

*We had some bandages for them though and they needed them bad so I started to carry them over on foot.*

*I got about ten feet and a whizzer [German 77mm] sang past.*

*I kissed the earth and as soon as the éclat had settled, I started. Three steps and another hit about 10 yards ahead of me. Down I went this time into a shell hole filled with mud and water.*

*My sterile bandages were a sight.*

*I made one more move attempt and lost my nerve beating it through shell smoke back to the abri regardless of how near the shells were.*

*Paul was there waiting.*

*I thought the situation over, wrapped my wet bandages in a piece of linen I found there and took them to the Post without kissing the earth more than 3 or four times.*

*When I got there all the Frenchmen had gas masks on. That was the worst of all. I spent an hour seeing if I couldn't cough and sneeze and then decided that it was only smoke and not gas in the end.*

*Paul says it was the worst night he's ever had.*

It was one of the worst nights Ralph ever had as well. Miraculously, neither shrapnel nor explosion injured Ralph on his two attempts to deliver the bandages. No gas disabled or killed him. He was totally unprepared for mustard gas. He had forgotten to take his M2 gas mask. No working spares were at the trench. Ralph knew that was a major screw-up and vowed to never let his mask out of his reach again.

On another hot night with Bantam Bunny Hunt, Ralph gave him a driving lesson. Mainly it was a lesson on how *not* to drive. Ralph had two dreadful accidents within hours. *Lizzie #2* was in her final days.

The worst part, to Ralph's horror, was his ambulance got a flat tire on the exact spot where Carey Evans had been killed by the artillery shell:

*I've been at Passel once since with Bunny Hunt. We didn't get much sleep either but it wasn't as hot as the night with Paul.*

The upper entrance to *le Poste*

*It was dark as the devil. The only way you could tell you were moving was by the sound of the motor. You drive by the feel of the road and instinct.*

*All what is wrong with that method is that instinct doesn't tell you about the shell holes ahead. You learn how to keep the road easy enough.*

*Once we ran into a field kitchen and then into a knocked down house.*

*We hit a nail in the wreckage and punctured a tire which I changed in the dark on the spot where Carey Evans was killed, without even the aid of a flashlight.*

*It was some job and every time a shell came over I'd lose my hold and to hunt for an hour on my hands and knees [looking for dropped tools].*

Bunny Hunt, a stoic intellectual, often spoke about murdering his parents for naming him *Bunny Hunt*. He got over it when he found the name Bunny to be a great opening line when meeting "attractive ladies and other female types." Like many Bantam rabbits, Bunny was a "ladies' man."

Ralph had been running with Bunny to prepare for new replacements. Their Sergeant Stevens thought they'd be the best to do the job. The two discussed what they would teach new recruits. They didn't relish the idea of dealing with new guys. Fortunately, no replacements had yet been assigned to the Bantam as their killed in action only consisted of Carey Evans. Their lack of casualties was short of amazing given the intensity of artillery barrages everyone had endured.

None so far had received disabling wounds. Ralph's first partner, Bill McClenaghan, however, was still missing from duty. His absence was odd. Nobody talked about it. Ralph didn't remember much of their final runs together. Being two men short, Davis in the hospital, Dick Brooke not doing well, and loads of sick and wounded, the remaining Bantams were drastically overworked.

To further muddle their situation, Bunny took his turn crashing Ralph's ambulance. They were riding along when Bunny hit a shell hole.

He didn't have the strength to control the ambulance at that speed. Plus, the brake failed.

So he headed for the softest obstacle he could see: a double wooden door.

*Bam!*

Bunny plowed right through the front door of a local dwelling. Without knocking, without a key, Bunny jammed *Lizzie #2*'s nose right through the door into the foyer.

Happily nobody was home.

The Ford wedged tightly through the doorway. The boys were okay but Ralph was not a happy hiker. They tried to pull her out by hand. She wouldn't budge. Reverse gear didn't help.

As they sat around, Ralph wondered what to do besides "tear Bunny's ears off." Then French artillery men on horses slogged by with several "155 longs" (155mm *Mle. 1917* heavy artillery cannons). Ralph flagged them down.

The lead caisson driver stopped. The amused Frenchie got down, came over, and pondered Ralph's dilemma: a car sticking in a house. He didn't speak English. Ralph thought he said something like, "*Comment diable avez-vous fait cela?* How the hell did you do this?"

Ralph pointed at a glum Bunny. The Frenchie nodded and instructed his men to unhitch his horses. They moved the horses to face away from the car. Tying the team to the Model T's rear axle, the horses heaved at the leather straps.

Ralph panicked. "*Doucement!*" he said. He wanted the Frenchie to do it *gently* so they didn't yank the axle clear off his machine. They tried slower this time. She budged. Once more. She inched farther out. The car finally worked loose with a little coordinated effort between the two countries: Ralph pushed from inside the house while they pulled from the outside. With a collective "heave ho" battered *Lizzie #2* was freed.

Job completed, the American and French boys shared good bottles of wine but second-rate cigars. Ralph didn't want to appear snobbish or ungrateful for the smokes. He took a few puffs and gagged. He tried again. Same result. A battle-worn Frenchie laughed and said, "*Je vais le prendre si vous ne voulez pas.* I'll take it if you don't want it."

Ralph gracefully handed the stogie over to him.

When the bottles were empty it was time to go. To Ralph's astonishment *Lizzie #2* hadn't driven her last. She was still travelable at ten mph. The boys set off bouncing down the road as busted sheet metal whistled in the wind.

Ralph drove this time. He scolded Bunny, "Remember, she ain't no tank."

Days later, Ralph lounged under an apple tree. Pestered by mosquitoes, he realized that summer had dawned. No more freezing cold! He rolled up a newspaper and swatted the bugs. It was the first time he ever appreciated blood-sucking insects.

Along with his newspaper, Ralph had received letters, a package, and "my pen that I've longed for." Now he had a first class writing instrument. His last one ran out of ink. He didn't like using pencil as it smeared on his often damp paper. Ralph spun the pen in his fingers as he got inspired to write. (His handwriting in the diary improved as well.)

When Ralph opened his diary, a 75mm cannon pulled by a truck speeded past followed by three ammunition wagons. He watched the noisy procession bound down the road. He hoped none of the shells popped off the wagons and flew into his lap. After the dust settled, he started writing. He had been through two dangerous weeks and filled in further details from the end of April into May:

*Saturday, 4 May 1918. Ribécourt*

*We've been through hot stuff.*

*On about the 25th of April the attack started. I skipped work on the abri and developed some plates and film.*

*The fellows said at supper that the Boshes had made an attack on Mont Renaud but hadn't gained much. The Lieutenant gave orders for inspection in the morning so I rose early and dress [sic] and shaved. But inspection never came.*

*At breakfast there was a call for 2 extra cars at Passel. They sent Hoffman and Harvey and Dennen and Hopkins [Bantams]. Then he put me in K.P. and told me I was next on reserve.*

*Afterwards he said he thought I'd be sore if he didn't send me. Soon I followed the other two cars. Jack Stearns was my pardner.*

*On every trip Jack would say as we approached the crossroads, "We can't get through!" but we do go through and all day we went time after time.*

*Towards the night the road became almost impassable but the shelling was so continual that we were not able to fill the holes.*

*Sarge Stevens [the Bantam's second American NCO] was changed to my car and Jack was relieved which was mighty good.*

*Stevens has good nerve but Jack hasn't the nerve of a flea and he gets excited, too.*

*It was stiff business all day and the shells literally rained on all sides of us. I saw one shell cross skipping on the ground ahead of us and exploded within a hundred feet of us. Three more followed it but I didn't look to see them.*

*I was wishing my Ford could bend its back like a snake in order to get between the holes faster.*

*But the day wasn't a beginning even for that night. Up till nine o'clock we got through well. Then they began to bring in the wounded that they were unable to reach in the daytime.*

*As fast as we could load we left and the shells fell.*

*Two or three hit on the shed where we had our cars.*

*One car was put out of commission.*

Obstacles continued unabated. Nothing was going right. Ralph nearly destroyed *Lizzie #2* for good after she just received substantial repairs. (Ralph said mechanics were "getting good and tired" of seeing him drive in to their depots.) To top it off, he almost ran over Sarge Stevens.

Sarge Stevens was a mild version of Sergeant Lee. He was not nearly as crazy and generally well liked. As far as NCOs were concerned, Stevens appeared competent. He was assigned to take Sarge Lee's place as Gabby was now Lieutenant Lee.

Ralph described his and Stevens's nighttime misadventure in remarkable detail:

*About eleven o'clock the thing was so dark we couldn't see our radiator. A cloud of fog hung so low that it couldn't have been darker.*

*They loaded Duke and Hopkins and started them off. Then they started to load me. I cranked up and waited. Duke came running back.*

*They had run into a wall that was knocked down on the road.*

*I went with him and help[ed] him lift the stones out of the way that were too heavy for one man. Then he went on.*

*He had a heck of a time he told me afterwards. They almost run off a bridge, got lost on the road and finally smashed the car so [badly] that they had to put it away.*

*When I got back they were wildly calling for me. They didn't know where I'd gone. Then we started.*

*We got past the wall but landed fair in the shell hole in the middle of the road. We pulled and pushed but to no avail.*

*Then I pushed and Stevens acted as engineer. But we couldn't go or come.*

*So after a council, Stevens started back to the post to get help.*

*Then all of a sudden how they did shell that place!*

*I had [to] beat it. But as I couldn't carry the couché alone, all I could do was stay and try to comfort him. How he begged to be taken away!*

*In a remarkably short time Sarge reappeared with six huskies [big men] and they backed us out of the hole.*

*As we started a star shell loomed up and I saw the other car coming like fools straight for us.*

*I yelled, whistled and blew the Klaxon [horn] but they came head on. Until about 20 feet away they attempted to stop.*

*They were on the left side of the road. There was a wall on the right side and a bank on the left. The only thing I saw to do was to save my radiator. I didn't care to be delayed there longer.*

Ralph floored it. He drove as fast as *Lizzie #2* could go, which wasn't very fast since she was literally falling apart and leaking oil heavier than a Pennsylvania well.

That was the right decision. He wrote:

*It would have been sure death, too, for two big shells fell within ten feet of the spot soon after [leaving]. I whirled my car to the left side and they saw me and started for that side, too. I got far enough over to partly miss them.*

*They knocked off my fender and gave me a side swipe [I] then went headlong in [to] the hole that I had just emerged from.*

*I didn't stop or at least didn't intend to but before I got my balance I went head over heels in another hole.*

*The Frenchmen were in calling distance and with their help we emerged again. Sarge got out and walked, I proceeded slowly behind.*

*I couldn't even see him and knocked him down four times. And with him leading we lost our way and passed our turning place. We proceeded all the way out of the village before we could make sure we were lost.*

*Then we had to turn on a road ten feet wide and a ditch on each side. My steering gear was bent double, too. A foot forward and a foot back a hundred different times we went before we got around.*

*Then we slowly proceeded till we got on the main road. There the machine gun bullets were putting up sparks on the stones. Some sang past us.*

*The Ford wouldn't run in high [gear] and it was too dark to run in high anyway.*

*So we proceeded in low. When we got almost in she stopped. We found that the hose connection was busted and we only had a little water. I poured in a can of fresh water and we were able to get in before she got over heated again.*

*We left the car at Ribécourt, the fourth [Bantam] car to be out of commission in one night. Bunny Hunt's car went out next and as the moon came up and the fog lifted the rest of the night wasn't so bad. It got beastly cold.*

*I was sweat wet but all went well.*

*I didn't sleep any. After daylight we had no more trips.*

*I collected an automatic [Colt .45 handgun] and a pair of field glasses.*

Ralph finally got his gun.

The Bantams had taken a beating. But still no serious, life-threatening injuries occurred during this chaotic episode. Ralph cleaned his Colt .45 then acquired *Lizzie #3* from a nearby depot. She was "used" but apparently in good working order. He grabbed her and launched back into the skirmish. At the end of immense disorder, he had one of the most unusual wounded he ever carried. He was one of the few German prisoners Ralph got to know personally:

*Our last trip we carried a bosh [sic] prisoner. His eyes were seared out with liquid fire. They said [from] his own [weapon].*

*His face was a scab and blood dripped from his nose.*

*He had two wounds through his chest which looked like a bayonet had tickled him. But he walked and talked showing no signs of pain.*

*His name was Wilhelm Kramer of the 209 Pioneer Liquid Fire Engineers.*

*He rode on the seat [next to Ralph].*

Kramer was lucky to be alive that day. His primary weapon was the despised flamethrower or the aforementioned *Flammenwerfer*. It was considered the first man-portable terror weapon. The contraption was hated more than the Maxim machine guns. A two- or three-man team carried the tanks and nozzle operating system. It contained about two minutes of pressurized fuel and had a standard range of approximately sixty-five feet (20m). The fuel tanks were a favored target of enemy riflemen. Watching the team burn to death by way of their exploding tanks seemed like a justified end to the defenders. Due to its dangers, few soldiers volunteered to employ the weapon.

During this time, the Bantam Boys received the first of many citations. There was some initial confusion as to what it meant. Ralph wrote, "This turned out to be a much bigger deal than we thought." Ralph copied the award in its original French into his diary. "Topped by one gold star," it looked supremely official. The colorful, grandly decorated citation roughly translated into the following:

*April 29, 1918*

*3rd Army,*
*33rd Army Corps*
*Headquarters*
*1st Office*
*No. 2320/1 Order No. 171*

*The General Commanding the 33rd Army Corps:*

*Service Sanitäre American S.S.U. 523*

*At the orders of Lieutenants Motte and Butkiewiecs during a severe*
*bombardment at Noyan and Mt. Ranaud on March 25 through April*
*8, 1918, the unit showed gallantry beyond the call of duty during the*
*evacuation of wounded.*

*Signed: Lecoute (General of the 33rd Army Corps)*

*Copy to the Chief of Staff*

The Bantam Boys were official French heroes. This award was a unit citation for the famous *Croix de Guerre* (Cross of War). The *Croix* was instituted on April 8, 1915, by the French government to recognize acts of bravery in the face of enemy actions that were "mentioned in dispatches." These were normally awarded to men of allied nations fighting in support of France.

*Mentioned in dispatches* meant those men whose names appeared in an official report written by a superior officer and therefore merited notice by the French High Command (*Commandement Supreme*). The report for the individual award had to specifically describe the unit or soldier's gallant or meritorious action in the face of implacable enemy fire. The actions had to go above and beyond the normal call of duty.

The Bronze Palm pin on the green cloth ribbon indicated that the gallantry of the soldier was worthy of the entire nation's gratitude. Every original Allentown Bantam got the unit *Croix de Guerre*. Many Bantam

One of two citations for Ralph's Croix de Guerres

Boys who survived the war got an individual medal as well. They were on their way to becoming one of the most highly decorated American units of the Great War.

All active-duty American Ambulance Corps sections received a large number of medals for bravery. Most every man was a volunteer or a conscientious objector. Conscientious objectors would not fight in the infantry but some entered the Ambulance or Medical Corps. One hundred and twenty-seven American ambulance men died in the line of duty. Many more, including Ralph, were wounded in combat. Every one of these men received the Columbia Scroll signed by President Woodrow Wilson (becoming the American Purple Heart awarded retroactively in 1932).

The Bantam Boys also received Campaign Medals for surviving the Somme, Marne, and other horrific battlefields all along the Western Front.

Ralph's two Croix de Guerre medals

American Ambulance Corps men were also sent to Italy. An eighteen-year-old Ernest Hemingway was wounded at the Piave Delta on the Italian front. A pivotal episode, it would provide the inspiration for some of his future tales. Another writer, John Dos Passos, a Bantam, would pen several stories including the novel *Three Soldiers* about World War I. (Ralph kept a written correspondence from John that he received from him in the 1930s.)

### Tuesday, 7 May 1918. Poste Ribécourt

Everything grew quiet. The calm allowed the boys to organize for repose on the 8th. They finished a new abri despite torrential

Ralph's Columbia Scroll

rains. Ralph made sure it was heavily reinforced—as thick as the walls of a bank vault. The awed Frenchies jokingly called it Ralph's petit garnison (little fort). Soldiers fought over reserving choice spaces inside. He wished he had raffled off tickets for the seating arrangements. He could have made some real spending money.

Despite generally respectable intra-squad relations, ongoing stressors caused Bantam tempers to flare. Before they left, two of them flew into a glorious fistfight. One unnamed soul "got his face pounded." Ralph stood in as boxing referee and eventually stopped the bout. Ralph pulled the victor off when he felt the victim "who had it coming" had gotten his due. "The boy should keep his mouth shut from now on," wrote Ralph. While generally uncommon, fights and arguments became more frequent.

Everyone fought exhaustion as well as each other. Ralph's sleep remained poor, his energy low. Despite eating, he lost more weight. His head ached and his stomach was sour. Nausea became a frequent bother. Ralph ate handfuls of aspirin as if it was a separate food group. He was bruised and cut from falling down while carrying litters. Cuts became infected. That "damn trench foot" was something nobody could get rid of "short of hacking his legs off."

One of the most bizarre symptoms in this panoply of misery was Dick Brooke reportedly seeing Carey Evans. Alive. Unhurt. Standing right in front of him close to the spot where Carey died.

The ghost sighting unhinged Ralph. "I don't want to hear no more!"

Dick never mentioned Carey again.

This type of event was more common than might be expected. Many trench soldiers reported seeing dead friends. A significant number said they had conversations with the dead on multiple occasions. Some front soldiers even saw angels or departed comrades fighting alongside of them in battle. Confusing at best, it was also comforting to many of the afflicted men. Some found consolation in the occult after the war.

On Wednesday, May 8th, Ralph left for a well-needed rest. It didn't turn out to be much of a vacation paradise, but it provided some historic sights to see. The relaxation was welcomed. He wrote about his self-guided tour of the area:

*Wednesday, 8 May 1918.*

*We are at Villers Cotterets. It's a measly little place. We have a barn with a hay loft to sleep in. Most of the boys slept in their cars. I slept in the hay and was cold all night.*

*I took a walk yesterday afternoon. I saw about 100 tanks hidden in woods near here. After supper, I walked with Herman Richter.*

*We visited a chateau near here . . . On top of a hill near is a stone tower with a gilded statue on top. We were able to get a fine view of the surrounding country. Near the tower are two statues of Joan of Arc—one mounted and one standing.*

*We have car inspection this afternoon. I've been cleaning the old girl up.*

*I took a bath and got a shave at the hospital near here, too, today.*

Ralph gathered his wits and renewed his strength while on respite. For about a week not much happened. But by the 13th, it seemed that some Bantam Boys had been vigorously sampling the local fare. Meaning they were sampling the local "fair ladies"—with the usual bad results.

Ralph said that four of his close friends (who shall also remain nameless) got "clapped." Ralph didn't mean they got standing ovations. But they sure were dancing as their equipment heated up from nasty cooties infections. He hauled them to the infirmary and en route gave them the ever-famous "Heller Condom Lecture." It didn't work the first three times he gave it. But Ralph could be stubborn and repeated his instructions.

These dejected clap cases were the high note. In a deplorable revelation, Ralph found out that Bill McClenaghan had left the unit to work in Paris. Ralph couldn't believe that Bill "walked away." The unwritten rule was "nobody gave up."

No able-bodied man left the unit. Nobody.

Ralph grew bitter. While the exact story was unclear, Bill apparently got a transfer because "he couldn't take it anymore." Ralph wrote, "He's such a coward that it is well if he stays away." Bill was *persona non grata*.

French Lieutenant Motte left the unit the same day of the discovery. That stifled some of Ralph's discontent. Motte helped get their unit *Croix de Guerre* medal. He was sent off to a higher command by a grand

Bantam dinner. "Huge" amounts of champagne were involved per proto-col. At the party, Motte told the boys individual awards were coming as soon as they were processed. He congratulated them all.

It was one of the few happy days left in the war for the Bantam Boys.

By June, the situation at the front had frayed faster than a burning rope. On June 1st, the French Army fell back in full retreat from the German offensives into Chateau Thierry and Belleau Wood. There was little to stop the Germans who were less than thirty-seven miles (60km) from Paris. As the retreating infantry passed through American lines, a French officer yelled, "The Germans are coming. The war is lost. Retreat! Retreat!"

US Marine captain Lloyd W. Williams, company commander of the 5th Marines yelled back, "Retreat? Hell, we just got here!"

The American 2nd Division moved into the French line with the Marines. This action became the Battle of Belleau Wood. On June 4th, General Bundy took command of the American sector of the front.

Over the month, American Marines and soldiers fought off six Ger-man assaults. French arrived to give General Bundy's 3rd Brigade sup-port so he could hold the southern section. A Marine brigade held the north. Together with the French, the Americans stopped the German advance on Paris. By the 26th of June, the Marines had cleared Belleau Wood in a fierce battle that completely destroyed the forest. It caused one of the largest losses of life in Marine Corps history. US forces suf-fered 9,777 casualties with 1,811 dead. Captain Williams did not survive the battle.

The Bantam Boys were recalled from repose and thrown into the battle. Attacks and counterattacks in their area left them exhausted. After days of continuous driving and rescues, Ralph was so tired he was making potentially disastrous mistakes. He later wrote about how confused he became in several detailed entries:

### Sunday, 2 June 1918. Poste Soissons

*. . . We've had some bit of hell for the last 60 hours.*

*At present it's quiet. We are in a dugout or old quarry. We have five Fords here.*

*We ran all night and all day without stopping. I stopped once. I was out of gas. It was queer. I went to work and didn't think I'd been at work an hour.*

*My auto stopped in a darn uncomfortable place. I tried the carburetor, it was dry. As I hadn't strained my gas, I concluded it was plugged. I started to remove the feed pipe. Then I found the tank was dry.*

*I woke up then and realized that I had been running over 18 hours.*

Ralph's loss of awareness of time troubled him. Nothing that extreme had ever happened before. In the wrong place and time, it could have gotten him killed. He knew it and tried to get some rest.

Ralph then described his next adventure:

*We stayed at Villers - Cotterets till about a week ago . . . All the time we were hearing the wildest tale about the Germans advancing.*

*. . . It was a wild drive at best. [Kid] Harvey was nearly killed by a camion [a motor truck]. One Frenchman was killed in the accident.*

*Dust, dirt, dust, so thick you couldn't see two feet ahead and the pace was terrific. With full speed one second and sliding our wheels the next.*

*Two cars were smashed out of four [in the] bunch.*

*But it's too long to tell all.*

The next day was even more serious:

*Monday, 3 June 1918.*

*We arrived by noon and six of us awaited orders.*

*Shells were falling everywhere and cutting the limbs of trees over us.*

*Avions were fighting and falling. I got a call. He died before I got in. Wounded along the road begged to be taken.*

*I took as many as I could. Sometimes ten on a little Ford. God bless her, she's never been good. She is Lev Hoffman's "old" car. He cast her off. He'd returned her and got a new one. The Lieut[enant] gave Lev a new one. The Lieut says he's going to give me a new one tomorrow.*

*He loves me up when ever we must and says pretty things like he did in the last attack. The medicine Officer took my name yesterday [for a Croix de Guerre]. I wonder who the Lieut will give the cross to this time.*

*After the attack I'll settle back to oblivion.*

*At present I seem to be swimming in luck.*

*Yes we're at the post. Richter, Pursell, Page, Clark and me.*

*The Lieut says he wants us five to get crosses [Croix de Guerres].*

Never say a situation can't get worse. It can and did.
Ralph tried to recall three more shadowy days:

*We've been here 60 hours and the chances are we'll be here 60 more. But I slept about 6 hours and feel all right.*

*So I don't care.*

*But it's been hot work. I've made 15 trips, carried 70 wounded and used 100 liters of gas.*

*As I've said, Lizzie [#3] never did me better. She only acted bad on one trip and that was because the Lieut [Lyon] was along and tried to tell me how to run a car.*

*One other trip John Litel went along. He tried to tell me too but I told him to shut his damn mouth and he did. He hasn't spoke a word since.*

*All other trips I've made alone. Two nights and two days. 15 trips and every one a hot one. I've had to change two tires.*

*Shells bust all around us. I don't think I've made a trip without have [sic] some explode in killing distance of me.*

*I saw one big piece of éclat strike a rock and glance over my head cutting the top of my wagon.*

*One trip a shell burst behind me. I set Lizzie spinning with a full throttle. I had three couchés in the back but it was fine road. I was putting down 40 miles an hour easy when one hit beside me. In the soft dirt thank goodness.*

*Had she been on the road I wouldn't be writing.*

A desperate situation deteriorated further. Ralph was nearly crushed by a transport truck. Then he received serious shrapnel wounds that took him out of action:

*Something struck my wrist and knocked my hand from the wheel.*

*My wagon swayed but I caught her. Then I felt the jar and heard the explosion. Four pieces went through my car and one cut a tire.*

*But I never even hesitated.*

*I left that country. I guess maybe it jarred me a little or else my luck seemed bad.*

*When I got almost in, I started to pass a convoy of busses which were making a sharp turn up the hill.*

*I waited and waited and would have waited longer ordinarily but my arm hurt and I wanted to get in. I shot behind one as it made the turn.*

*A black [colonial trooper] was driving it. He stalled the engine and his brakes couldn't hold back he came and caught me in the middle.*

*I felt my wagon going over, under the thing and attempted to get away by cutting and driving over a bank. I got half way around and then got caught on an iron and could go neither way.*

*My Ford was [trapped] between a telephone post and a bus. I thought my blesses were goners when a Frenchman jammed a big rock under the wheel of the bus and stopped it. I got out and away with only a busted side.*

*The black [trooper] cried like a baby and went all to pieces.*

*When I finally got in, to this triage, my radiator was boiling like a steam engine. I started to take off the cap and it blew off and threw scalding water all over me. I had on my overcoat and only got a few drops in the face.*

*My gloves saved my hands.*

*My overcoat and some of the other clothes I had on save [sic] my arm, too. It struck {I mean the éclat} the flap on my sleeve went through 4 thickness' of my overcoat 2 of common coat and one of my shirt.*

Ralph had a three-inch piece of jagged shrapnel blown into his left forearm. Several other smaller pieces peppered his upper body. His coat stopped the large shard from going completely through his forearm muscles. He was so hyped on adrenaline, and since he couldn't see it, he didn't know how serious it was.

When Ralph got to the aid station, he couldn't pull his coat off. The shrapnel pinned his sleeve to his arm. A French army surgeon, a captain, cut open Ralph's greatcoat and removed the heavy splinter. A local anesthetic of a cocaine derivative decreased the pain but was not enough. After receiving several indistinct pills that he thought were opium, his pain finally faded away.

Feeling good and filled with fascination, Ralph watched the surgeon at work. Ralph even offered to help much to the consternation of his doctor. In his dreamy state, he wanted to see how his pork chop suturing technique compared to a real surgeon's knot. Ralph concluded he had more to learn. No matter! With the aid of the opium, he said he didn't care about "any-goddamn-thing."

After the surgeon finished forty stitches, he told Ralph, "Stay down for day or two."

Ralph saluted. "Order heard and obeyed, General."

The next treatment was the really fun part of Ralph's personal battlefield medical training. The infection prevention medication for his wound was almost worse than the *éclat*. Most victims of artillery were at risk of developing tetanus or "lock jaw." The infection arose from spores in dirt that entered the wound on the shrapnel. It could be fatal in some cases. An effective tetanus vaccine didn't come along until 1933.

Ralph was in for a treat.

Before Ralph left the aid station, a nurse came in to the medical tent with a mammoth syringe of over eight thousand units of antitoxin. It was so large it might have been as many as sixteen thousand units (because Ralph was big). Usually a nurse shoots it intramuscularly in multiple doses and sites. For some unknown reason, Ralph got all his shot right into his abdomen. All of it. Ralph's opium effects faded rapidly.

Fortunately the injection didn't kill him. He stumbled away from the medical tent in a daze. Lev saw him and he made Ralph lay down on a cot. Later he finished his long diary entry with the following passage:

*They made me take anti-tetanus serum at the hospital. They shot about a quart into my belly. It was worse than the wound. A lot.*
   *It gave me a heck of a headache!*
   *A dozen [shells] hit just as close afterward but I was lucky.*
   *I know darn well that all the boshes can't kill me.*
   *They [Germans] are starting [the artillery] again.*

It took him two days to recover from the shot. His belly hurt worse than his arm.

Ralph said to Lev, "The Bochies can't kill me. But the nurses shore will."

Other Bantams would not be so lucky.

# CHAPTER 13

# I'm Not Going to Make It

The 1918 German Spring Offensive or *Kaiserschlacht* (Kaiser's Battle) rained flaming hell down on the Western Front starting March 21st. After four summers of unrelenting war, legions of dead lay on top of one another like corn stalks plowed under in a farmer's field. The Huns sought to reap a final crop of destruction by launching a last attempt to prevail in their failing military crusade.

Fifty divisions were freed up from the Eastern Front when Russia signed the Treaty of Brest-Litovsk on March 3, 1918. Russia capitulated to remarkably harsh terms and exited the war. The Germans transferred their eastern soldiers to France. They had to act decisively and prevail quickly before "the damned Americans" flooded onto the western battlefields. The Boche had to win now or they could lose the war.

The first attack nearly broke the Allied lines at the Somme. The Boche main thrust erupted between the French and British Armies in an action known as Operation *Michael*. By April, the Huns had not accomplished a breakthrough. Casualties and matériel losses were massive during the back and forth battle. Nothing of strategic value was gained by either side. The effort, essentially, was a German defeat. It achieved the same perpetual attrition that characterized the war. Thousands of infantrymen were ground into the dirt like manure.

The Boche next attempted to split the Allies on the Lys River. While the United Kingdom and Portuguese forces took heavy casualties, the month-long German attack was also unsuccessful. With the situation growing increasingly desperate, the High Command in Berlin decided to

Carey Evans's ambulance. Ralph refused to touch it.

launch a third attack on the French lines on May 27th in the Chemin des Dames. This operation, named *Blücher-Yorck,* was meant to open a direct line of vulnerability toward Paris.

Germany's General Ludendorff reasoned the Allies would concentrate their defenses around Paris and not let it fall. The movement of Allied reserves to the city would allow a new attack against the British previously weakened in *Michael.* This supposedly would collapse the British front before the Americans could plug the breach. The Allies would have to surrender or make a peace offering.

The angst-ridden Ludendorff worried his legacy as a commander was on the line. A loss would bring the German Empire to ruin; millions dead for nothing. Billions of dollars in matériel destroyed. An evolving workers' revolution would demolish what little of the Empire remained. The monarchy would fade forever, and the dastardly Americans, through their President Wilson, would impose democracy on their country. All of it, he believed, would be Ludendorff's fault.

Also called the Third Battle of the Aisne, *Blücher-Yorck* started with one of the most concentrated artillery barrages of the entire war. Two million shells began to fall on the morning of May 27, 1918. The world erupted into fire. Smoke and gas blotted out the sun. The earth shook like a never-ending earthquake. Frightened birds were blown from the sky. Soldiers disintegrated in artillery explosions. Tens of thousands of wounded bore remarkable suffering as their friends died around them.

Ludendorff extended *Blücher-Yorck* west in Operation *Gneisenau*. He tried to pull the remaining Allied reserves to the south. The intent was to extend the German salient and link up with his forces near Amiens. The French called this the *Bataille du Matz* (Battle of Matz). The artillery bombardment started on June 9th. The Germans advanced with twenty-one divisions over a twenty-three-mile (37km) front along the Matz River. The Huns captured nine miles (14km) in their deepest penetration. A French counterattack on June 11th with infantry and over 150 tanks stopped the attack. *Gneisenau* failed.

Causalities were enormous during the Spring Offensive. Up to June 6th, there were 137,000 Allied and 130,000 German dead, wounded, and missing in action. The European armies were literally bleeding to death. Infantry soldiers' morale was dying as well. Their intellect, endurance, and will to fight eroded away.

In front of this Boche steamroller drove the Bantam Boys. They carried their share of the *blessés* in a confused, bloody effort. Half a dozen boys had nearly been killed by artillery. A 77mm shell narrowly missed Ralph, skipping along hard ground like a flat stone across pond water. He could see it as clearly as if he held it in his hand. Much to his relief, the dud never exploded. A detonation would have blown him apart and destroyed *Lizzie #3*. After the immediate carnage he wrote the following entry:

*Sunday, 9 June 1918. The Marne Department, Poste Unknown*

*We layed around trying to sleep but without much success during the morning. We had a few trips.*

*About noon we heard the lines were giving way and we took our wagons over to the other side of the valley.*

*The machine gunners and the others slowly retreated.*

*I never saw such heavy shelling of the valley. Such big shells. One shell failed to explode. It was more than a foot through and 3 1/2 or four feet long. They had two guns playing on the turn of the road.*

*We waited an hour while the Lieutenant got drunk.*

*Lev Hoffman went to sleep. Then the Lieutenant went to the chief and sent two men back. Richter and Clark went. I followed about a half hour later.*

*We had one trip apiece with the wounded.*

*I stayed up all night and made three trips letting the others sleep. Most all night I was forced to run in low [gear].*

*Once I took a trip for Jim Clark. I thought I'd be good to him. He had to follow me a half hour later and was nearly killed.*

*A big piece of éclat went through his radiator.*

*I knew full well that there would be a scrap that day. Three lines of ammunition went up all night and they had 75's [mm cannons] placed everywhere.*

*I told the doctors that it would be such a battle as we hadn't seen before.*

*It was, too.*

The next weeks were chaotic and bewildering. On an early run, Ralph was loading a young *poilu* when a wayward piece of *éclat* slammed into the boy's head. Blood and brains sprayed all over Ralph in a sickening moment of disbelief. He nearly passed out. It was a one in a million chance the poor kid would get struck squarely in the temple right before he was rescued. *I shoulda been quicker*, Ralph chastised himself.

As more artillery exploded around him, his mind went blank. Ralph took several deep breaths as he put the body down on the ground. He covered what was left of the boy's face with a blanket. Ralph wiped the kid's brains from his face with his hand and grabbed another man who was still alive. He clumsily loaded him into his ambulance.

Shrapnel flew around the ambulance with the force of hurricane winds destroying a town. Ralph wasn't sure how he got out. Luck kept him and his few wounded alive. He drove off feeling as if stuck in one of his recurrent nightmares. *When will I wake up?*

Ralph wiped off the remaining blood with his favorite handkerchief. He threw the linen hankie out the door. The bloodstained fabric floated down on the side of the muddy road as his ambulance disappeared into the cordite smoke.

Ralph was on another close run to the front the next day. While loading the wounded several shots zinged overhead. Once again he wasn't sure if they were strays or snipers. Then two bullets slammed *Lizzie #3*, shredding a plank of her composite body. Ralph got hit with multiple, jagged splinters as the composite material shattered. They felt like bee stings when they cut through his ragged undershirt. He sped out of there without assessing his cuts.

Later, he had to dig the shards out individually with his Bowie knife. It was akin to doing plastic surgery with a pick axe. He was delighted that he had practiced surgical knots on pork chops as he stitched his wounds. *Not bad*, he thought.

Jim Clark, looking supremely seasick, was watching him. "Dammit Ralph, see a real doctor," he said. "You could die from an infection."

"Unless your leg is blowed off, you ain't gonna see one out here." Ralph took a long swig from a wine bottle, spilled some on his wound and continued stitching himself.

Ralph kept busy with his Frenchies. He lost count of the number of runs and wounded he carried. He even forgot where he was.

"The crying and dying" was heartbreaking. He tried to reassure and comfort the boys hoping to ease their passing. He wasn't a chaplain, but at times he wished he knew more about religion so he could answer their questions. At times he wished he had more faith. His beliefs were shredded; his idealism crushed.

The war was winning on all fronts.

Ralph's *blessés* now seemed to be younger and younger. He felt he knew who would live and die: "Hollow cheeks look like a dead man. He got bad hollow cheeks and the boy probably won't make it." Every face held a story. One kid begged Ralph to shoot him, to put him out of his misery. He couldn't do it. "I'm sorry," was all he said.

The entrance to an unnamed post

Another anxious kid told Ralph his name was Andre. He was sixteen years old. He said he lied to get into the service saying he was eighteen. The kid looked twelve. He weighed 130 pounds only when clad in thirty pounds of battle gear.

Andre was lucky. Ralph thought he was going to live. But he would be scarred for life with probable paralysis of his left arm. The shoulder damage from a rifle bullet looked bad enough Ralph didn't think he'd ever use it again.

Andre kept up a crooked smile. He had done his duty. "*Mama sera fier. Mama will be proud,*" he said.

Ralph just nodded and patted the boy's head. Later in the month the Bantams settled in Florent. The bottle fly swarms were horrendous. "Always so many goddamn flies." The smell wasn't as bad as on the front. The smell at the front was worse than falling into an open septic tank.

They made camp in an old laundry. Civilians were still using it to wash clothing. One especially pretty girl reminded Ralph of Edyth. He didn't think he would ever see Edyth again. Loneliness now hit him extra hard and added despair to his chaos. He read and reread some of her old letters. No mail had arrived for weeks. Her letters were falling apart from so much handling. Many had been lost to artillery. He still had no picture of Edyth. He felt desolation like he had never experienced before.

The boys erected a dining tent and managed to have regular meals. Despite eating, they continued their weight loss spiral and loss of strength. They ate as much as they could hold down but nobody looked healthy. No ration of wine, however, went unconsumed. Everyone forced himself to eat at least twice a day. The French food was usually excellent and it rarely disappointed. It was one bright spot in all the darkness.

As a further diversion, Ralph hunted rats with his handgun. He decided to take in some target practice with his Colt .45. Despite his best efforts he wrote, "So far, no rats have been killed." There may have been a double meaning here. The "rats" he referred to could have been Germans.

Ralph ruminated about killing the enemy. He still couldn't contend with his anger over Carey's death. Given the opportunity, Ralph decided he *could* and *would* kill armed Huns. Aunt Bea's ideal about "every life is sacred" was demolished. Ralph was no longer confused on that matter. He agreed with the British that "a good Hun is a dead Hun."

The Bantams had eleven cars on duty but only ten men in camp. Lucius Cook was missing in action. Ralph hoped that they would find him. Nobody knew where he could be. No one knew if he was alive or captured. If he was captured, he was likely being tortured. Ralph couldn't fathom that possibility. "Lucius is a good guy," he said.

Ralph felt helpless and depressed that Lucius might be suffering untold abuse. He viewed their situation as increasingly hopeless with his own survival unlikely. One night he bowed down on one knee next to his cot and made peace with "his Maker."

A common Bantam worry was that one of them could be hit by heavy artillery and nobody would ever know what happened. He'd be gone. That was it. No funeral. No grave. Missing in Action (MIA) would be all the report would say. Ralph had nightmares of being consumed by artillery fire. He'd see himself running away in slow motion, only to be blown apart in a roiling blast wave. On many a night he woke up sweating. (His dreams did not ease until years after the war.)

The remaining boys limped their way back to the aid station at *Poste Saconin*. Shortly thereafter, it happened. Ralph's dream came true.

Two more Bantams were dead—their bodies blown to pieces.

Bill Purcell and Paul Hargreaves had gone off duty. Both were exhausted. They entered a small post *abri* and went to sleep on cots. They had not been asleep long when they were stuck by German heavy artillery shells. A 240mm trench mortar firing a 220-pound (100kg) shell made direct hits. Twice. A near impossibility, it was overkill of the highest magnitude. The poor boys never felt a thing. The shelter was crushed beyond all recognition.

Had no one seen Paul and Bill enter the *abri*, they would have been gone forever without a trace. Their families would have never known their fates. Even the Bantams would not have known. Everyone was in shock. Ralph and Paul had been friends ever since their wacky blind night-ride together near Chartres on the way to the front. Grief hit him, like Carey's death, extremely hard. He wrote about the tragic loss with shaky handwriting:

*Sunday, 23 June 1918. Poste Secours*

*It was coming daybreak when I got back to the post.*

*Things were still as death.*

*They loaded me up again and I let the boys sleep. Richter and Clark were the only ones with me.*

*Bill Purcell had asked to be relieved. He was all in [i.e., exhausted]. He said to me that "he couldn't stand it any longer."*

*But though we spared him from our post he was called later to help Paul Hargreaves out.*

*They were sleeping in a dug out when two 240's [mm shells] struck it. You couldn't even see where it had been.*

*Good lads they were. I guess they are rested by now.*

There wasn't much of anything to bury in Bill and Paul's graves. Ralph and the boys gathered remains of what they could. They put up crosses on the spot where the boys were killed. Nobody spoke. Everyone looked immensely disheartened. Even Lieutenant Lyon didn't know what to say. All shared several bottles of wine and loads of grief.

Ralph took a picture of the grave but couldn't write anymore about the deaths. He felt too heavy for words. He just wanted to go home to Ohio.

Bill Purcell had been suffering from shellshock. It seemed especially unfair to Ralph that Bill had to die in a confused state. "It's wrong." He kicked around empty oil cans and sobbed for half an hour.

Ralph then wiped his eyes and went back to work.

The boys didn't have much time to philosophize over their loss. Their position was about to be overrun by heavily armed Hun storm troopers.

Lyon ordered an emergency evacuation of the camp. They took everything they could carry, packing men and medical supplies into the backs of their ambulances. They burned what they couldn't carry. The boys blew out of there as fast as their damaged ambulances could drive.

The evacuation soon deteriorated into abject chaos. They tried to follow each other as artillery threatened to wipe out their only roadway. And them along with it. Somehow all the Bantams made it through an

Bill and Paul's gravesite

intense barrage. Many cars took shrapnel. Amazingly no man got hit. They stopped their tattered convoy on the opposite side of the valley. They needed to regroup and rest, and wait for orders.

Caves in the hills provided some protections from falling shells.

To stop was a mistake. This area, too, was soon taken by Germans in a decisive push. Ralph and a few Bantams were almost left behind in the confusion. Ralph narrowly averted being captured or killed. He explained in bleak detail:

### Tuesday, 25 June 1918. Full Retreat

*... when I left the post they told me not to come back but to stay on the other side of the valley. The stillness only meant that they [the French] were holding their fire for what they knew was to come.*

*It wasn't long in coming either. The bombardment soon was at full blast.*

*I found the other boys trying to sleep in a cave in the hill side. The post of Secours was a little ways off.*

*I got a stretcher and layed down in the doorway of the cave. Then I looked around. If a shell should strike the houses opposite [us] I'd sure get smeared. I tried to bluff it off but it wouldn't go [away].*

*I got up and hunted a more safe place.*

*I soon found a cave where there was plenty of room and even a bed. I tried to sleep but I was too nervous and uneasy.*

*I was laying there thinking when some one came past and yelled [an] alert. I couldn't figure it out but thought he meant gas. The more I thought, the uneasier I got.*

*Then a French soldier ran in and grabbed his gun. He asked me if we hadn't been warned.*

*I couldn't make out exactly what he said but it didn't make me any more at ease.*

*Bill Porter had relieved Clark. Jim's machine was hit. So I went in and asked Bill if we hadn't better investigate. He agreed and I went.*

*I saw the [French] Major and all his bunch beating it.*

*When he saw me, it was easy to tell that he had forgotten me.*

*He told me to get out as fast as I could. I told the other boys. He said to turn our wagons around and go up an old abandoned road.*

*I told him I didn't think it possible. But he said come. Bill and Rich beat it down the hill and up the other way. I tried to head them off but they were too far gone. I turned the wagon and climb such a hill as would do a goat justice.*

*At the top of the hill I got on the road again. There I waited till the other boys came out. Both came out safe.*

*The Major had rode with me to the top of the hill. Here he left me. I tried to make him understand that I was game to stay with him.*

*I showed him my automatic [Colt .45 pistol]. He said, "No, no, no!" And motioned for me to go on. I went as far as the farm on the top of the hill and waited for results.*

*The bumble bees were singing on all sides. Soon a man was hit near me. I loaded him up. Then a fellow came running up the hill, blood all over. He wanted me to get some blesses down the hill.*

*So we got them.*

Seven filthy, wounded French soldiers were crammed in the back of Ralph's ambulance. Another clung to the right running board. A boy bleeding profusely from a bandaged facial wound sat next to Ralph on the passenger seat.

As they scurried down a cow path, they passed an armed French soldier. The man threw away his *Lebel* rifle and ran to the ambulance's sideboard. To Ralph's disbelief, the soldier jumped on his car. The added weight made the ambulance impossible to steer.

"Get off my machine!" Ralph said. The man did not react. Ralph tried using French, "*Descendre!*"

Ralph rocked the steering wheel but could not turn. Artillery shells flew overhead. Bullets plummeted down. Desperate, Ralph shook the soldier and said, "You ain't hurt. Walk! *Marcher!*"

The frightened soldier did little but mutter in French. Ralph pushed him. The boy tensed his grip on the vehicle. Ralph grabbed him by the collar and pulled him closer. Ralph said slowly in French, "We'll all die!"

The boy cried for his mother.

Ralph said, "I'm sorry!" He wound up and cold cocked the soldier. The boy tumbled off the ambulance, splashing into the mud.

Ralph cranked the steering wheel and turned down a small ravine. It provided respite from the bullets. Artillery felt less lethal as it exploded overhead.

Ralph drove on. He searched the banks for an escape route. Nothing looked familiar. No retreat seemed feasible. Moments later Ralph saw hazy figures scurrying out of whitish smoke at the distant end of the gully. *Is that gas?*

The heavily armed figures had their faces covered by gas masks. The point man signaled them to stop by raising his fist. The German storm troopers froze in their tracks.

Ralph jammed the ambulance reverse pedal and shredded the transmission band. *Lizzie #3* would retreat no further.

The soldier jumped from the right running board. "*Les Boche! Les Boche!*"

Barely finishing his shout, bullets struck the soldier's body. The next shot exploded his skull. A blur of red engulfed his head as he twisted to the ground.

The German storm troopers scrambled in all directions.

Ralph saw soldiers on the flanks shoulder their rifles. A tall sergeant glanced up over a stump at him.

Ralph continued to fight his transmission. Frenchmen scattered off the ambulance. The wounded man in the seat next to Ralph dismounted and walked toward the Germans. Ralph called to him. As the man turned, he took gunshot wounds in each leg. Falling to his knees, a bullet exploded into his sternum. He slumped into a muddy shell hole.

Ralph howled in frustration as more bullets whizzed past. A bullet skimmed off the hood. A submachine gun stitched the ground in front of the ambulance.

"You stupid bastards! I'm Red Cross!"

A wounded Frenchman in the back of the ambulance struggled to get up. A stray bullet tore open his chest and killed him. Two other wounded men in the rear watched the widening blood pool beneath the dead man. One lit up a cigarette and took a long drag.

A bullet struck the radiator of the battered little Ford. Steam spewed from the overheated engine. Ralph pounded on the backboard. "She's done for! Get out! *Sortez!*"

As Ralph spoke an air burst artillery shell flashed overhead and stunned him.

Slow motion seconds passed. His eyes could not focus. His bleeding ears could not identify muffled sounds. Looking to the sky Ralph said, "My fault boys . . ."

Ralph pulled a rabbit's foot out from the upper pocket of his soiled Army blouse. He dangled it in the air. Overwhelming fatigue gripped him. He didn't know what day it was. He had forgotten the names of the last towns he had driven through.

Ralph slumped in his seat as he dropped his rabbit's foot onto the mud-covered floorboard. He casually flipped off his dented helmet.

Suddenly, to Ralph's left, a German private jumped up. He thrust the bayonet on his Mauser rifle directly toward Ralph's face.

Ralph didn't move. The two men watched each other.

Colors faded away. Sounds grew nonexistent.

The private's bony finger closed on his rifle trigger.

Ralph sank lower and bowed his head. He thought, *I'm not going to make it.*

With his remaining strength, he closed his eyes and conjured up a picture of Edyth in his mind.

"Love ya, Edyth . . ."

Ten meters away, the Boche sergeant jumped up and pulled his gas mask down revealing a disheveled, gray handlebar moustache. He dashed ahead, grenade in his left hand as he fired a shot into the air from a 1908 Luger 9mm pistol in his right.

*Bang!*

The sergeant yelled in German, *"Feuer einstellen! Er ist ein Sanitäter.* Cease fire! He is a medic."

Ralph opened his eyes to see what was happening. He did not understand why he was not dead. Or was he? How do you know if you're dead? he wondered.

The thin storm trooper cautiously lowered his rifle.

Nearly out of breath, the old sergeant ran up between Ralph and his soldier. The sergeant breathed hard as he looked Ralph over head to toe.

Seeing no weapons he said, *"Lassen ihn.* Leave him." Then he waved his men ahead as he shouted, *"Vorwärts!"* (Ralph had hidden his Colt .45 under his seat. He never made any attempt to defend himself, which saved his life.)

The Huns had no time for prisoners. The aged sergeant would not, however, let his young trooper kill a medic doing his duty. *Der Feldwebel* still possessed humanitarian restraint in allegiance to his old Prussian military code of honor.

The three men looked at each other again. Nobody said anything that Ralph could recall. The sergeant nodded. Ralph nodded back. The sergeant replaced his gas mask and ran forward. He dragged the thin trooper up the ravine and into the roiling artillery.

It looked like they were charging into the gates of Hades.

The remainder of the German squad stumbled past Ralph's ambulance under the cumbersome weight of worn rifles and grimy stick grenades. Ralph could see vacant, dark eyes behind the dirty glass eye ports of their gas masks. They walked but they didn't appear alive. He sensed that these wretches would die that day.

Ralph didn't know it at the time, but he was saved by storm trooper tactics. These men were the "attack element" to be followed by the "mobile units." In what would become known to the Americans as "haul ass and bypass," attack element storm troopers raced through weak points to flank their French opposition. They left prisoners and pockets of heavy resistance behind for the mobile infantry to "mop-up." These Germans were considerably ahead of their flagging support troops. Ralph had time to escape.

After they struggled past, Ralph bent over and picked up the rabbit's foot off his floorboard. He smiled and put it back in his pocket. *Maybe my luck didn't run out,* he thought. Then he jammed down the low gear pedal.

His luck hadn't run out. *Lizzie #3* moved.

He goaded her down the ravine. Several of his hiding wounded Frenchies rejoined him further downhill. Ralph was glad to find two more men were alive.

How long Ralph's wagon radiator and transmission would hold together, he did not know. He drove as deftly as possible avoiding obstacles. He feared she could give out at any moment. But the old girl kept going. She hissed and steamed and groaned in protest. The transmission rattled but she would not stop. It was one of the most outstanding performances of a Ford Model T in the entire Great War.

Low gear held up. She did not explode. The engine did not burn up. *Lizzie #3* got her boys home.

Ralph wrote this about his propitious escape:

> . . . *I drove through the German lines. They were shooting at me, I know, but none got me.*
>
> *We didn't let any more [grass] grow under our butt on the way in. On one special down hill stretch of smooth road I know I made fifty miles an hour.*
>
> *We were in the heart of the battle.*
>
> *I remember seeing one battery desert their guns and beat it [run away]. Another place I passed two staff cars in flames, well burnt.*
>
> *I guess maybe the boshes were a little closer than I thought.*

*I took them in {the blessés} and started back.*

*I passed everyone even the Leut but he signaled to some French men and they got in the road and stopped me.*

*I went back to where the Leut was and he told me of Paul's and Bill's death.*

*I already knew.*

*[Sgt.] Stevens, Duke Dennen and Bunny Hunt are missing.*

Surviving his incredible dash through the German lines left Ralph utterly worn out. How he found his way back to Allied lines is unclear. He couldn't remember much. In the simplest of terms his luck held up. He apparently followed the first road he could find. He had to refill his steaming radiator with water from numerous shell holes. He packed mud-covered rags around the leak as a "radiator bandage." She hissed back at him but it worked well enough to drive. The steam dried the mud into a hard patch after several heavy applications. His medical training paid off: Medics tended bad wounds by piling on bandages until the bleeding stopped. It worked for *Lizzie*'s radiator, too.

Ralph drove until he came upon a temporary French staging area. He sputtered in out of gas and his radiator having cooked off its water for the second or third time. The oil reservoir was fried. He didn't understand how the engine hadn't melted or froze up.

He refueled and refilled his red hot radiator. The first tin *bidon* of water boiled away and scalded his fingers. He added three more. Oil sizzled as he added lubricant to the crankcase. The engine radiated extreme heat. To Ralph's amazement, the transmission low gear held together when he jammed on the pedal. Reverse and high gear were useless. Driving as fast as he did should have been mechanically impossible.

By some divine act, *Lizzie #3* refused to die. He felt affection toward her as horsemen felt toward their prized mares.

Looking around the staging area, Ralph couldn't grasp what to do next. He realized he was washed out, lost in a mental fog. He needed to lie down. A French mechanic volunteered to further look over his car. Orderlies tended to his wounded. Ralph drank wine and found a cot. He grabbed some peace for a few minutes.

Awaking later, he felt better and loaded up with wounded. The mechanic said there wasn't anything more he could do. She was too damaged. He gave Ralph directions on where to go for help. He drove off.

Unfortunately, Ralph took a trip into the realm of the bizarre.

His next drive was nearly as deadly as his last. Although it lacked the threat of German infantry or artillery, he endured a spate of strange accidents. It was as if he had entered a demolition derby. The war was determined to destroy his barely functioning ambulance. Ralph continued his long entry:

*After lying around a while, I picked up [another] blessé and went in.*

*The farm house at the top of the hill [used as camp] was deserted with all its things as they were. It was some classy place once.*

*When I got almost to camp I saw a horse and rider ahead of me. I blew my horn. He looked over his shoulder and apparently thought he had as much right to the middle of the road as I.*

*If he had stayed there it would have been all right but he didn't. As I got up to him he dug his spurs in the horse and she jumped astraddle of my radiator. My clutch froze fast and I couldn't stop the engine. My brakes were long since worn out. I should have used my reverse but it didn't [work].*

*We headed for the bank and [we] were close to it. I couldn't steer the wagon. Then we hit a ditch and the rebound threw the horse rider and all head long over the bank. My one wheel went over but I brought it back and got stopped on the other side of the bridge.*

*All the spunk went out of me for I thought I'd killed the man.*

*He wasn't hurt in the least and was on his feet before I got to him.*

*I thought it was my own fault, got in my wagon and started for the triage. I was going up a hill passing an ammunition train going the same way as I.*

*All was well till a truck came towards me. I drove in between two 75 [mm cannons] and the same thing happened. I couldn't stop to save my soul. I almost caught a man, too.*

*I rammed that 75[mm] and I rammed her hard. I knocked her about six feet ahead.*

*When I got loose I ran in on low. My radiator was bent back to my engine. She still held some water. I busted off a lamp and bent my fenders.*

*When I left the triage she again got out of my control and I smashed her into a bank and left her there and went to camp for a mechanic.*

Ralph was not sure exactly where he was, but for now he was on the Allied side of No Man's Land. Peculiar events continued. A window opened up from which Ralph viewed the mounting absurdities of the Great War. He had nearly been killed several times in the previous twenty hours. After all of his effort, an officer proceeded to chastise him for being obnoxious to a haughty camp mechanic.

Neither the officer nor the mechanic had any idea what Ralph had been through. And Ralph was in no state to take any guff. The American mechanic said his ambulance transmission "was just fine." Incredulous, Ralph went to work on the mechanic with verbiage stolen from the venerable Sarge Lee. He said, "Fix her or I'll tear your head off and piss down your spine."

Apparently, the mechanic didn't like intimidation.

*Wednesday, 26 June 1918.*

*Bucksnyder [the mechanic] came [out] and we ran her to the shop. There he insisted nothing was wrong except my radiator needed changing.*

*He still argued and I wasn't in the humor to argue.*

*I told him frankly and not softly that his breaths were numbered if he didn't open that transmission [and fix it] while I got a little sleep.*

*I meant business and I didn't need to repeat [myself] either. He had it open in less time than it takes to tell it.*

*But all he did was to fill it up with oil so it would run and change the radiator.*

*And while I slept he told the Leut a string of stuff and the Leut came and gave me hell.*

No good deed goes unpunished. The transmission was the lesser of many evils as the tactical situation deteriorated into full-throttle mayhem.

Bandages were nearly gone. Fuel was short. Oil stocks had been exhausted.

Hundreds of wounded, however, still needed transport.

The Bantam Boys carried on.

Frantic, hardcore German troopers were near and intent on destroying everything in their path. Their own supplies were dwindling so they made serious efforts to capture Allied equipment. Anything on the road to Paris was targeted for exploitation or destruction. Nothing was spared. Rumor had it prisoners were executed. The dead were looted. The front burned furiously as Germans, drunk on captured wine and gorged on stolen food, set fire to anything of value that they couldn't carry off.

Ralph continued his story as casualties mounted. He struggled to maintain a sense of hope despite a greater sense of doom. He continued to write on the 26th of the craziness that erupted in a world gone starkly mad:

*I slept a couple of hours and ate some dinner.*

*All the Frenchmen were busy picking chickens and pigeons. We ate chickens for some time. Someone killed a deer, too, and I butchered him.*

*I didn't go out any more.*

*They soon evacuated the triage. While we waited there we saw the Legion of Honor [an elite French force] go out as a reserve.*

*Jess Clayton took a notion to join it. He was drunk as a fool. I told him he'd be shot for a desertion if he went and he wanted to fight me.*

*Jess has been court marshaled since and got two months [in the stockade]. What he was sent up for, I don't know . . .*

*The evacuation went on in good shape.*

*Ten French cars came and relieved us of some of the evacuation work. We stayed there and watched the battle through our [field] glasses. The bosh [sic] were stopped.*

*We went to Mont Fontaine for several days as a half reserve, half run.*

*There some of the fellows came down [ill]. I slept good in spite of avions and shells the first night but I worked all the next day with sick men.*

*I didn't feel very good myself.*

*Jim Clark's nerves gave way and I lost a night's sleep [assisting] with him.*

*John McCune was sick and I work[ed] with him. I doped myself with all the salts [possibly Epsom salts] and aspirin I could find.*

*Then the Leut came and asked for volunteers for 72 hours more.*

*I was first to volunteer but dought [sic] if I would have come through it.*

*Thank the Lord the Bosh[e] didn't attack again.*

The Bantams were coming apart at the seams. But they continued working harder than ever. The entire unit had been sick multiple times. They continued to suffer from dysentery, lice and trench fever, respiratory and wound infections, Spanish influenza, and trench foot.

Three were dead.

At least sixteen suffered significant crash injuries and/or clinical concussions.

Twenty-one had artillery wounds that required medical attention.

Over half displayed various symptoms of shellshock.

Four were missing in action, assumed to be prisoners of war.

One was in jail after a court martial.

Bill McClenaghan disappeared to Paris.

Sarge Lee transferred to command another unit.

Lieutenant Lyon was despondent and drinking heavily—as were all his Lobsters.

French commanders presumed forty-one Bantams were still alive.

How many would remain alive was questionable.

# CHAPTER 14

# All Dead on the Western Front

The boys continued to suffer. Influenza ravaged Europe in 1918 and the rest of the world thereafter. Over one hundred million people perished across the globe and five hundred million got sick. With a world population of 1.8 billion people, 5 percent of all human beings died. It was one of the deadliest pandemics of modern times.

Due to its unusual virulence, unlike with most influenza strains, young healthy adults were more likely to die than small children or the elderly. The over-response of their immune systems killed them. They'd drown in lung secretions much akin to the effects of mustard gas. Weary soldiers were an easy target for infection. The Bantam Boys' situation became so critical the remaining survivors were pulled from the front near the end of June. They were dispatched to L'Isle-Adam for a needed rest and ambulance refitting. Their cars were virtual wrecks.

At Adam, Ralph received "fine quarters in an old ballroom." After relaxing for a few days, several of the boys went with Ralph to Paris. They needed to exchange their damaged ambulances for new ones. Ralph was first in line to get *Lizzie #4.*

For once, a leisurely trip awaited them.

Their first stop was to get rooms at the Paris YMCA. The boys took hot baths until their skin wrinkled and turned beet red. The Lobsters boiled themselves and they loved every second of it. It was their first bath in months. Grime peeled off bodies like old paint from sun-bleached doors. "I shore am clean!" Ralph yelled to his roommates.

His filthy bathwater nearly glued him to the tub. He didn't get out until the water was ice cold and he ran out of soap. Ralph liked French soap. "I smell like a petunia!"

Believed to be one of Ralph's three destroyed *Lizzies*

Lev puffed on a cigar and said, "You smell like a tuna."

Ralph climbed from his bath and looked into a mirror. He saw what looked like an oversized, wrinkled, and red newborn wearing the scraggly remains of a Mohawk. He used dull scissors to unsuccessfully tidy his hair. The resulting coiffure was a lost cause.

Jack said, "Good thing you ain't a barber."

Looking the part of military hobos, the boys were off to a bistro where they stuffed themselves until they could barely walk. They waddled back to their rooms resembling a flock of lethargic penguins after a successful hunt. They appeared to be brain damaged, and not even the low-rent hookers propositioned them on the return trek.

The idea of going out for drinks after dinner was never even discussed. They were soon fast asleep at the YMCA, most not bothering to fully undress. Fitful snoring replaced the sound of machine-gun fire. Respiratory infections kept some of them awake because they continued to hack up copious amounts of green phlegm.

Lev was miserable but he smoked cigars all night "for good health."

The next day the Bantams nursed their wrecks over to an "auto park" to get new cars. The officer in charge gawked at the old ambulances when they drove in. He shook his head and directed them to the scrap heap.

Maybe the mechanics could cannibalize some of the ambulances' innards. If so, then this mass of machines might not be a total loss. There were always too few replacement parts available. They'd be stripped to their bones then dumped in the trash heap. The new ambulances weren't perfect either. One didn't have a muffler and according to Ralph "sounded like a rancor."

Getting new ambulances was the least interesting of their discoveries. While they were getting ready to leave the auto park, Bill McClenaghan, missing for weeks, walked in to see what was going on. He said "he heard the Bantam Boys were in town."

Ralph was in shock. Here Bill appeared in the flesh. He wasn't injured. He wasn't sick or obviously shellshocked. In fact, he was pretty damn fat and happy compared to their wretched state. All gawked at Bill.

"What the hell?" asked Ralph.

"Hell yes!" said Bill. "It's me."

Bill looked at Ralph and appeared taken aback. Bill said they "looked like they'd been dragged by wild horses." He was clearly uncomfortable with their poor condition. He tried to avoid eye contact as he straightened his posture. He kept his demeanor affable. But Bill looked nervous as he put his hand out to shake.

Ralph would have none of it. His anger boiled over faster than a punctured radiator. He grumbled and turned away.

Bill lowered his hand.

Ralph felt betrayed. He turned back to Bill and said, "You don't walk away from friends. You just don't!"

Bill's unexpected appearance caused a bigger rancor than any ambulance muffler:

*Saturday, 29 June 1918. Paris*

*. . . He was listening to the reputation I was giving him to the sergeant. I started low and worked up.*

*When I finally said, "that if you'd put Bill in the sunshine, you wouldn't see him."*

*Well, that was too much for Bill. He came out from behind his door and stuck his paw out to shake.*

*If floored me. I couldn't even start the speech I'd planned.*

*All I said was, "You got in a colder climate didn't you, Bill?"*

*And Bill planned revenge. Bill owed me 70 francs.*

*He figured that saying would cost me 50 francs. But I collected Bill's wages two months back, a thing he wasn't aware of.*

*So Bill invites the Leut [of the auto park] over and tells him [about Ralph].*

*[Ralph tells Bill] Give me 20 francs that he owed me.*

*If Bill ever denies owing that 20 francs when I'm around [without an officer], God pity him is all I can say.*

*Bill's got a job in the park now.*

*I'll add one more compliment to Bill. It's a pity he couldn't get it in the neck instead of somebody like Carey or Paul or Purcell . . .*

A happy reunion it was not. Ralph and Bill, former partners carrying hundreds of wounded and loads of anguish, walked away forever.

They never spoke to each other again.

Ralph strode over to inspect *Lizzie #4*. Or maybe she was #5 if he included the loaners. He couldn't exactly remember. He crashed, trashed, and smashed so many cars it was hard to know how much damage he'd been a party to. Either way he was too angry to care. *I don't have to pay for 'em*, he thought.

When the incredulous American officer in charge learned that this was Ralph's fourth vehicle he asked, "Private, are you unlucky?"

Ralph thought a few seconds. Then he answered confidently, "I shore am lucky, sir. My machines are not."

The boys lined up their new vehicles and left for Versailles. They spent several days on site at Versailles because they couldn't get a commissioned officer to ride with them. They learned it was illegal for a military convoy to drive to the front without a commissioned officer. Why? Nobody knew. Maybe it was the French officer corps' paranoia that "reprobate enlisted men" might steal these "valuable" ambulances.

The "stupid regulation" was fine with them. The pause gave more time to sightsee and eat. Then eat more. "This stinking Frenchie food is so good I got my appetite back," said Ralph. He crammed his mouth full of *pâté de foie gras* while lingering at a sidewalk cafe. "What is this stuff anyway?"

Jack said, "It's goose liver."

"You are so full of crap, Jack. This ain't liver. It actually tastes good!"

They then took the grand tour of Versailles. The caretakers let the Americans in for a free excursion around most of the palace. Ralph even learned the meaning of the word *boudoir*. Unfortunately the Royal bedroom was off limits—much to Jack's disappointment. He said he wanted to see where "noble happiness was made."

Versailles was something the likes of which Ralph had never seen before. While touring and gawking at its splendor, Jack recounted what he read about it in one of his French history classes. What he didn't know, he made up. Because that's what men do when absent of facts. Jack was "a master of the black art of deception and brown art of bullshit," according to Ralph. "You shore could be a propaganda agent."

Jack rendered thanks for this supreme compliment.

His fuel tank overflowing with wine, Jack proceeded to recall Versailles's role in the French Revolution. He spun quite a yarn. True or not it was an amusing distraction from Ralph's fervent desire to "beat the living hell out of Bill McClenaghan."

Jack told the boys about Marie Antoinette's inaccurate but famous misquote "let them eat cake." Since the peasants "had no bread and were starving, she said they should gobble cake instead of bread. Or some snarky thing like that. So the hoi polloi chopped her head off," said Jack.

"Let them eat cake?" Ralph asked. "Let them eat U.S. Army rations. That's cause for revolution."

Everyone clapped in agreement.

After their tour, the Bantams hijacked a weary French officer so they could return to their aid station. The officer slept in the back of an ambulance with a bottle of *Pernod* for company. He slept all the way to L'Isle-Adam and never woke up.

Upon their arrival, the boys were presented with new orders. Now they needed to go to Meaux. Their section had left several days ago. No one relayed the change of *Poste* to them in Paris. Their new orders were days late. It was no big deal to Ralph. "More play time for us." The group decided to set out at first light without an officer.

"They gonna arrest us?" asked Jack. "Maybe we can room with Jess Clayton."

The boys left the next morning on a restful journey.

Ralph daydreamed on the drive. He wanted to leave all the craziness and war behind. He had fantasies of driving to Switzerland and staying there the rest of his life. He thought he could work on a Swiss farm and make cheese. *Making cheese couldn't be that difficult,* he decided. Or he could make clocks. He could build cuckoo clocks! *Nothing's more cuckoo than this war.*

The drivers arrived at the new staging area without damaging a single new ambulance in route, despite driving through unusually heavy military traffic. They grabbed some intermittent sleep. They had a few interesting exploits over the next several days. The time away allowed Ralph to take stock of the Bantams' situation. He wrote about their effective status as it appeared to him at that moment:

*Wednesday, 3 July 1918.*

*I rested and went to the triage for three days and now I'm at Croix de Pierre for [the next] two days.*

*This is as pretty as any park. It's in a beech forest and three miles from the front.*

*At present we have nearly 50% of our small band on the casualty list and almost 20% on the mortality list.*

*The Ambulance [Corps] is Ambuscade [ambushed] without a doubt.*

The Bantam Boys had been ambushed. The 50 percent casualty rate was correct. Fortunately, Ralph's 20 percent mortality assessment was triple the actual figure of 7 percent. Only three men were killed in action (KIA). None were officially designated as permanently missing in action (MIA). All the "lost" drivers were eventually located and returned to the unit. Some missing actually had been seriously injured and taken to hospitals for recovery. Communication was slow, which led to the boys needlessly worrying about Lucius Cook's fate. He was injured not captured. Others went missing periodically.

Three Bantams—Sarge Stevens, Bunny Hunt, and Duke Dennen—had been taken as prisoners of war (POWs) by the Huns. They were not executed. If they were tortured, it was not disclosed in any documentation. Ralph didn't know they were alive. In his pessimism, he thought they were dead. (They were released at the armistice.)

No matter how the number was calculated, the Bantams registered one of the highest casualty rates of American units in the war.

But the war wasn't close to being over.

The first week of July remained calm. Ralph's handwriting became very small and difficult to read. He couldn't sleep despite being "used-up." The situation was maddening. He ate. He drank. Enough wine would put him "out" for the night.

He thought they had been relocated to a safe area. It was not. No matter how many moves they made, the war would not let the Bantam Boys out of its grasp. Ralph worried more were going to die. The war hunted them as fervidly as a deranged stalker:

*Saturday, 6 July 1918*

*We are at Les Islettes. We thought we had a quiet sector but at present it looks as though we would be in the center of another Verdun.*

*We have been on the alert for several days. All preparations for heavy work are going on all sides . . . We are waiting and wonder what will come.*

*We had a great dinner on the fourth [of July].*

Ralph didn't write again for weeks. The front lines were changing daily. After years of static trench warfare, nobody was ready for the extreme fluidity of the Allied defenses. In later writings, Ralph at times could not recall where he had been. Sometimes he was too tired to care. He was hit with minor shrapnel wounds again. *I feel like a goddamn pin cushion,* he thought.

On July 15th, twenty-three German divisions attacked the French Fourth Army in the *Bataille de Champagne* (Battle of Champagne). The

A street believed to be in Soissons

US 42nd Army Division was attached to the French. Meanwhile, seventeen divisions of Germans fought what was known as the *Bataille de la Montagne de Reims* (Battle of Reims Mountain). They hoped to split apart the two French armies and wipe out the Americans.

The attack on Reims unraveled quickly. The inadequately supplied Germans bogged down and got nowhere. The French on the south Marne took far greater casualties but succeeded in a more resolute push to destroy their enemy.

This was, unfortunately, right where the Bantam Boys were arrayed.

German storm troopers used boats to cross the Marne and strove to erect bridgeheads in the Bantam sector. Allied units, including the US 3rd Infantry Division (called the "Rock of the Marne"), held their positions against the initial attack. The Germans captured a bridgehead despite French *Caudron* and *Breguet* bomber aircraft dropping forty-four tons of ordnance on storm troopers and construction battalions. British XXII Corps and eighty-five thousand additional American infantry joined the French in the fight. Together they halted the advance on July 17, 1918.

The failure to break the lines led to an Allied counterattack on July 18th. French divisions accompanied by the US 92nd and 93rd Infantry with 350 tanks attacked the German line. It was another bloodbath. But the French and gritty Americans refused to stop regardless of casualties. On August 2nd the Allies recaptured Soissons.

During this frenzy of combat, the Bantams got hammered on the campaign anvil. Seeing maimed and mutilated men in pain was soul destroying for Ralph. Now he was carrying Americans. He tried to reassure the wounded that he would get them to aid stations. When his first American soldier died in transit, "an Ohio boy," he felt terrible. To continue coping, Ralph built an emotional brick wall.

He no longer learned names, units, or took a personal interest in any of his wounded. Work became a stark, mechanical routine. To put more energy in made the task debilitating. Falling apart didn't help anybody. A job had to be done. He did his share.

This was the low point for Ralph. He simply completed his bloody trade. What he needed was months of recovery time. That would not happen anytime soon.

The Bantam Boys had been on a long, rough ride and pushed to near collapse. The unit had been spread thin across a wide area of the battlefront. In a conservative estimate, Ralph traveled over five thousand kilometers (thirty-one hundred miles), as did many veteran drivers during their year of front duty. Much of it was a fatigue-filled blur under a rain of steel. Ralph longed for the end so he could go home to be with Edyth.

On Thursday, August 15, 1918, Ralph wrote that he was on station at Aix les Bains. He said that he had been there "several" weeks. Davis, a Bantam, had been wounded but "nothing of consequence" had happened in the last few days. There were several gas attacks that were more harassing than effective. Tensions remained high. A substantial German infantry force was believed to be right across their wire defenses.

Ralph said he liked this area for its beauty. It was nothing like the old wastes of their first No Man's Land where he almost got himself shot in the head. Given his apparent exhaustion, he was ordered to take repose at a nearby YMCA, a small but friendly place. French officers recognized that he was not well.

For once, Ralph did not protest their decision.

On leave his favorite activity was getting warm showers. He talked with a number of American and Scottish female nurses who were assisting the wounded. Seeing the women made him long for Edyth. He desperately wanted to hear from her. Ralph had no letters left to read. The last ones had fallen apart or disappeared under shellfire. Mail was behind schedule. He eagerly went to the post office every day. Nothing arrived for him.

Ralph took bicycle trips into the nearby mountains. The exercise invigorated him and time alone renewed his optimism. During his tours he could see the picturesque range. He had never seen "real" mountains before, certainly none as big as these. The peaks were a contrast to the squat mountains he saw in Tennessee when he rode the train to visit his Aunt Bea in Maryville. That summer he volunteered for the Ambulance Corps. It seemed a century ago.

Ralph thought about Bea. As a pacifist, he remembered she was not happy when he told her that he had joined the Army. She threatened to "lock him in the woodshed 'til it's all over." Remembering her words made him smile.

The fresh alpine air and pedaling did Ralph well. He wished he could put its therapeutic effects in a bottle. While viewing the mountains, he suddenly yearned to climb them. *Could I run away and become a mountaineer?* Switzerland sounded even more inviting. He wanted to disappear from the face of the earth. In all this emotional turmoil Ralph questioned his future.

*What do I do after the war?* he asked himself.

He had seen so much blood, it now made him physically sick. That, he decided, did not bode well for a medical doctor's career. He couldn't stand to see other people's pain. It distressed him too much.

*Do I go back to medical school?*

Ralph barely had time to wrestle with this conundrum when his repose was cancelled. The war yanked him back into its relentless grip:

*Friday, 23 August 1918. Poste Breteuil*

*We didn't go south. We stayed several days at Grange au Bois then went to Brieux for two days then we took a two day drive for a place near Amiens.*

*We are at Breteuil now and expect to move again soon.*

*The drive was hot and dusty. We passed through Chalons, [unreadable], Meaux, Senlis, Clermont, St. Just [-en-Cheaussee] and Breteuil.*

*I was lost most of the time.*

*Wood [a Bantam] road [sic] with me the last day.*

*We have been here two days. Last night was [a] full moon and we had some air raids. They blowed Breteuil to pieces.*

*They hit an ammunition factory and killed about 60 people.*

*There is an old castle here [Château de Breteuil] with a tower over 100 ft. high. I took some pictures of it yesterday.*

That was all Ralph wrote in this entry. The war raged through its final destructive phase. Many more American and French soldiers were going to get wounded. Bantam Boys would try to save them.

On the previous August 15th, the Allied attack at Amiens halted. They then executed a plan to open an offensive at Albert on August 21st. The main attack was launched by the British Third Army and the US 2nd Corps. The effort drove the Huns back thirty-four miles (55km). Albert was taken on August 22nd.

On August 26th, the British furthered the extent of captured territory by seven miles (12km). In what has been called the Second Battle of Arras, the city of Bapaume fell to the Allies on the 29th. Few buildings remained. Fewer soldiers remained alive.

The Australians crossed the Somme on August 31 and shattered the German defensive lines. On the morning of September 2nd, dogged Canadians seized control of the western end of the Hindenburg Line. The carnage was incredible. Thousands of men were dead, wounded, or dying. Suffering was on a scale beyond comprehension.

Their sacrifice, however, breached the last major line of defense for Germany. The Huns withdrew behind the Canal du Nord. Soon afterward the Canadians also penetrated the Hindenburg Line at Cambrai. Germany could not win this war.

Only the Boche Kaiser would not acknowledge their hopeless situation.*

Ralph filled his new notebook pages with an extensive, detailed entry, the longest of the war. It contains confusing recollections of his experiences, some likely before August 24th and others possibly all the way up to September 12th. He started with, "We are in Rethel on repose. We have just finished our third battle of the year. It was the third battle of the Somme."

Being the good farm boy, Ralph sidetracked himself from the carnage by first focusing this entry on a description of the village and its surrounding farmland. Rethel was a small community of about six hundred inhabitants, most of which were evacuated or dead. A few had returned in an attempt to take care of their crops and harvest any plant worth saving. "The town is situated in a large valley which is not very deep but had considerable swampy marshes running along the creek that drained it. The water is fair and we find many springs. The land is fertile and contains lime stone," he wrote. Ralph drank all the fresh water he could hold.

He loved the horse teams as they reaped the fields. Feeding young ponies apples, he wished to take them home with him. He liked to watch them run free. That was better than anything he could imagine. Ralph vowed to raise horses when he got back to Ohio.

Soissons was not far distant. Between Rethel and Pierrefonds was a fertile plateau covered with wheat fields, trenches, and barbed wire entanglements. "An aviation camp and wireless station are visible, too," he wrote.

Lieutenant Lyon and Bantam Bill Porter went to Saconin that week and found the place where Bill Purcell and Paul Hargreaves were buried.

---

*Author's note: For some unknown reason Ralph added loose leaf pages and purchased a notebook to write new diary entries. Few had dates. He did this despite having plenty of blank pages available in his leather diary. This made his timeline impossible to accurately decipher. He may have been temporarily separated from his gear. He also likely damaged or lost his second camera at this time. The first camera was irreparable and discarded months before. Many of his photos and negatives were destroyed during this episode as well. Over one hundred original photographs and twenty nitrate negatives managed to survive. The delicate, curled negatives are highly flammable, and subject to chemical off-gassing and spontaneous explosive ignition. They even burn underwater.

Ruins of an unnamed cathedral

Also they went "to see our old scrapping grounds." The pair placed a wreath on the double grave and paid their respects.

At the aid post *avions* bothered Ralph nightly. "They wounded a fellow in an anti-aircraft battery two nights ago. But no serious damage has resulted." To Ralph, the irrational Boche tenacity signified that this fight wouldn't end well or soon.

Pierrefonds was about two or three miles from Ralph's location. He had gone to see it three times with Bantam Joe Swan, Dick Brooke's first partner. Few places were as stately as this. Other than Versailles, it was as opulent as anything Ralph had ever seen. Its beauty, however, was not enough to diffuse Ralph's anger. He allowed himself to wax ironic on the meaning of the war for the crumbling "Hun Empire" and the destruction it had wrought:

*Date Unknown, 1918. Pierrefonds*

*The Chateau at Pierrefonds it is the most magnificent I ever saw. It was there that the [German] Crown Prince made his quarters in 1914 and was nearly captured by the French in the first battle of the Marne.*

*A few bombs have damaged it to some extent but as a whole it is unharmed. They say the reason [it was bombed by the French] is that the Prince expected to abide there.*

*It's too bad that God's chosen [the Germans] can't have what they want. It looks, too, as if the Salt of the Earth had lost its or their savior.*

*Fritz has had the worst of the deal lately.*

The Bantams soon left the Pierrefonds city limits. They passed through many small villages on their way to relieve Canadian ambulance drivers on the evolving front. The Bantams headed through many areas that had seen intense combat and sustained considerable damage. Ralph wrote about the horrors and curiosities he found on one extensive Somme district battlefield. He continued the undated entry:

*After we passed Attichy, we could see the results of the scrap. We saw all sorts of affaires [gear] both French, English and bosh [sic]. The trenches and barbed wire entanglements were knocked to pieces, clothing, guns and even dead Germans were scattered about.*

*We saw many tanks both large and small of the British when they had met their fate. All had caught fire and burned.*

*At one place between Attichy and Berneiul [su–Asne] we stopped and hunted souvenirs. Some found guns and bayonets and all sorts of clothing.*

*I noticed that some of the shells for the lighter guns were made of steel or some kind of alloy that rusted.*

*The machine gun cartridges were possibly made of aluminum.*

*We found many sandbags made of woven paper that look much like gunny sacks. Afterwards I found even hand towels made of woven paper. Some where [sic] good but some were very harsh.*

*Everywhere were piles of captured ammunition mingles with the fragments of skin and bones of horses.*

*And sometimes men.*

The Germans were running out of resources, especially vital copper-based alloys and cotton cloth. The sight of all these inferior materials must have given Ralph hope for victory. The sheer amount of captured material was astonishing as well. He thought that Germans had to be near the end of their rope. By fighting on, the Huns were only going to hang themselves.

The Bantams continued on their relentless journey. Tons of abandoned matériel littered the ravaged countryside. French villages were nothing but stark rubble:

> *Just before we reached Berneiul we saw a pile of captured guns.*
>
> *Berneiul was the first city I've seen in such condition. It was hammered down in a manner hard to describe.*
>
> *It looked as if forty most violent earth quakes had shaken it for months. Each house and building was simply a pile of debris dumped in a heap. Most of the homes were of brick and no two bricks hung together.*
>
> *The coolies [Chinese] had shoveled a one way route through the town and we followed it through and out the other side.*
>
> *That whole country look like hell and smelt like a slaughter house.*
>
> *The trees of the forest look much worse than a pine forest after a fire has swept it.*

The boys drove into the village of Le Quesnay in a small valley. They took up station in an old German hospital. A Boche doctor and two or three male nurses or orderlies had remained and formally surrendered under a white flag. Above the hospital was a vast graveyard "decorated with German [Iron] crosses." Ralph complimented the Boche on their sensitive attention to their graves. At least the Huns did something right. "If a man gives his life, give him a decent grave," Ralph said. The site was poignant:

> *Date Unknown, 1918. Le Quesnay*
>
> *They take far more care of the graves than the Allies do . . . Where they buried the boshes they stuck their guns in the ground at the head of the grave.*
>
> *The French as a rule are very careful to keep the graves in good condition and well marked. Even when burying an enemy they put a black cross up for him and mark it.*

*As I have said the Germans put large painted crosses made of hard wood and well set. All decorations are painted on them with the name, date and rank.*

*"Hier ruht in Gott ließ Heinie." [Let him rest in God.]*
*One place they had buried an Englishman beside a bosh.*
*"Hier ruht in Gott," said Heinie's cross.*
*"Here lays an Englishman," said the other.*
*C'est le Guerre.*

The Bantams took over the German hospital from Canadian combat troops. The Canadians captured it intact with little resistance. The wounded Germans were left in their beds, although they were officially prisoners of war. Canadian guards kept watch over the pitiful lot of their dying enemy. Many begged for water. The guards fed them.

The Bantams stocked the facilities with familiar American-made supplies in preparation for the arrival of US doctors and nurses. Until then, they worked with the Canadian doctors. Allied officers allowed the Boche medical teams to continue to work on the wounded without interference, as long as they treated men from both sides "equally." The German staff was grateful for the freedom to continue and avoid a worthless existence in a prison camp. They worked diligently with the Canadians and Americans to save lives. It was a tiny island of sanity in an ocean of lunacy.

This hospital posting kept most of the Bantams on site until further notice. Ralph observed the colorful Canadian combat soldiers in the process of regrouping on the hospital grounds. He ran out to talk with them like greeting old friends. "Michigan is right next to the Cannucks," he said. "I been across the border to Toronto. It's beautiful." He continued his entry:

*Their artillery was moving in all directions. Everywhere in the abris and in little scooped out holes in the fields, the boys were camped.*

*Some wore Kilts like the Scots. They crowded around us eager to swap tales. They had surprised Fritz and their losses were comparatively light.*

*They had him running for fair.*

*Most of them were very young and some were homesick.*
*Some were new troops.*

The sector remained quiet. Only the night held much danger from the last airworthy German *avions*. It appeared as a last act of resistance by the few surviving Boche aviators. Allied planes ruled the daytime. Dogfights ceased. Germans only came out after dark and rarely hit their intended target. Even so, their numbers dwindled by the day and the German air force was shot from the skies using high-intensity spotlights and skilled American anti-aircraft artillery—otherwise known as "Triple A."

Their mission accomplished, the Canadians mounted up and left Le Quesnay in an elegant procession. Ralph enjoyed the grand show:

*Occasionally a shell hit in the valley but they were rare and we seldom saw an aeroplane except at night they flew over and bombed every-thing in sight.*

*The whole country was full of search lights and a dozen or more streaked the sky all night long. They told us of a bomb hitting a hospital and killing a bunch of wounded prisoners.*

*The second day we were there our troops began to replace the Canadians and by the fourth day our division held the line.*

*Then the Cannucks started to leave. The Scots went first. Just after dark they started marching past with their pipes and drums. The pipes play a ditty like Fisher's Hornpipe [by Johann Christian Fischer].*

*The high tenor drum beats a tattoo. The large drum sounds like a kettle drum and comes in every other time.*

*It makes good live music and sounds as weird and romantic as a mandolin on a moonlit lake.*

*The moon was full. Fritz was burning all over the skies like a mad hornet.*

*The search lights were running opposition to the moon.*

*For several hours I had laid there listening to each regiment as they came and went. Coming up with a faint squeak and beat getting louder and louder. Then fading out of our hearing.*

*Once or twice a Regiment of straight Cannucks passed with their band playing. One played the Long, Long Trail [There's a Long, Long Trail by Stoddard King] and one or two of them sang as they played. It reminded me of when we left Halifax harbor and the moon was just as bright. That band on the ship played the same piece.*

*The boys said that they had been over just about a year.*

*I wondered if it could have been the same band.*

*I went to sleep some time late and the next I knew Jack Stearns was shaking me.*

*We had a trip.*

Ralph then had one of his most unusual experiences. He was clearly exhausted and groggy. (He may have been hallucinating. Distorted visual and auditory experiences were common in men with shellshock.) His experience was disconcerting as he thought his Bantam Boys were shot-up and dying. He continued writing about the odd event:

*I got up and went into the triage.*

*It was full of wounded, both Canadian and French.*

*I was too sleepy to think much and I came to the conclusion that the boys in khakis were our boys.*

*One I saw lying there. I thought [he] was Joe Swan.*

*"Are you hurt?" I asked.*

*"Got it through the back," he said.*

*I saw one next to him who I thought was John McCune.*

*"Did you get it, too?" I asked.*

*"Yes," was all he said.*

*I went out and got my wagon ready then I asked Jack how bad the boys were hurt.*

*He told me I was asleep and I wasn't sorry to find out that it was true.*

*A captain, a major and two or three Lieutenants got theirs.*

*Several Frenchmen were killed, too, and a heap of wounded.*

None of the wounded were Bantams. Not knowing what had happened, Ralph believed that he dreamed it all. He said he was "still asleep" while he walked and talked to the soldiers. It bothered him, however, for days. He obsessed about what had happened to those men. To find out, Ralph queried several officers trying to get the story straight. He discovered that the incident leading to the wounded was stupidly tragic.

Apparently, the wounded Ralph spoke to had been the Canadian men marching away from the hospital the previous night. They were the procession he so much enjoyed watching. Apparently the luckless infantry came under attack by Boche night bombers. Their band was playing and "Fritz spotted their instruments gleaming in the moonlight."

This was an enormous security error. A group of American anti-aircraft engineers had a German *avion* spotted with their searchlight and tried to "shoot the bastard down." Why the Canadians didn't scatter to cover on the aircraft's approach is a mystery.

"Fritz dropped his tail gait and dumped his whole load on their heads." The men were slaughtered where they marched. Ralph said Canadian medics "buried 20 bodies." But someone told him at least forty-five were killed and it could have been as high as sixty. The Bantam Boys carried upwards of 120 wounded. These poor Canadian infantrymen had survived the worst combat only to be struck down as they retired from the battlefield. Ralph couldn't comprehend the futility of it all.

To make things worse, he suddenly came down with another illness:

*All night I carried wounded. We had to go all the way to County with them and they took them to Beauvais.*

*I pitied those poor blesses for the road was like the ocean waves and it took at least two days to get where they could lay still.*

*Though I had some chance to sleep the next day I didn't sleep and that was my last chance for a week.*

*I had a cold, then belly ache and the heart ache and felt tough all over.*

*After I'd worked two days [the] Chief gave my car to Donald Burrows and let me have a night off.*

A bombed Somme cemetery

*Then Kid Harvey got sick and I took his car. It wasn't in very good shape to start and on a camion [truck] crowded [road] ran into a ditch and I broke the front spring and brake.*

Ralph put Kid's ambulance out of commission. Ralph's machines continued their bad luck. Kid had extra days of rest while the unnamed "Chief" tried to get the ambulance repaired. Ralph had creamed it royally. He was later jokingly credited as one of America's most prolific World War I ambulance "collision experts."

The boys moved their triage *Poste* to a location the Americans code-named *Rosco Roy*. There an American army division attacked the Germans and drove the Huns backwards for miles. It was bloody, awful work in which the weather could not have been worse. The Germans faltered in the morass. The Americans took the remaining Huns as prisoners. Thousands of Boche were captured as they threw down their weapons en masse. They had had enough. Four years of war was too much. What were they dying for?

The Bantams didn't fare much better than the Germans. They hauled hundreds of wounded. Ralph wrote, "We were almost dead after several days. It rained most every night and was cold as ice." Even though it was only fall, the weather was horridly bitter.

In desperation, the Boche sent their frayed, residual *avions* into daylight raids. Now, again, no front location was safe. Anything that moved was targeted. Boche despondency appeared to become angry homicidal and suicidal gestures. Pilots died.

The boys changed their triage station to Hattencourt as the Allies forced Fritz back across the Somme. The village Somme Suippes had been pounded to the ground. A few heavy shells fell as the boys arrived. The most forward operating area outside Hattencourt was termed "Post 123." It wasn't much of a hospital base or an aid station. It was quite literally a hole in the ground:

### Date Unknown, 1918. Poste 123

*We were cached in an old road way and had a few holes dug in the near side of it where we stayed.*

*Those [last shells] were the only near shells I heard in the whole battle.*

*I had a trip and returned to the reserve post of 123 and tried to sleep in my car. A heavy English gun some few yards away kept booming every ten minutes and I couldn't sleep worth a crap.*

*The avions worried me, too, though no bombs came near.*

*I had a trip and a little [rest] after daylight. So I filled my guts with eats, coffee and Pernod at the reserve post.*

*We always ate there and took no grub with us. I had several cans of beef, sardines and hash in my car that I ate when hungry.*

*Next, I went to the post of 57 and there saw [French] Major Ferron. He was very nice and gave me his pen and a post card to write on.*

*We didn't get any rest there either for this regiment attacked every day. We had all the available cars carrying wounded.*

*There was a bunch of prisoners, too, and many were wounded.*

Ralph had his second and rather sad encounter with Boche prisoners. The vaunted and bellicose Hun ranks were now packed with fearful teenagers. While quite worried about their immediate futures, these near children were happy to be captured and not be dead. Even an impassive Prussian officer had had enough of the fighting. Ralph wrote in the same entry about brief conversations with two Hun prisoners:

> One flaxen haired kid looked scared to death. They put him on the side of my car. He grinned friendly enough and said, "So."
>
> I said, "Ja, so."
>
> Some were officers, too. I carried one who spoke good English.
>
> I asked him how long the war would last.
>
> He said he thought this winter would finish it. "You may think I like this war," he said, "but I don't."
>
> He didn't express his views as to who would be victorious.
>
> Most of them say in reply to the question of the number of Americans [they think are] over here: 3000.
>
> If there are only three thousand now I pity them when we get an army.

As an organized fighting force, the German Army's days were few. Their main function now appeared to be a rear guard defensive action. If they could hold out long enough, they had slim hope for a peace treaty. At least, that's what the diehards believed. They didn't want other nations marching on their soil.

Ralph's Boche prisoners were very wrong about the number of Americans in France. If they knew the true extent, the morale of the average German enlisted man would have been shaken if not destroyed.

By June 1918, ten thousand American troops were arriving by the *day* into France. Four battle-ready American divisions were already getting experience with French and British armies. This was over forty thousand American combat soldiers alone. But even Ralph had no idea how many were already in depots or embarking on troopships. A million-man American Army would be on European shores soon enough.

Ralph and the Bantam Boys soldiered on. During this time, Ralph slipped up and made a big mistake. He relearned a disgusting lesson on where not to sleep. As unexpected punishment, he proceeded to slap himself silly:

*Date Unknown, 1918. Poste 123*

*I worked that post [123] two days and nights. Lev Hoffman was chief of the post.*

*The first night I tried to sleep in the abri. It was an old German dugout and about thirty or forty feet deep.*

*It was a long narrow passage way tunneled under the street. The sides were boarded and braced and the gang ways had slats to keep from slipping.*

*The floor was lightened with moldy, damp straw and the walls and ceiling were covered with sickly fat grease flies that crawled about all night over your face and hands.*

*I smashed so many that I had juice all over me. Then I went to sleep.*

*A French soldier awakened me by gently placing his hobnailed boot on my face. He skinned my nose all up.*

*Then I started scratching.*

*It felt like I'd been rubbed with red pepper. I couldn't stand it any longer.*

*I was lousy from head to foot.*

*I went out and poured a gallon of gas over my blankets and went to sleep in my wagon regardless of shells or avions.*

Flames were the only sure cure for a lice infection. Ralph reluctantly burned his favorite blankets. The cold was still unusually intense. He rolled up in his overcoat looking like a hibernating squirrel wrapped in its tail.

Work was as hard as ever. Bloody wounds, one after another, never ceased. Ralph tried comforting the dying the same way he succeeded with the banker's baby back in Allentown: He'd rub their shoulders. He arranged the bodies of the dead to give them some semblance of dignity. To him they only looked like sardines ready for a can. He made sure their

An unknown post

faces were covered with some cloth or piece of clothing. He toiled up to twelve hours per day and many hours of the night.

"You got a little sleep on the front. But you didn't get any on triage," he wrote.

Soon their division attacked and that night Ralph got hit with a salvo of gas. It was supposed to be Joe Swan's run, but Ralph took the trip out of pity for him. Ralph drove down to a place near the Somme across from what he called "Rory le Petite" (he perhaps meant Roye).

While loading their cars, the Huns fired seven tear gas shells. Fortunately, stocks of more lethal mustard shells had been exhausted. Nobody got hurt in the attack and, ironically, the Boche got the worst of it:

*They lit beside us in a field and their pieces whirred over our head. Bullets and [artillery] fire, too, for that matter.*

*We were kissing the ground and hugging mother earth. I don't want to be hit even with a piece of gas shell éclat. The gas rose like a fog but a friendly breeze drove it the other way. And none of [us] even got a breath of it.*

*The next day I went on triage duty again at Hattencourt. For these days I never had a single night trip and as the hospital had moved from Cutry to Le Cruesanet {sp?}, we had an easy time of it. About this time the 144 Regiment relieved the 57th and went in repose. 144 pushed them back and some distance, too.*

*We evacuated our casualties to Vaux.*

Outside of Vaux Ralph said, "Them Boche boys was on horse back. I saw the sparks from their horse shoes on the cobblestones right in front of me."

Jack said, "Ralph, those were Hun machinegun bullets. You nearly got your head 'blowed' off. Again."

"You're making that up."

"Nope. Sorry old boy."

About the middle of the month the boys moved their triage to Nesle and several other outposts. Ralph went on duty at the advanced reserve post at Toul. He crossed canals on several pontoon bridges and took rough roads until he managed to find a big sign in English on a sugar beet factory. It said: "This is Toulle" [sic]. (The British Army left these signs in many small villages to guide their fellows during the retreat of 1916.)

The boys "ate up heavy" in Toul. When Ralph came in on late-night trips, he stocked up on canned food, just in case he'd miss a meal or get lost. He wasn't going hungry. He had dropped considerable weight and hot meals were now inconsistent. But crates of American canned goods such as fruit cocktail, vegetables, and lowly British bully beef (affectionately known as monkey meat—basically dog food rejected by mongrels) were available. Ralph ate whenever and whatever he could choke down. His stomach had been bothering him for months so smaller, more frequent meals stayed down better than heavier fare. He ate a little bit five times a day to keep his weight up.

The boys had some rough times in villages after Toul. Ralph wrote about their route in detail previously lacking in earlier entries:

## Date Unknown, 1918. Poste 088

*The first two days I worked the reserve and advance post of 088. The reserve post was in [Villers] St. Christophe.*

*In wandering around through the village I visited the church. It still contained some paintings that were not half bad. The outpost was at Aubigny. Jack Stearns was chief of the post.*

*I slept in my car, or tried to, for I couldn't find the dugout. The Avions bombed all night. I got lost trying to find the place and wandered for an hour or two among the ruins. I had no more trips that night.*

*The next day I was with the [post] 123. The work was not bad but the abris were so lousy that I couldn't sleep in them and the avions worried me when I went into the car.*

*In a day or two we relieved [post] 044 again and did some heavy fighting. The advance post changed to Villers St. Christophe and from there to a quarry on the next hill. This was the most dangerous post we had.*

*Don Casto was wounded there. The same shell killed the medicine chief.*

*I went to relieve Casto but they changed the post and I only stay an hour.*

*Kid's car was badly shot up. Murray Smouse lost a car at Vile, too.*

*The post was changed to another hole in the ground further up. It was not any slouch either. Section 288 relieved us and they had a man killed there.*

*About the 23[rd] our division was relieved and went on repose at Nesle and around it. We did evacuation work for section 288. We had our triage at Vertus and evacuated through Aine, [unreadable], Moutdidier [sic] to Ribécourt.*

*I worked the triage two nights and had two trips. The first one and the second: It was more than 140 kilometers each way.*

*Montdidier was a good sized town but is only a mass of ruins now.*

*Then we were relieved for all duty, given the high sign after supper to pick stakes and be ready to move by daylight.*

*We worked like the devil and about midnight [we] were ready to move.*

The summer and early September of 1918 were continuous slogs from one triage station to another. Ralph lost count of all the moves he made. His writing took on a preoccupation with graves. Death occupied his thoughts more than ever before. He devoted much time writing descriptions of the German markers. Perhaps it was easier to concentrate on the dead than to triage the wounded:

*Date Unknown, 1918. Nesle*

*Our place in Nesle was about as dirty a place as we ever housed in. I worked all my spare time but it was stinking as a manure heap anyway.*

*We had an awful amount of rain, too. The water was rotten and made me sick every time I tasted it.*

*One of the main features of the town was a German graveyard. They had it fixed up in a great stile [sic] and must have had a lot of dead to bury in that spring drive. They had learned English, too. I guess there was more than a thousand single graves and many marked like this: Here lies 30 German soldiers.*

*The avions had the best graves. One or two were covered with hard wood shrines varnish and carved. Most however had crosses made of broken propeller blades, varnished and shored up. More than 20 aviators were buried in this one graveyard.*

*I took several pictures of this country.*

The next move started at eight o'clock in the morning via a convoy. Along the way Ralph found ripe apples in an orchard. He gave them to the ever-present and excellent Frenchie cook, Jarlaud. The cook was more important to them than their officers. Ralph asked him to make applesauce, one of his favorite foods. Ralph also found and shot a British Small Magazine Lee Enfield (SMLE) bolt action rifle. It let him blow off a little steam. He decided to keep it for self-defense as well as a souvenir.

The lack of Boche offensive activity indicated that the war might be over soon: less shooting, little Hun artillery. Given the fact that the war could be winding down, the Bantam Boys didn't want some Hun blasting them to heaven now. They became even more cautious and slightly hopeful as they continued gathering the sick and wounded.

Ralph gathered several hundred rounds of .303 caliber (7.7mm) ammo for his SMLE rifle. He considered it an insurance policy. He oiled the gun and made sure it was perfectly clean and operational. Ralph was determined not to be a casualty after all he had been through. He was going home no matter what, even if he had to kill *Frontschwein*.

Ralph thought to be the last man to die in a war was an especially cruel joke. He later found out, Pvt. Henry Gunther of Baltimore, Maryland, Company A, 313th Infantry, 79th Division of the US Army at Metz, was the last American listed as killed in action in the Great War. He lost his life on the last day of the conflict. It made no sense at all. He pitied the poor boy's family.

Following several additional moves, through previously occupied German territory, the Bantams ended up at Lassigny. Only Ralph could explain the folly there:

> *It was a sight. It looked like it had a bad case of small pox. Not an inch wasn't torn with shells and bombs.*
>
> *We only passed around the edge of town. Lassigny is placed on a rounding raised piece of ground probably seventy five feet at the highest point.*
>
> *From our point of view on the road it sloped towards us. This slope was cover [sic] with ruins of the town's barbed wire entanglements, trenches and concrete gun pits and machine gun forts which commanded the roads.*
>
> *The buildings had been constructed mainly of brick and stone with the tile roofs. These were completely raised. An occasional wall, a chimney, and a pole of debris marked the sight of each.*
>
> *Even these piles had been pitted and scattered by shell fire.*
>
> *Lieutenant stopped the convoy and we explored the ruins. Some of the boys took pictures. I didn't have film or a plate.*
>
> *Most of the boys stood still and looked with out a word, some swore and Hank Gilland took his shovel and started to fill shell holes.*
>
> *He made a picture too deep to laugh at.*

*The road was yet one to be remembered but even at this time showed much evidence of filled shell holes and bomb craters.*

*Along its sides were scattered piles of shells both German and allied . . .*

*Once we had gained our fill on the ruins of the town, we parked farther up on the scene. All the fields near showed the same shell pitting and desolation as the town.*

*At the top of the hill, off toward the right, stood the stumps of a forest, stripped bare of limbs and branches. Some shot completely in two at the waist part of the trunk. Trenches and fields of wire wound themselves among the trees . . .*

*The whole thing was the completest [sic] picture of annihilation I have ever seen anywhere.*

*Not a crow perched on the stubble or the trees could I see and not even a rat crossed the road ahead of us even though the putrid smell of dead horse and even unburied men still hung to the place and there was plenty of skin and bones laying scattered everywhere.*

*I've heard that the gas used in these battles kills the birds and rats.*

Lassigny was an apt symbol for the Great War. In one passage, Ralph summed up the entire conflict. He didn't know why it started. But this is how it was ending:

Armies were annihilated.

The Bantam Boys were decimated.

Even birds and rats were exterminated.

*All dead on the western front.*

More were soon to die.

# CHAPTER 15

# From Hell and Back

On September 12, 1918, US forces began their first large-scale operation, known as the Battle of St. Mihiel. The attack at the salient was designed to break the German lines and capture Metz. Fortunately, sections of Germans were out of position and unable to mount a full defense. The effort by US infantry proved highly successful and shocked the Boche High Command, who did not think lowly Americans could defeat their expert soldiers. Even the Allies were surprised at the scope of the triumph.

Doughboys swept into the Huns using French-made tanks. Colonel George Patton directed 114 American-manned Renault FT light tanks. These men were supported by an additional 275 French-manned FT and Schneider CA medium tanks. The latter vehicles were cumbersome with low clearances, but they carried effective 75mm howitzers. Nearly three thousand additional artillery pieces laid a welcome mat of flames at the feet of the Boche.

The ensuing combat was bloody. The motivated, but inexperienced Americans fought valiantly, being all too willing to expose themselves to machine-gun fire. Before night fell on the 13th, however, all primary objectives had been captured or destroyed. The doughboys took thirteen thousand prisoners and seized over 250 field guns. The Germans lost five thousand soldiers killed or wounded. America suffered nearly seven thousand casualties in the battle. In comparison, this casualty number is twice the 3,466 coalition deaths in Afghanistan for the thirteen years from 2001 to August 17, 2014.

### Saturday, 14 September 1918. Lassigny

The Bantam Boys knew little of the American assault. They left Lassigny and headed for Compiègne. Their convoy retraced many of the steps they had taken on their way to the front weeks before. Ralph didn't know if they were looping around a salient for another battle or going on repose. Nobody knew anything.

"Back in the mushroom business," Jack said. "We're fed shit and kept in the dark." Such was, and always has been, the conduct of war for the plucky enlisted man.

"After we'd eaten up on bully beef, baloney, cheese and bread we didn't care where we were going," wrote Ralph. Food was still his primary solace. Sleep, his second favorite activity, didn't offer much relief. "Dreams are not good . . ."

The usual sequence of an enlisted soldier's needs, often said in jest, was rest, food, and then women. Few could sleep well but everyone ate. Nobody gave a hoot about women at this stage. Going home to Edyth was Ralph's only obsession.

After leaving a damaged and virtually uninhabited Compiègne, lacking proper resupply, they again headed for Pierrefonds. Along the road Ralph spied an old French refugee wandering along with a small pig in her arms. Ralph hit his brake pedal. The other boys slowed to a stop behind him. They all got out and looked around.

Lev asked, "What's up, Ralph?"

"I want that piglet," he muttered.

Ralph raised pigs when he was growing up. He apparently envisioned this pig as a sign that harkened back to a normal life. With the help of their French cook, Jarlaud, Ralph negotiated a trade for the porker. He passed the thrilled refugee a big handful of francs. While overpaying, Ralph felt he got the better deal.

Jarlaud asked Ralph, "You want me make ham?"

"He shore ain't for dinner."

Ralph put his pig on his passenger seat. He used his belt as a collar and leash so the porcine partner wouldn't hop out. The little thing settled into the worn-out passenger seat. As the boys resumed their travel, it snored as it took a snooze.

Ralph petted him like a rescued bulldog.

At one stop, everyone got out to stretch. Ralph told Jack he was going to name his pig "Bill" in commemoration of Ralph's most infamous partner. Jack interrupted the exchange and said Ralph should name the pig "Marius."

"Why?"

"It's a joke." Jack went on to explain that the whole Princeton Philosophy Department would find it uproarious that their Bantam Boys named their porky mascot after an Epicurean character in an ancient novel. Jack laughed.

"That's goddamn hilarious," said Ralph with a blank face. He didn't have a clue as to what Jack was talking about.

"No, really!" Jack droned on. The essence of his explanation was *Marius the Epicurean* was a protagonist in an historical philosophical novel. Because Epicureans were associated with pleasure, including eating, and you could eat pig, and since pork was delicious, the name would be apropos . . .

Ralph stopped him and said, "Jack, you dream-up shit wilder than Mark Twain on an opium binge."

Jack swore his story was true.

Ralph said if Jack would shut up, he'd name his pig Marius.

The boys drove on with Marius as mascot and navigator. He sat shotgun on the lead ambulance. A different ambulance led the convoy each day so everyone shared the risk of being up front and getting sniped by stragglers or setting off an artillery dud. Drivers tried to keep within established tracks or the tracks of cars in front of them. To ease the first driver's mind, Ralph consented to let Marius be onboard his car. Everyone wanted a turn chauffeuring their cute, new lucky charm. He was a welcomed companion even though Lev joked that he wasn't kosher.

At various stops Marius garnered lots of attention and eager offers of purchase from hungry soldiers. Ralph refused to sell his "puppy."

At one stop on an old battlefield, Ralph cut up a damaged gas mask and made riding goggles for the little guy. Road dust was thick. Ralph also made a pair for himself. With two long strips of white bandages as sporty driving scarves, Marius and he resembled members of a pre-war British racing team.

Jack whispered to Lev that Ralph had "finally driven over the edge."

Once again they came upon the old château at Pierrefonds. All stopped and filled with liters of oil and gasoline. Ralph visited the château. He took Marius around, now on a proper leather leash like a canine, and explained the various sights.

Jack asked Lev, "Did you hear *Raff* talking to Marius?"

"Better than talking to himself."

After Pierrefonds, the Bantams passed on to Rethel where they went into full repose. Everyone appeared relieved that they hadn't been tossed onto another battlefield. *How many has it been?* Ralph couldn't remember.

Unfortunately, at this point their quarters were so bad they slept in their ambulances most nights. This led to major ruckus. The boys fought over who Marius slept with. Live pork was a highly effective bed warmer. Marius was sought after more vehemently than the ever-present Moet champagne. Since nobody could beat Ralph in a fair wrestling match (Lev and Jack once undertook a tag-team ambush—to their dismay both got body slammed half-senseless and never tried that stunt again), the boys resorted to hands of poker to win the nocturnal warming privileges of Marius.

As rightful owner, Ralph received 50 percent of gross winnings as a pork chop rental fee.

While there, Boche Richter decided to sleep in the basement of a ruined house. He was too cold in his car. Several boys decided to join him and sleep upstairs, carving out canvas-covered niches in the rubble. All their first floor clearing activity weakened the remaining stone walls and floor supports around them. In the middle of the night, the center collapsed and fell directly on Boche. The force of the impact was so great Ralph thought they'd been hit by *avions* or artillery.

Bantams flew into rescue mode. This was for one of their own! Ralph thought Boche was dying for all his pitiful groaning below. The boys on the floor above were not badly hurt and struggled out on their own. The rest formed a bucket brigade and passed debris out from the basement. They levered out concrete chunks using wooden beams. As long as there were sounds, Boche was alive.

Hundreds of pounds of wood and stone had to be manhandled out of the cellar. Underneath it all, Boche was a pulpy mess. His upper lip was flayed open, he was black and blue, and he had received a concussion. After being carried out of the basement and hurriedly assessed, they slid him into Ralph's waiting ambulance. Boche was bandaged and on the road to a hospital thirty seconds later. Lev stayed in the back to tend to him.

Boche muttered for a while. When he finally "woke up" he had no idea where he was or what had happened. Ralph wrote, "It is a wonder he wasn't killed. The floor was made of stone four inches thick. The joist rotted through and let the whole thing down on him."

Boche recovered in the hospital and soon returned to their unit. He was, however, disappointed to find he had chipped his two front teeth. The only consolation was that Lev said his "overbite had been cured." Boche didn't appreciate the joke. But all were relieved to have "that Kraut bastard back in one piece."

### Wednesday, 2 October 1918. Rethel

The Bantams remained on repose. The local sights did not inspire Ralph. The boys had no access to bicycles, so strolling lanes was the best exercise. Ralph took frequent naps. He noticed that his hands shook when writing. He burned off his nervousness by taking long hikes. "Snaggletooth" Boche went with him on most trips.

Returning to duty, periodic emergency runs filled the boys' nights and days. It turned out to be a routine week compared to the stark thrashings of the past months. German artillery was scant in their area. French and American guns, however, sent the Germans plenty of HE rounds at all hours. The constant noise grated on nerves.

Jack asked, "How the hell are we supposed to sleep?"

Ralph said, "I'll call Pershing. I'm sure he'll stop the war for your beauty rest."

Generous supplies came to the Bantam Boys via American Army G.M.C. trucks. Ralph was delighted to receive "new clothes and dress uniform, a pair of shoes, 2 pair pants, 1 pair gloves, three pairs of socks, leather vest or jerkin, 1 pair puttees, and six bars of soap." It was their biggest resupply of the war. Ralph finally got a spiffy new pair of boots. Christmas came thirteen weeks early.

A haul this spectacular meant something "big was in the works." *Why do I need a dress uniform?* Ralph wondered.

Spirited conjecture grew among the boys. What was the "big event"? Maybe the end of the war. Maybe generals were coming to conduct an inspection. *More medals? Maybe Pershing himself will shake our hands!* thought Ralph.

The Bantams had been in the field longer than most American Army groups. They had "official Frenchie hero status" with their *Croix de Guerres*. Despite this, nobody was in the mood for a dress parade. No matter what was going on, Ralph took the opportunity for a long, luxurious bath in a horse trough filled with boiling water. He used an entire bar of soap in a wholly decadent action. Marius, just field promoted to sergeant by Ralph for "Outstanding Leadership and Keen Heating Skills," took a swim in the tub. He never smelled finer as Ralph buffed him dry with a scratchy towel.

With new uniforms in hand, the team engaged in a sartorial transformation. Their old clothes were so torn and "lousy" that they were not salvageable. They'd worn the old uniforms for months. Now comparing their new clothing, they realized how filthy the old ones had become. Donning their new clothes, they looked top-notch for the first time since leaving Allentown in the United States more than a year ago.

Jack lit a majestic bonfire. Champagne in hand, they flung their tattered uniforms into the flames. Old socks, underwear, and ratty puttees were next. The experience had a mental cleansing effect. Dirt disappeared. Splattered blood from wounded burned away. The boys' low-quality, hand-stitched repairs went up in flames. The most outstanding result was that lice exploded in the heat like miniature popcorn being popped for the party.

"Take that you blood-sucking bastards," Jack yelled as he raised his glass.

Clinking their glasses together, the boys toasted their recent good fortune. Nearly a barrel of "outstanding libations" disappeared. Ralph's optimism had rarely been higher in the last six months.

He wrote, "Lev felt so good he went to sleep eating his supper."

Lev said days later, "I been drunk as a *Son of Bitch* for four days and I gonna stay that way four days longer."

Lev kept his promise. He remained so deliriously happy over those days he brought Ralph a solid gold pen for the outrageous sum of 25 francs. Ralph had saved Lev's skin once or twice. Or more. But who was counting? The pen was a token of his gratitude and a first class admission ticket to the Princeton inner circle.

*Raff* was now a full-fledged Bantam.

Unfortunately, Ralph found the pen "isn't worth a damn" and wouldn't write well. When Ralph got the pen working he wrote, "The Lute [Lieutenant] assured us that we'd get our Croix de Guerres."

The Bantams, including Ralph, who had not yet gotten their individual medals, would soon have it. (This was in addition to the unit medal.) Ralph felt proud and his hopefulness rose higher for the first time in a long while. He might actually survive!

The *Croix* award announcement required a whole new Bantam celebration. The boys had another bang-up party worthy of a footnote in Princeton history. Pre-1917 university fraternity bashes were considered merely "little girls' tea parties."

With such a rumpus affair going on, French civilians thought the war was over. They were disappointed when told it was not. Still, they enthusiastically joined in with these happy American soldiers to celebrate this small but noteworthy victory.

The town butcher brought out a tabletop 1910 Victrola to play music. Although he had few recordings, they were enough. He played them over and over again until the needle started skipping. Dancing was lively if not wobbly. Even Ralph "cut the rug" as they partnered up. This sparked a conversation about the boys' hope that Duke Dennen, infamous for the drunken kissing episode, was still alive. They talked about their fears that he had been tortured or executed by the Huns after being captured.

Ralph didn't want to hear it. "Dance ladies!" was all he said.

More pent-up Bantam steam needed a vent. Innocent, empty wine bottles were lined up on the top of a stone fence and sentenced to death. The unfortunate jugs were snuffed out with captured Boche rifles shooting poorly manufactured aluminum-clad ammunition. Every cartridge misfire required the marksman to drink a shot of wine.

Some boys' rotten aim got better as the night progressed.

Amazed by their inaccuracy, Ralph, relatively adept with firearms and hunting as a teenager, was pleased that they were not an infantry platoon. "You boys couldn't hit the ground with a pea-shooter," said Ralph

"I can hit the ground with my pee!" said Jack as he opened his fly.

"That little thing is smaller than a 7mm cartridge."

"Edyth didn't think so." Ralph chased Jack for about fifty yards and then gave up.

Marius was party to the festivities as well. He got more than a tea-cup full of red wine and maybe some surreptitious champagne. After all, he was one of the boys. And he liked it! Because of their inebriated states, they pressed Marius into service as a dance partner. With four legs, he was one of the more stable dancers present. Ralph rescued Marius at Lights Out before his suddenly attractive pig got any marriage proposals.

It was cold that night. Ralph needed the warmth.

Unknown to all, on October 4th, the German and Austro-Hungarian governments sent a request to President Wilson proposing an Armistice. On the 8th Wilson replied that enemy forces must withdraw as a first condition of an Armistice and that he would only deal with a democratic government. On the 20th, the Boche accepted his terms.

Peace negotiations began. German nobles were now fighting for their futures and the future of their nation. Monarchical structures were crumbling like so many ancient dynasties had done before them. Their economy was in shambles. Workers were starving and in armed revolt. Allied soldiers, especially the growing American forces, were poised on the frontier ready to invade the country. And burn it to the ground—if that's what it took. Germany had to obtain a treaty.

### Monday, 11 October 1918. Poste Ognes

The Bantams re-provisioned and moved to Ognes via shattered roads through multiple villages. They left Breteuil days before the 11th, passing through the old battlefield of Soissons. They parked two days in the town square. On their way up they passed through Montdidier, Lassigny, and old aid posts. Some *Postes* still functioned as secondary aid stations. War flooded toward the German border. Newer Allied aid stations were being established daily. American boys were increasingly filling their wards.

Despite all the enlisted men's sacrifice, military "chicken shit" (unreasonable or irrational discipline) still managed to drop from "echelon assholes" above. Along this journey, a French major noticed the dapper Marius, wearing scarf and goggles, heading up the convoy. The Frenchie got offended. He failed to see the humor in "Colonel Marius." (Ralph had given Sgt. Marius a second field commission to brevet colonel for "Uncompromising Leadership and Outstanding Dance Skills." He used his pen to gently draw full-bird American eagles on Marius's shoulders.)

The pedant major did not agree with Marius's grade. (Being outranked by a hog, he must have felt insulted.) He said they must remove him from their unit. He cited pigs were against military regulations unless they were "in a tin can or on the menu."

Ralph thought the major was joking.

He wasn't.

The potential loss of their mascot stoked Bantam Boy anger. They argued to save Marius. Other units had dogs as mascots. "Mammals were mammals. Pigs were as intelligent as canines and could be found in every country of the world. They did not sweat and were cleaner than most animals," Jack lectured the increasingly annoyed elitist major. The team begged to keep their little *Frontschwein*.

The major would hear none of it. Rules were rules.

Ralph felt this was petty in the scheme of the war, especially after all the Bantams had done. "Goddamn Croix de Guerre winners should have any mascot they want."

That sentiment didn't translate well into French. He was overruled.

A Bantam wondered aloud about assassinating the major. "It wouldn't be difficult." Several heads nodded in agreement. They had been practicing their aim. Killing a lone officer was simple. "Blame it on a sniper."

Reason prevailed over violence. An un-judged execution was determined by the pre-law boys as philosophically immoral and wholly dishonorable.

And it could get them shot by a firing squad. That was the worst part.

They turned their discussion as to what to do with poor Marius. Some thought about releasing him. But they worried that someone would grab and turn him into stew. Or worse, he would starve to death alone in some barren field. There wasn't much fodder out there. They couldn't hide him forever.

And what would they do when they shipped home?

Ralph was angry at Jack because he thought he "jinxed" Marius by naming him after that "stupid Epicurean fellow." The philosophical joke wasn't so funny right now.

By show of hands they decided to butcher Marius. Jarlaud agreed to do it.

On October 14th, Ralph took Marius for a final, pleasant walk. He fed him a carrot. He then took him to the cook station and handed Jarlaud the leash.

Ralph petted Marius a final time and walked away.

He heard a squeal but never looked back. After all, Marius was just an animal.

Jarlaud fixed a meal including *saucisse* (sausage). Ralph ate a little and tried not to think about it. He had to admit the old boy tasted pretty good. Jarlaud was the best cook in the French army and the Bantam Boys had pulled tricks and clever subversions to keep him from being transferred to other units (one cover story was Jarlaud was suddenly dying from influenza—for more than six months).

At the end of the meal, Ralph collected and buried the bones.

The next day the boys loaded up. They were ordered back to Soissons. Ralph felt as if they were on a merry-go-round, driving in so many circles. He never knew where they'd end up next. But then again, he didn't really care about anything anymore.

Fortunately wherever they stopped, there were fewer wounded and the wounds were not as horrendous as in past battles. Gas cases were minimal. Most of the scant German artillery was the smaller 77mm whizzers that didn't contain large amounts of shrapnel. Heavy guns had been oddly silent.

Local trade and economic activity picked up as well. Photographic film was more available than in the past. Ralph took pictures. Shops stocked additional luxury and consumable goods. All were encouraging signs. "Something was going on."

In Soissons, Ralph bought a newspaper. The headlines were optimistic. He hoped it wasn't propaganda. A soldier's rule of thumb had been to believe anything verbal, even wild rumors, before one believed what was printed or approved by the government. That included newspapers. Ralph wrote:

> *The papers speak very favorably of peace. Germany seems to have accepted and intends to withdraw from the conquered soil.*
>
> *As yet our [American] division has not found them.*
>
> *One solitary [German] avion disturbed our dreams during the evening but he didn't drop anything.*

> ### Friday, 15 October 1918. Poste Unknown
>
> *We are quartered in ruined houses, some of which still have comfortable rooms with large fire places.*
>
> *We had a roaring fire all evening and I wrote a letter to Ma and Edyth.*
>
> *The main event of the trip was a party we held in an old house the night before last when we stopped at Dreslincourt.*
>
> *We built a roaring fire in the fire place and Pernod flowed freely. I never had a better time at any party.*
>
> *Each one spoke his piece or sang a song.*
>
> *The lieutenant made a speech saying that five more men had been called for commissions.*

Ralph quietly refused his officer's commission. After all the applications he sent out, he decided he did not want to command men. He did not want to tell a kid to do something that might get him killed. Being promoted to private first class was enough responsibility. He was tired. Lieutenant Lyon understood and did not press the matter. He tore up Ralph's commission decree. (From available records, it is not clear who accepted or declined the four other commissions.)

Ralph spent his time catching up on his neglected diary:

*Sunday, 17 October 1918. Poste Breteuil*

*After the Somme we went into repose at Breteuil, some of the boys remembered the village from spring, but if I ever passed through it I had forgotten.*

*It's a small country village of four or five hundred inhabitants, contains a church and a few small stores.*

*One old lady on the corner of main street had the best store and it was there I spent many a franc buying a half penny's worth of candy.*

They were on the move again. This time it was back to Pierrefonds for a third or fourth or fifth time. The merry-go-round continued unabated. Wounded runs were few with even fewer hurry calls. The war moved into the last French frontiers or stalled dead in some contested sectors.

Ralph revisited the château and recounted his fascination with it. He carefully explored it more fully than ever before. It was fun setting himself adrift in the maze of the castle. Like a kid running around a museum, he opened every door that was not locked.

*Tuesday, 19 October 1918. Pierrefonds*

*. . . the Chateau is well worth seeing. It was built first by some of the older Roman Emperors, restored by Charlemagne and rebuilt a third time by Napoleon third.*

*The Chateau is a massive fort in itself surrounded by shallow moats. The building itself is practically untouched save for a bomb or two. The tower however, is badly demolished especially around the Railway station.*

*It was in this castle that the Crown Prince had his quarters and narrowly escaped capture in 1914. It was said too that he expected to make the place his permanent headquarters when he was emperor of the world. It's too bad. I wouldn't mind having that place for a summer cottage myself.*

*Under the chateau is a large dugout or bomb-proof. All the civilian population congregates there about dark to sleep. They all sleep together.*

*On one occasion I brought some writing paper and once Alex and I went in search of a chicken to have a feed on.*

*We found one but it cost us 15 francs. We had the wash woman cook it for us but I've eaten a bit more other times for 15 francs.*

*We had an air raid while we were there. An artillery man got a broken leg out of it. No one else was hurt.*

*Most of us slept in our cars and it was cold as sin, the last day there I slept in a house.*

Little rescue work fell into their hands. The Boche only attacked once. Bantams saw it as an indication that the war was either coming to an end or soon to explode into a major new offensive. Everyone rested. One Bantam Ralph didn't know well began to have overwhelming anxiety attacks. He tried to comfort him but wasn't sure what to do.

Ralph then visited Bill's and Paul's graves and took more pictures. The photos turned out strangely distorted and it bothered him greatly. He felt it bode for bad luck. *Maybe the boys are trying to tell me something.* He threw the negatives away.

Bill Porter and Ralph went to another section to bring back Les Gardner and Ben Goodale for a Sunday dinner. Their unlucky Bantam section was in a "scrap ahead of Soissons and were steadily advancing." Some sectors were still quite "hot" with pockets of resistance. Storm trooper stragglers, not knowing diplomats were working on a peace agreement, would not surrender. Some enemy diehards fought to the last man. Many American soldiers were happy to shoot them.

Ralph met Ben on the road on the peaceful side of Soissons. Ben was having auto trouble. He tried to fix Ben's machine but couldn't get it to run correctly. He didn't know what was wrong. Ralph took his load of wounded on to the main hospital at Soissons. There Ralph encountered a "section of Americans and they looked as though they had seen tough work." Ralph talked with them. They said they took heavy casualties but were advancing against the remaining German resistance.

Ben finally made it back to the hospital. Ralph asked him how well they were eating. Ben said a little better now but at times they hardly got anything at all. Ralph tried to get him to come to his aid *Poste* for a decent meal. Ben said they were on the move and he couldn't go. Ralph wrote, "So we went back disappointed." Ralph gave him all the provisions, water, fuel, and oil he kept in *Lizzie #4.*

Ralph restocked and moved once more. He stopped in a town, ironically, named le Braine. Apparently the town was staffed by a number of not very intelligent, less than competent civil servants. Life *was* getting back to normal. He wrote:

*Friday, 25 October 1918. Le Braine*

*We parked there on a square and had quarters for eating and sleeping a couple of squares south. There was a Y.M.C.A. at the corner where you could buy coffee and matches.*

*The lady was some relation to the boob headed jam that stayed at the information desk at the YMCA at le Braine. The bunch I was with called her the rag doll [stuffing in her head—i.e., she was an idiot].*

*We didn't have any dangerous raids while there.*

*The thing that impressed me most about the place was a fourteen inch American gun just back of us.*

*It was manned with American Marines and when it let loose, which it did about every quarter of an hour, my hair left my head and my heart left my mouth.*

Ralph was frustrated by one of the new guys he had worked with. He was "pretty slow on the draw." New driving partners weren't much appreciated. To the veterans, they could be a liability rather than assistance. Ralph continued writing:

*We prepared to pull out after dinner and every one was in his car when we found George Glace changing a spring.*

*I tried to hurry him up and then [I] put it in myself.*

*I'd sooner try to hurry a French Poilu than George.*

*But we left soon by the same road that we entered on then branched to the left and landed after passing a lot of bad road in Dreslincourt. The town was a heap of cement and stones and not a soul in sight.*

*The ground had recently been retaken and was a mucky sight to behold. We found one large room in a house that was still inhabitable and it had a great big fireplace. There we made a roaring fire and with a big ten gallon bottle of Pernod we had one glorious party.*

*Each spoke his piece or sang a song then the Chief gave us a spiel saying that nine names had been asked for commissions.*

*Yes, we fell [for it] as usual and all washed and shone our cars up the next morning.*

*I went to bed late and woke up early with a headache.*

*C'est le Guerre.*

They continued on a seemingly endless trek to places known and unknown. Ralph wrote two days later:

*Sunday, 27 October 1918.*

*We left Dreslincourt for Ognes about noon. The roads got worse and worse. Ognes was a small village near Chauny.*

*Chauny was the largest town I saw in ruins. It showed many ruined factories and foundries and had lots of coal scattered about and if you got lost in those ruined streets you had a hell of a time finding you[r] way out.*

*I got lost several times.*

*The town was completely wrecked. All the bridges were down and the ones temporally [sic] constructed were always jammed and broken by camions. A continual stream of ammunition flowed both ways.*

*Gendarmes were on every corner and all they knew was to make you go to the right, they didn't know where they were or what was next.*

*Most everywhere we went we could see Tirailleurs or colonials in kaki [sic] suits. They were a wild bunch and had done their share of fighting.*

*The foreign legion has been in every battle we have and I guess a lot more.*

*Our cantonment at Ognes wasn't bad. We had three houses each of which had at least one good room with a fire place.*

*We had it nice and comfortable there and we all wished we'd spent the winter there and wondered if we wouldn't.*

*The colonial troops had taken up the scrap at [Chateau] Thierry and had pushed them back about fifteen kilometers.*

*Our troops took the lines first near Catigny. And pushed them about twenty kilometers past Noyon and Crisollis.*

Ralph and the boys soldiered onward. They anxiously awaited news of peace or a Boche surrender. Rumors flew in flocks in every direction, never landing anywhere or making much sense. Ralph occupied himself by taking pictures of the destruction:

*Thursday, 7 November 1918.*

*We moved from Ognes to Sinceny and there for a week or more. I did evacuation work to Crouy. At Sinceny we had fair quarters and not very much to do. But the roads got worse and worse.*

*I took some pictures of the church there and I developed some in an old wine cellar.*

*The avions didn't bother us much.*

*We moved in a day or two to Lassigny and there Whitbeck [a Bantam] broke his arm. I still did evacuation work.*

Then the impossible happened. The war was over.

*Armistice. Monday, 11 November 1918.*

Guns fell silent on the 11th hour of the 11th day of the 11th month.

Ralph did not believe it. He didn't know what to think.

Church bells rang across Europe. Soldiers laid down their rifles.

The silence on the front was deafening.

Few combatants, so long in the trenches, grasped that it was over. Men walked around in utter astonishment. Others danced in the trenches.

Upwards of sixteen million human beings were now dead. Twenty-one million were wounded. Unknown millions were shellshocked or psychologically traumatized.

The Great War officially started on Tuesday, July 28, 1914 and ended on Monday, November 11, 1918. It lasted approximately four years, three months, and two weeks. The Great War died with a whimper as politicians negotiated its burial with a written agreement. It was over.

Of the Americans in Europe, over fifty thousand would not go home. (Killed: 37,541. Died of wounds: 12,934. Total: 50,475. From: *War Casualties* by Albert G. Love, 1931. Later estimates from the US Department of Justice placed the total at 53,513.) In comparison, this is roughly fourteen times the number of Americans killed in Iraq for eleven years from 2003 to 2014.

Many more died of diseases and non-battle injuries. Full American losses were variously estimated at 63,000 to over 116,000. Many boys died in the 1918-1919 pandemic Spanish influenza. The epidemic was so severe that the average life span in the United States decreased by ten years during the 1920s.

No war is simply a male enterprise. Upwards of twenty-five thousand brave American women served in the war as nurses, civilians, and in military support positions. Several hundred hard-working women died overseas including 111 US Army nurses.

After three weeks of acute and brutal symptoms, Edyth survived Spanish influenza, which spread through Camp Upton, New York, in the summer of 1918. During this time she dictated to a friend a goodbye telegram for Ralph.

Fortunately, her letter was never sent. Its content was never revealed.

Nearly 4.3 million Americans served in the Armed Services throughout the United States's involvement in the Great War. Less than half of those men deployed to Europe before the war ended.

The cost of the war was staggering. Converted to 1919 American dollars, Germany exhausted $37,775,000,000. Britain depleted $22,625,253,000 and France spent over $24,265,583,000. America added $22,625,253,000 to the total. That year an ounce of gold cost approximately $20.72 and Keds revolutionary new rubber sole athletic shoes, that every real American boy had to have, were only a dollar per pair.

Europe was on its knees. She owed America over $10 billion. Old empires of Germany, Austria-Hungary, Russia, and the Ottoman Turk, ceased to exist. Many new hopeful nations would emerge from the death

Tired French soldiers watch German prisoners disembark from their train.

and destruction. Self-rule and democracy now seemed possible for the common man.

America was the major creditor nation to the world and was an industrial superpower. It had the largest and only fully battle-prepared army of all the combatants. And it had the second largest navy on earth behind the British Empire.

Western civilization had forever changed.

But little had changed for the Bantam Boys.

After the Armistice, the Bantams were better fed but work was as hard as ever. Many wounded still needed to be moved. They drove steadily ahead as the armies withdrew behind. Ralph had been on reserve for two days and had a couple of short evacuation trips directly after the Armistice.

On Friday, November 15th the boys were called to evacuate the injured from a railway accident near Montmacq. Twenty French soldiers were killed and about seventy injured. "Talk about bad luck," said Ralph.

These troops were returning to Paris after years of fighting. They were on their way home. "To be killed in a damn train crash. Unbelievable. Just unbelievable." Ralph thought the gods of war were merciless. To him, enlisted men were pawns in a bleak cosmic game of chance and could rarely, if ever, win a wager.

Ralph hated the recovery work. Pulling mangled bodies out of the wood and steel cars was backbreaking. They'd have to pry apart crushed sections with crowbars. Then pull out the man. Or more likely pull out his severed and mangled body parts. In Ralph's estimation, the carnage indicated there were more than twenty dead. Many unknown men must have hitchhiked a free ride on the train. And arrived at their graves.

For Ralph's frayed nerves, the recovery felt as bad as being in the front trenches. The boys and their French assistants emptied bottles of wine while performing their distasteful work. Days passed before many could eat solid food.

The Bantams moved out the next week and had nothing to do but fight the rain. On Monday the 25th, Ralph received his individual *Croix de Guerre*. He was pleased but would have "rather have gotten a ticket home." He desperately wanted to see Edyth.

During Thanksgiving Ralph thought deeply about the last eighteen months. He remembered Carey Evans's twenty-first birthday party alcohol ambush. That gave him a big smile. He wondered why he was alive and Carey, Paul Hargreaves, and Bill Purcell were dead. That brought tears to his eyes. He asked himself, *Why did I volunteer? What did we accomplish? Was it worth it?*

His thoughts and emotions whirled in a confusing vortex.

Sorrow ran down as tears on his cheeks more than smiles lifted his lips.

Ralph had few rational answers.

One thing he knew for sure: He was glad it was over.

In the middle of December, the boys quartered at Foyer du Soldat at Héricourt. The Bantam Boys rested as best they could. Ralph received large dosages of medications from French doctors trying to help him sleep. During those blurry and difficult days, Ralph thought long and hard about what to do with his diary.

*Why would anyone ever want to ever read it?*

*Should I throw it away?*

*Should I burn it?*

He walked up to the bright and warm hospital fireplace. Diary in hand, he flipped through the pages. He smiled. Edyth told him to write down "everything."

He realized that he did the best that he could.

Ralph turned and walked away. *Maybe it'll help someone someday*, he thought.

He sat down at a splintered wooden table, pulled out his gold pen and wrote:

*Monday, 16 December 1918. Héricourt*

*This book was written word for word as it happened. Some days I filled in detail. The worst and the best are with without deceit.*

*So if anyone should try to follow in my footsteps, as I have done with others, he will find here my life as it is. And will not as some point have revealed to him that he has been fooled and has been attempting to pattern his life after some who has deceived him.*

*My advice is for them to take another path. For I have led a fool's life.*

*NOTICE, Attendervous:*

*Abandon hope all ye who enter here.*

*When I was a youngster I believed in Santa Claus. Finally someone thought me old enough to understand that mystery.*

*And as I grew old here my faith began to weaken and I felt that life was a lie.*

*Other things have turned out in the same manner. The men and women I have trusted most have deceived me.*

*I am now on slippery ground . . .*

*I feel many stories in the Bible were from vivid minds of the Hebrew race.*

*But since I had been where I was going to die, I know from experience that there is something, somewhere beyond this life.*

Private Ralph Heller closed his diary and never wrote another word.

Ralph's diary with inserted pages

### *April 1919. On board the USS* President Grant, *Atlantic Ocean*

The regimental history described the *Grant* as a "whale of a ship." It was not a compliment. The boys were disgusted at the overused, poorly maintained accommodations. The "smelly old ship" was nothing like the *Baltic*.

But they were going home. That made up for many of its deficiencies.

The food onboard was so meager that some of them joined the firemen and worked menial jobs on the ship. They could eat in the "stokers' mess" and not the main mess. "Scraps of meat were better for the stokers."

This ship started its life in the US Navy as USS *President Grant* (ID-3014). It was later turned over to the US Army and renamed the *Republic*.

A total of 37,025 servicemen took her on westbound returns to the United States. These Bantams were just one more load of weary soldiers heading home.

A peacetime transatlantic voyage took about a week on a luxury liner. This likely took longer on an unhurried, underpowered troopship. The extra time onboard with nothing to do gave the boys an opportunity to talk about their experiences. They spent their days swapping war stories with other soldiers. They siphoned off their mental dross.

Few tales could beat Ralph's near fatal jaunt down the ravine through the platoon of German storm troopers and across enemy lines.

Jack said, "You're lucky you ain't dead."

He advised Ralph to become a New York taxi driver.

Ralph said, "Thanks. But cities shore ain't for me."

The time crossing the ocean helped them to recover. They tended their wounds with marginal shipboard first aid kits. They shared good-byes. A final toast, with canteens of fetid water, to those not returning, left no man without sorrow or abundant tears.

All onboard activity stopped when land was sighted.

Quiet embraced the ship until she docked at Newport News, Virginia.

An unknown Princeton author (possibly John Dos Passos) wrote the following untitled poem onboard *Grant*. It was on the last page of the regimental history. (A personalized copy was given to every Bantam Boy at a reunion during World War II.)

> *We had learn to love France,*
> *That is, all but Jess Clayton.*
> *We'd seen and encountered*
> *The wiles of Old Satan.*
> *We will never forget*
> *The old Call of "voiture."*
> *The dug-outs, the whizz-bangs,*
> *The "vin rouge," to be sure.*
> *When we take our last trip,*
> *Which'er place we seek,*
> *May the Brown Derby gather "Au moins" twice a week.*
>
> *(Voiture = car. Vin rouge = red wine. Au moins = at least.)*

After reaching the shores of America, the boys hauled themselves and their gear out of their dreadful ship. They then marched over to Camp Gordon.

Few dock workers took any notice of their arrival.

None cheered their return.

The Bantams could not believe they were home. Some kissed the ground. Many sobbed. All shook hands and slapped each other's backsides.

They were alive.

They traveled on to Camp Lee. "The red tape ran without kinks," the regimental history reported. The boys were processed and discharged on Sunday, April 13, 1919. The entire crew departed company for a last time. They wearily sought trains home.

For civilian Ralph Heller that meant returning to Marietta, Ohio.

Back in his now "foreign" hometown, Ralph paced its clean, wide streets while awaiting Edyth's return. *The homes have walls. And roofs.* He felt bewildered.

He drank cold beers with high school friends. But he never talked about the war. Ralph got free meals at the diner but was aggravated by constant, inane questions about France. Walking down the streets he got too much ogling from enthralled teenage girls and flattering old women. They seemed to want to take him home and display him on a shelf like a rare bauble or cheap knickknack. After all, Ralph H. Heller was a hero.

He didn't feel like one.

Each night Ralph trudged back to his family home as if in a fog. His ma seemed not to know him as he slipped through the front door like a wraith.

"What's wrong son?" she'd ask.

He didn't have an answer.

Sometimes, after midnight, Ralph wandered out of his bedroom and marched on the cold ground in leather slippers. He then sat alone in the cornfield until the sun rose.

He didn't know why he did it.

On May 17th, Nurse Edyth Sarah Lemmon was discharged from the US Army. She left Camp Upton via the Long Island Railroad. (Her train ticket home, number 47217, punched at each stop on the railroad line, still exists.)

She hopped several trains on her way back to Marietta.

Scheduled to arrive on the 20th, the trains ran on time.


### Tuesday, 20 May 1919. Marietta, Ohio

This quintessential midwestern town still showed scars from the 1913 flood. Union Depot and Front Streets, however, had been repaired. The

Ralph and Edyth meet for the first time since 1917.

Masonic Temple had been cleaned up. Most of the damaged homes were either repaired or torn down.

Ralph and Edyth met for the first time in almost two years. When they first saw each other both had on Army dress uniforms, the best clothes they currently owned.

He had the remnants of his Mohawk haircut tidied up for the occasion.

She looked "prettier than a postcard."

They grabbed each other under an elm tree. They hugged for a long time. As they parted, Ralph's ma took a picture of them with her Kodak camera.

Ralph smoothed down his wrinkled uniform. He hated his gaunt, tired appearance. Tiny shrapnel wounds and various infections left small scars on his arms and neck. He had lost thirty pounds. His stomach hurt. He was as nervous as if under artillery fire.

Ralph said, "I shore look bad."

"You never looked better to me," said Edyth.

Ralph took her left hand. He gazed into her eyes as he got down on a knee.

After a moment, he pulled from his pants pocket the plain gold band that he bought in Paris. He slipped it on her finger.

"Edyth . . . will you marry me?"

A tear came to her eye. She cupped his trembling face.

"Yes."

*La Fin.*
*C'est la Guerre.*

Presenting Mr. and Mrs. Ralph Heller

# World War I French and American Casualties

American Battle Deaths: 53,513
French Battle Deaths: 1,357,800
Americans Wounded: 204,002
French Wounded: 4,266,000

Estimated Total Deaths in the Great
War for All Countries Combined:
21,228,813

The Bantam Boys' self-published
newspaper, *The Exhaust,* recounts the
Death of Carey Evans.

*Hear the pitiful screams of the wounded and dying. Smell the butcher-house smells of feces, blood and burned flesh, and rotting decay, which combine into the awful stench of death. Feel the shudder of the ground as the earth groans at the abuse of artillery and explosives, and feel the last shiver of life and the flow of warm blood as friends die in your arms. Taste the salt of blood and tears as you hold a dear friend in mutual grieving, and you do not know or care if it is the salt of your tears or his.*

—Lt. Col. Dave Grossman
From his book: *On Killing*

# Providence

After the Great War, Ralph locked his diary, photographs, and medals in a wooden steamer trunk. My family doesn't know if he ever opened it again.

After their wedding, Ralph did not return to medical school. He and Edyth stayed in southern Ohio where he struggled to find work. Edyth found employment as a doctor's nurse. They eventually leased a farm. Times were difficult but they did their best to raise horses and produce. On the farm they birthed my two uncles, Ralph and Marion. Several years later, one of his horses kicked Ralph in the head and nearly killed him. He never fully recovered. He and Edyth continued to struggle financially. The Great Depression of the 1930s nearly wiped them out.

Ralph fought psychological depression after the war. He was admitted to several veterans' hospitals. Treatments there were crude and failed to help him.

Apparently, he was difficult to live with. No longer able to continue a tumultuous marriage, Edyth periodically separated from Ralph in the late 1930s after my mother, Martha, was born. Doctors had told Edyth years before that she could not get pregnant again. Martha's arrival was, therefore, quite a surprise.

Her birth could not mend the fraying marriage.

Drifting through jobs for a number of years, Ralph sent money back to Edyth when he could. World War II provided Ralph steady employment building military transport ships in Elyria, Ohio. He continued his life working as a machinist. In 1946, the divorce was final.

Ralph returned to Cambridge to ask Edyth to remarry him in the early 1950s. She refused. Ralph passed away several years later, essentially alone.

Cousin Lew, "Lew's girl," Edyth and Ralph in 1919

I believe he died of a broken heart.

The Great War finally claimed its casualty.

Ralph passed away before I was born. Nobody ever spoke of him as I grew up. I knew almost nothing about him. I always wondered why most of my friends had two grandfathers. But I only had one.

Ralph's leather-bound diary lay forgotten in Edyth's attic for nearly forty-five years. When she passed away in 1965, Ralph's personal effects and the trunk were given to the eldest son, my late Uncle Ralph. Then he rediscovered the diary. The diary stayed with Uncle Ralph until 1999 when he presented it to my mother, Martha. She couldn't bring herself to read it, so she gave it to me.

I transcribed the diary for my family. As a psychologist, I then tried to write an academic manuscript about it as an analysis of the development and early treatment of post-traumatic stress. I had treated Vietnam veterans in the 1980s. I wanted to see how far we had come in helping our returning war fighters. Most of all, I wanted to know who Ralph was. But I did not have a clear story of his experiences. The impasse was frustrating. I didn't know what to do.

Several years later, my Uncle Ralph, Aunt Cloé, and their daughter Jenifer Heller gave me critical information and photographs. The regimental history helped me to fully understand the timeline and circumstances of my grandfather's enlistment. Subsequent interviews with my Uncles Ralph and Marion, and my mother, gave me additional "family lore" that helped make my grandfather a real person replete with quirks, flaws, and a spiritual but not religious outlook on life. Then I had the details I needed for this book.

I am proud to be Ralph Heller's grandson. He was a first-rate medic, skilled driver, and excellent mechanic. He saved hundreds of lives and won numerous medals. Ralph was one of the most highly decorated American medics of the Great War with two French Croix de Guerres (Cross of War) with Bronze Palm, the American Purple Heart (awarded in 1932), a French Citation for Valor, the Victory Medal with four Battle Claps, and a citation signed by President Woodrow Wilson. He also won a dramatic, color illustrated French combat scroll for bravery that now hangs on my office wall.

In writing this book, I found my grandfather. I discovered that despite his anguish during and after the Great War, Ralph was thoughtful and sensitive. He was a good athlete. And he had a wry sense of humor. As Sarge Lee once said, "Heller, you're funnier than a one legged Boche trying to hop a ten foot trench."

Most of all, Ralph never gave up. Despite the consequences, he kept fighting against unbelievable odds.

This book is dedicated to you, Grandpa. And to my Princeton Bantam Boys.

These kids were a quiet band of American heroes who did what was right.

Writing this was an emotional journey as Ralph and *my* boys carried me through those dreadful battlefields. This book was one of the most difficult challenges of my life.

I would not have missed a moment of it for the world.
Rest well, Bantam Boys. You won't be forgotten.

Dr. Gregory Archer
May 20, 2015

Want to know more about Ralph and Edyth?
Or learn about post-traumatic stress?
Visit my website at drgregoryarcher.com.

# Acknowledgments

Writing a book is hard work. Writing a good book is even harder.

Many people helped me write this book. I wish to thank you all.

Most importantly, I thank my wife, Linda Searfoss, for her support, feedback, editing, and caring. It was a lengthy haul—over ten years to write this book. Thanks for hanging in there with me, laughing and crying on that long, winding road of discovery.

I love you.

Special thanks go to Laine Rountree Walter. Her suggestions and line edits helped me so much I can't estimate the impact. Laine cleaned out excess verbiage like a literary samurai chopping away at rogue sentences. My book vastly improved because of her efforts. And also to Trevor Thomas for relaying her edits over the Internet to me.

Thank you both so much!

Many thanks go to historian David L. O'Neal in Kansas who I believe is the top authority on the mechanics of the Ford Ambulance. Dave's knowledge was endless and I pestered him with an immense number of technical questions. He also edited the book to ensure mechanical and historical accuracy. Thank you! Readers should see his hand-built M1917 ambulance at ww1history.com/Model_T_Project.php.

Thanks go to readers including Marsha Sturla, Madeline Stillwell, Dr. Ray Valle, and a host of others who over ten years helped shape and reshape the tone, and the content of the book. I really appreciate the feedback.

Thank you Patrick de Haan for the 1:48 scale M1917 model based on David O'Neal's ambulance. Pat gave it to me the very day I first talked to Dave. That was a surreal experience and more than a little spooky. But I took it as a very good sign!

More thanks go to my agent Doug Grad. He helped me improve the book when it most needed it. His suggestions about adding detail and his insightful edits helped make this book a reality. I am lucky to have him represent me.

Thanks go to Rebekah Tabah at the Arizona Historical Society. She gave me direction on how to safely copy and preserve the over one hundred photos that my grandfather took in the war. Since many of the photos were in poor condition, I was quite concerned about how to handle them. She helped put my fears to rest.

Final thanks go to my publishers, Lyons Press, and Rowman and Littlefield, for taking on this project. Editors Mike Urban, Keith Waldman, Eugene Brissie, Joshua Rosenberg, and Ellen Urban, and layout artist Adam Caporiccio were immensely helpful in putting the polish on the book, and getting the photographs transferred for proper page placement. They helped to make this World War I venture a success. Thanks!

Without all of your help, this would not have been possible.

Again, I sincerely thank each and every one of you.

# Appendix

Below are the names and addresses of Ralph's Battle Creek Ambulance Corps friends. This is exactly how they signed his diary at the huge Red Cross party in France in late September 1917. I removed the street numbers so that current occupants of the properties may avoid curiosity seekers. (BCM is Battle Creek, Michigan. RFD is rural free delivery via the US Postal Service.)

I'd like to hear from family members of these or any other persons with knowledge of the Allied or Central Powers Ambulance Corps.

Go to my website at drgregoryarcher.com. I will publish on my webpage the history of any relative you find in this book.

Feel free to e-mail me questions or comments.

I may not be able to respond to every query. But I will do my best!

Keith Schroder Fremont St. Battlecreek
James B. Baker North Ave. Battlecreek
Daniel L. Sageant c/o Sanitarium
Clarence Olsen Clark Street Neenah, Wis.
Edward A Moore E. Michigan St. Marquette, Mich.
Elmer M. Noyro Cedar Street Marquette, Mich.
Ladd T. Rattenbury E. Cass Street Cadillac, Mich.
Geo. D. Hickman Pennfield, Mich RFD
Horace W. Mechen Majale St. Battlecreek Mich
Geo. W. Toeller Freemont St. Battlecreek Michigan
Charles Beyers c/o San Battlecreek Mich.
Gus Hart c/o San Battle Creek Mich
George Miller Battle Creek Mich
Henry B. Muldery Zeeland Michigan

John H. Hoeketra Hanover St Battle Creek Mich
H.P Myler N. Jeff. Battle Creek Mich
Otis A. Ketcham East Ave. So. Battle Creek Mich
Schuyles Heilner Harvard City Michigan
Joseph M. Boos Battle Creek Mich
Carelton G. Geneback Battle Creek Mich
Fred L. Strong Battle Creek Mich
LaVern A Weickgenant Battle Creek Mich
A. L. McComas Branchland West VA.
James R. Wells Howard St. Battle Creek
Wm. M. Miller Chicago Ill
Afton Phillips Ann Ave Battle Creek
Billy William Milwakee Wisc
Phil Brewer Battle Creek
DeVille Hubbard Mashall Mich
Clarence E Thorne Cadillack Mich
Franz J. Toeller Battle Creek
Rex J. Brown Battle Creek
Geo. H. Hickwam No. Division St Battle Creek
George I. Butler Manchester St. Battle Creek
J. Authur Redner Fremont St. Battle Creek
Donald Hoelkel Marshall Mich
Authur C. McHart Seymour St. Lansing Mich
G.M Spatitalis Battle Creek
Chas. N Pouton Sherman Wesford Co Mich
William E. Dunlap Battle Creek
Carelton S. Ellsworth Oneida St. Battle Creek
Morris H. Tichenar Lash St Battle Creek
R.K Cunningham Harmon St Marshall Mich
R. Donay Ravenna Mich
Carey L Roberts Gobles Mich
Leon D. Jones N. Wash. Battle Creek
Jospeh J Rohimove RFD
J.K Klonskey Carolina Freeway New York
Daylight Lemon

W. Chester Rasmussen Wright St. Oskosh, Wisc
Leroy F. Sparks Marian St. Columbia S.C.
Paul d. Holder E. Jackson St Battle Creek
Stt. Walker N. Jay St. Battle Creek
Edwin O. Ashley Okego Michigan
W. C. Adams Battle Creek
J,. Clarence Soutose N. Huron St Ypsilanti, Mich
Clanence L Andre Battle Creek
A.E. Shultz Rumsey Ave. Lansing Mich
H.H. Baves Mary St. Battle Creek
C.F. Tuttle Oyster River West Hanover Conn.
Chas. Don Palm East Lansing, Mich
Claude Eppley Lansing Mich
Leo R Wolff Lansing Mich
J. Harold Stevens Lansing Mich
V.E Boyd Lansing Mich
Carl M. Austin Kalamazoo Mich
R. T. Dobberteen, Stugis Mich
Leighman M. Bright Battle Creek
Roy S. Westerman Battle Creek Mich
A.F. Bloese Battle Creek
Roger B. Kellogg B.C.
G. Raymond Derby, Battle Creek
Harry D. MacCreery Stockbridge Mich
J. Frank Stapleton, Washington D.C.
Robert I. Baker Albrair Mich
Taylor P. Reynolds Booneville KY
O. Wesley
Haley G. Melvin Battle Creek
Russell F. Estell Battle Creek
Ray L. Henrich Battle Creek
Loran J. Clay Battle Creek
Nils Ol Byland Battle Creek
Theodore R. Cox Marshall Mich
Wm Dale Horeful Marshall Mich

D Hubbard Marxhall Mich
C. A Werner BCM.
A. L French BCM
Lairg E. Paquette Cadillac Mich
J. E. Hodson Marquette Mich
R. H. Rerbel " "
W. J. Morrison Jr. " "
J. P. Case Marquette
L. B. Benson B.C. M.
H. B. Seager Ferina Ill
John K Kellogg
Frank A Allwaldt BCM
Laurence H. Allwaldt BCM
H. A. Rice Blanche, Ky

# United States Army Ambulance Corps Service World War I Memorial

## Placed at Allentown, Pennsylvania

*To The Memory Of*
*The USAACS*
*Trained At Camp Crane*
*To Serve With The French*
*And Italian Armies*
*Who Gave Their Lives*
*In The World War*
*"In A Righteous Cause They Have Won*
*Immortal Glory And Have Nobly Served*
*Their Nation In Serving Mankind."*

—Woodrow Wilson

*This Memorial Presented To*
*The City Of Allentown*
*1927*

# Index

200; Clark, 207–8, 214, 223; Clayton, 222, 274; cold weather and, 52–53, 73, 127, 158–59, 244; Cook, 91–92, 101–4, 211, 229–30; cook for, 142, 250, 254, 262; Davis, 143, 173, 232; Dennen, 92–93, 230, 259; discharge of, 274; Dos Passos, 13, 194, 274; dreams, xii, 124, 166; evacuation of, 212–14; Evans, 91, 166, 176–78, *179*, 180, 196, *205*; fatigue of, xiii, 100, 108, 166, 196, 198–99, 216, 232; fights among, 38–39, 196, 256; Gilland, 251; Glace, 266; Goodale, 265; grandparents and, 137, *137*; guard duty for, 72–73; Gunther, 251; handguns for, 147, 171, 190–91, 217; Hargreaves, 62–63, 182–83, 211–12, *213*, 235–36; Harvey, 27–28, 103, 243, 249; Haupt, 27–28, 103, 141; headquarters for, *93*, 135–36; Hoffman, 37–39, 54, 91, 166, 199, 225, 255–56, 259; Hunt, 183, 185–87, 230; illness of, 9, 11, 19, 25–26, 127, 149, 158, 197, 223, 242–43; injuries of, xii–xiii, 201–2, 208, 223, 229–30; Kirkjian, 38–39, 54; Litel, 139, *151*, 152–54, 157, 161, 200; locations of, 58, *93*, 100; McCune, 223; MIA, 223; money for, 150,

161, 227; Porter, 214, *265*; as POWs, 230; priest of, 181, *182*; primary camp post for, 64–66; Purcell, 211–12, *213*, 235–36; request for, 12; Reynolds, 88–89, 94; Richter, 168–69, 197, 256–57; roadwork for, 155; self-published newspaper of, *279*; shortage of, 12–13; Smouse, 249; snobs among, 18; Snyder, 116, 118–19; Stearns, 20, 31–32, 36, 39, 77, 160–61, 188, 228, 255–56; Swan, 46; trench orientation for, 66–68; triage instruction for, 149–50; venereal diseases of, 9, 11, 149, 197; work after Armistice, 270–71. *See also* Lee, "Gabby"; Lyon, Lieutenant; McClenaghan, Bill

barbed wire, 64
barrage balloon, *52*
bathing, 224–25
Battle Creek, Michigan, 1–4, 286, 289
Battle Creek Ambulance Corps, 2–4, *16*; to Allentown, 5–7, 9; signatures of, 286–89
battle deaths, 232, 269, 279
battle fatigue. *See* shellshock
Battle of Belleau Wood, 198
Battle of Champagne, 230–31
Battle of Matz, 206
Battle of Reims Mountain, 231
Battle of St. Mihiel, 253
Battle of the Avre, 176

# About the Author

Dr. Gregory Archer is the maternal grandson of Private Ralph Heller. He is a licensed clinical psychologist, nonprofit consultant, writer, and public speaker. He has consulted to various charitable organizations in the American Southwest. He also moonlights as an actor in television commercials and movies. He is a member of the American Psychological Association and Screen Actors Guild.

Dr. Archer is an avid hiker, backpacker, mountain biker, and devotee of nonfiction. He lives with his wife, Linda, near Phoenix, Arizona.

You can follow him on Twitter: @DrGregoryArcher.